THE
SCHOOL
ADMINISTRATOR
AND
LEARNING
RESOURCES

THE
SCHOOL
ADMINISTRATOR
AND
LEARNING
RESOURCES

A HANDBOOK FOR EFFECTIVE ACTION

ROSS L. NEAGLEY
Temple University

N. DEAN EVANS
Burlington County College

CLARENCE A. LYNN, JR.
Burlington County College

PRENTICE-HALL, INC., ENGLEWOOD CLIFFS, N.J.

Library of Congress Catalog Card Number 77-82704

Printed in the United States of America

Current printing (last digit):
10   9   8   7   6   5   4   3   2   1

PRENTICE-HALL INTERNATIONAL, INC., *London*
PRENTICE-HALL OF AUSTRALIA, PTY. LTD., *Sydney*
PRENTICE-HALL OF CANADA, LTD., *Toronto*
PRENTICE-HALL OF INDIA PRIVATE LTD., *New Delhi*
PRENTICE-HALL OF JAPAN, INC., *Tokyo*

to

ISABEL

JACQUELINE

CATHERINE

Preface

The fascinating and provocative media revolution is a fact of life for educators and their students. It is increasingly apparent that newly-developing technology offers significant and exciting challenges to the schools of the present and the future. Talking typewriters, computer-assisted instruction, dial access systems—such is the current vocabulary for those who are interested in improving the learning process for pupils. The new learning resources do not mean the end of the old ones, such as textbooks and filmstrips, but these and many other traditional instructional aids will have a vastly different role to play in the "schools" of tomorrow.

How do teachers and administrators plan pupil learning experiences today, especially in light of the variety of media that are available to enrich the curriculum? Certainly bold and innovative approaches are needed in the process of curriculum development and in planning effectively for learning resources. The variety of choices alone demands that we approach the entire teaching-learning process in a logical manner. We need some definite guidelines and criteria for selecting and developing those methods and materials of instruction that will best meet the objectives of the curriculum.

The tasks ahead, though extremely challenging, promise to be equally exhilarating. The reader is invited to join the authors on a daring journey into the future. Let us see if we can together capture the vision necessary for educational leadership in the 1980s and beyond. Let us further pledge ourselves to bridge the present with the future. This is the immediate task, and we hope that the following chapters will assist the reader in moving from current practice to the best that creative learning research and educational technology are producing for his pupils.

R.L.N.
N.D.E.
C.A.L.

Contents

1   A New Age of Media and Learning—What's Ahead?   1
     The School of Yesterday and Today   *1*
     The Media-oriented "School" of the Future   *2*
     Organization of the Handbook   *8*
     Summary   *9*

2   Administration and Learning Resources   12
     Administration as Leadership   *13*
     Educational Administration as a Process   *19*
     The Team Concept   *25*
     Administrative Theory   *26*
     The Systems Approach and Educational Administration   *29*
     Community Support for Learning Resources   *32*
     Summary   *35*

3   An Integral View of Curriculum Development,
     Learning Resources, and Instruction   38
     The Relationship of Learning Resources to Instruction
     in the Local School District   *38*
     Media and the Process of Curriculum Design   *40*
     Identifying Sources of Media for Instruction   *45*
     Learning Resources and the Instructional Program—
     Selection, Use, Adaptation, and Production   *47*
     Summary   *51*

4 ORGANIZING THE STAFF FOR EFFECTIVE ADMINISTRATION
OF LEARNING RESOURCES   54
The Chief School Administrator   54
The Assistant Superintendent in Charge of Instruction   54
The Assistant Superintendent for Business   59
The Subject Area Curriculum Coordinator   60
The Principal   62
The Teacher   63
Summary   64

5 LEARNING RESOURCES AND THE EDUCATIONAL PROCESS   67
Teaching, Learning, and Learning Resources   68
The Total Learning Resources Center   71
Summary   80

6 PLANNING THE SCHOOL PLANT FOR OPTIMUM USE
OF LEARNING RESOURCES   83
Cooperative Planning of Facilities for Learning Resources   83
*Designing School Buildings for Optimum Use
of Learning Resources*   86
Space Requirements, Locations, and Affinities   99
*Adapting Older Buildings for Modern
Educational Programs*   115
Encouraging Proper Use of Facilities   117
Summary   117

7 ORGANIZING COOPERATIVE INSTRUCTIONAL SERVICES   120
Determining Necessary Cooperative Services   127
Summary   133

8 GUIDELINES FOR FINANCING EDUCATIONAL
MEDIA PROGRAMS   135
The Budget as the Key to a Quality Educational Program   135
Financing the Educational Media Program   142
Summary   153

9   EVALUATION AND THE LEARNING RESOURCES PROGRAM   156
Evaluating the Learning Resources Program   157
How to Evaluate Specific Aspects of a Media Program   161
Summary   165

APPENDIXES   167
INDEX   193

1

A New Age
of Media
and Learning—
What's Ahead?

The great playwright, George Bernard Shaw, was more of a prophet than he realized in 1949 when he told the writer that radio had revolutionized the education of the masses and brought the world into little villages like his Ayot St. Lawrence, nestling in the Hertfordshire hills some twenty miles from London. As Shaw alluded to the electronic infant, television, and spoke of his belief in the effective use of educational motion pictures and other audio-visual aids in the classroom, he was indeed anticipating a technological explosion which was to transform society and the educational process in the second half of the century.

Whereas Shaw referred to the great changes in his village, Marshall McLuhan proclaimed some twenty years later that man lives in a global village created by the instantaneous world of electronic media. From relative isolation in many separate cultures and societies, man has dramatically and rapidly evolved to an awareness of the other "villages" in his world. He has been thrust into involvement with peoples and lands once quite distant from his own both geographically and culturally.

If one accepts to some degree a major McLuhan premise that "any technology gradually creates a totally new human environment,"[1] then there are serious and challenging implications for all educators. In a world which has suddenly become much smaller and more intimate through the development of communications satellites, intercontinental color television, and supersonic jet airlines, many traditional concepts of the school and the classroom are rapidly becoming obsolete.

The School Of Yesterday And Today

Educators, like all human beings, find some comfort in reverie about the "good old days." In terms of teaching, learning, and curriculum, this

[1] Marshall McLuhan, *Understanding Media: The Extensions of Man*, 2nd ed. (New York: McGraw-Hill Book Company, 1966), p. viii.

means an era when almost everything a pupil was expected to know could be found between the pages of a basic textbook. After this major resource was selected, the administrator could rest secure in the thought that the teacher, dutifully following the text, and supplementing it from his own background, would probably succeed in covering the required material. The pupils were required at intervals to regurgitate selected facts on a test paper, and the "learning" process continued into the next chapter. George Bernard Shaw was speaking of such an environment when he said that schools are prisons for children. He spoke of being locked up in one for many hours and not learning anything worthwhile. Simply digesting facts from a basic text was thought to be adequate education at one time, but any modern-day proponent of such a curriculum would face a formidable task indeed. With the sum total of man's knowledge doubling every few years in most academic fields, it is impossible to catalog all facts, let alone teach them.

By the 1950s and 1960s, many schools had thrown off the shackles of a rote curriculum designed for group consumption. Research into the learning process made it apparent to more educators that all students did not learn at the same rate and could not profit from the same curriculum. "Individual differences" and "individualization of instruction" became popular terms in the professional literature. Learning aids such as supplementary books, filmstrips, motion pictures, and recordings were used by many teachers; however, it was still difficult to help the individual student to learn according to his needs so long as children were in groups of 25 to 40. The teacher who understood that he should individualize instruction was really unable to do so. Then came the various organizational patterns, team teaching, non-grading, and other innovations, which gave some promise of breaking down the artificial grade and classroom groupings. Large group lectures were planned to free more teacher time for smaller seminar discussions and some individual work. But always the problem of the teacher-pupil ratio really prevented the individualization of instruction until the technological explosion of educational media in the late sixties. Here was a breakthrough in methods and materials of instruction that held the promise at last of Mark Hopkins on one end of the log and the student on the other.

The Media-oriented "School" Of The Future

One of the massive problems facing the curriculum worker and the learning resources specialist is the fantastic information explosion that continues unabated. In fact it is predicted that the sum total of man's knowledge will be doubling every 90 days or less by the turn of the century. Marshall McLuhan has stated that the information level in today's

classroom is considerably below that of the electronic environment outside, and another problem occurs for the educator as the impact of present-day media helps to cause much greater individual differences among
children. For example, some view television more than others; the intelligent child involves his mind and senses and learns much from the
programs he sees. Travel, the telephone, the movies, radio—all of these
influence the child who is involved with the medium.

How can the educator make sense of these developments and harness
the media to the teacher and student? Achieving the elusive one-to-one
teacher-learner relationship will require another revolution—in "schools"
and "classrooms" of the future.

EDUCATION IN THE TWENTY-FIRST CENTURY

Although long-range predictions are a dangerous game, there are
enough clear signs to enable us to chart the path of education for the
next few decades. And remember, the buildings on the drawing boards
today will serve the twenty-first century student, for better or for worse.

The school of the future will not be a school at all as we know it, but
a learning center. There will be no standard classrooms, but rather a
few large group instructional areas and some seminar rooms. Most of the
space in the learning center will house individual carrels equipped with
the latest in learning aids. There will be full-time teachers in the center
but only part-time students. Each family will have a learning center in
the home and much of Johnny's learning will take place there, although
he may spend two or three days a week in the community learning center
with the schedule geared to his particular needs. Let's join twelve-year-
old Johnny in his 1998 home and see how he learns.

At 9:00 A.M. after breakfast Johnny proceeds to the home learning
center, seats himself before the console, and turns it on. By placing his
identification card in the appropriate slot, Johnny establishes his identity
with the central computer at the learning resources center downtown.
Looking at his programmed lesson sheet for the day, he presses the digits
3–1–2 on the console, and instantaneously a program in space biology
flashes on the screen. Since his last test yesterday the computer has tabu-
lated his responses, they have been verified by his teacher, and the program technician has inserted the proper sequence for Johnny's new
lesson this morning. He now proceeds to interact with the program,
which incidentally appears on the screen in color. Since it is programmed
for branching, Johnny is able to work at his own pace. If he makes an
error, he is told by the computer and is routed into a series of alternate
problems that will help him discover his mistake. He writes on the screen
with a "light pen" or electronic stylus and erases his work before pro-
ceeding. At 10:10 A.M. Johnny completes this sequence and turns the

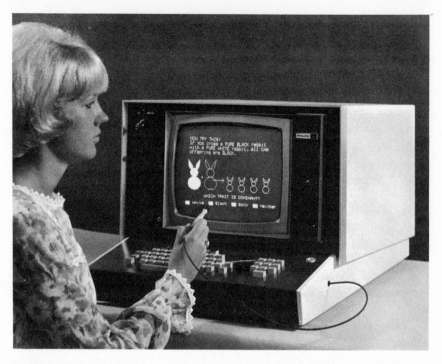

FIGURE 1.   Student audio-visual interface unit. (Courtesy of Philco-Ford Corporation, Communications and Electronics Division and Education and Technical Services Division. Equipment presently in operation within the school district of Philadelphia.)

console over to his six-year-old brother, Jimmy, who is ready for his reading lesson.[2]

After a snack, Johnny catches the bus downtown where he joins a group of fellow students for a concert by the Philharmonic Orchestra. This is part of the fine arts curriculum. Following lunch with his friends, Johnny is off to the community learning center for a conference with one of his teachers.

At the learning center, Johnny's teacher, Dr. Jones, is waiting with an analysis of his progress compiled from the computer, which can tell her or the guidance counselor or the psychologist almost anything they want to know about Johnny's interaction with his programs and his progress toward the goals of his curriculum. Johnny always enjoys his conferences with Dr. Jones; she is so helpful in focusing on his learning problems, if any, and she seems to understand so well his interests, abilities, and aspirations.

[2]Elementary school pupils were first taught reading and mathematics by computer in a program conducted by Stanford University in East Palo Alto, California.

A group of 220 students, including Johnny, gather in the lecture hall at 2:00 P.M. for an introduction to the next unit in space biology. The age of the pupils ranges from 10 to 15 in this large class, and they all have been evaluated as ready for this next unit. A brilliant, personable, scientist-teacher, Dr. Thomas, conducts an illustrated lecture, using the large color screen and many of the automated audio-visual devices under his immediate control at the master console. At appropriate intervals, Johnny and his fellow students respond to questions posed by Dr. Thomas, using the electronic styli and small screens at their seats. Quickly surveying the sum total of pupil responses, Dr. Thomas either continues on his main track or switches to one of the branching programs available to him before returning to the basic lecture. In every respect this one hour presentation rivals in production techniques and technical quality the best commercial television available. And it has the added learning advantage of direct student participation.[3]

At 3:00 P.M. Johnny checks out a wireless headset from the learning resources center and asks the technician for a replay of one of the orchestral numbers he heard live at the morning concert. He walks over to a large window overlooking a patio garden, sits down in a comfortable chair, and enjoys once again the strains of Debussy's *La Mer* in stereo.[4]

A joint United States-Russian space launching is scheduled for 3:45, and Johnny joins a large number of young people of all ages in the learning center lounge. On TV sets spaced throughout the area they informally watch this live coverage beamed from the USSR via one of the communications satellites.

Home again at 4:40 P.M., Johnny checks with the home console for a set of exercises suiting his present physical condition as recorded on his master health record. He then goes off to the home gymnasium for a workout.

After dinner, brother Jimmy, Dad, and Mother vie with Johnny for the console. They all want to do some research or get some information from the learning resources center. (Pupils used to call this "homework.") Father, resigning himself to a later evening hour when the children are in bed, vows that next year's family budget must provide for a second learning console.

There is no such thing as a "typical" day for Johnny. In addition to the activities outlined briefly above, he sometimes joins in seminar discussion groups with a small number of his colleagues at the community

[3]Several electronic response systems have been successfully demonstrated in university lecture halls and large-group instruction areas throughout the nation, *i.e.*, Oral Roberts University, Tulsa, Oklahoma.

[4]A wireless audio system has been used at the Learning Resources Center, South Campus, Miami-Dade Junior College, Miami, Florida.

learning center. Teachers and pupils request such sessions when there is a problem in pursuing a particular learning goal or when there is a controversial issue to be explored.

Large areas of the learning center are arranged in attractive groupings of carrels completely equipped with the latest learning aids involving audio, visual, and tactile stimuli. By touching several digits on the terminal control, Johnny can gain immediate access to films, tapes, slides, and other instructional materials programmed in the learning bank. He selects pertinent programs from the printout provided him for each of his learning sequences. In addition, master teachers are always available in an individual learning area to assist students, to monitor the programs, and to discuss any points that Johnny wants to raise. At the master console the teacher in charge is alerted if a student is experiencing difficulty with any material that has been programmed into his carrel.

When does Johnny visit the library? He doesn't. The traditional library finally gave way to the concept of the comprehensive learning resources center by about 1985. Schools found that they could not possibly keep up with the burgeoning number of books that were being published in all fields. Even the largest libraries were able to maintain only representative collections. And the smaller ones were completely lost in an attempt to maintain current book inventories. Then one day the obvious solution was suggested and finally adopted, after many bloody battles in the stacks and reading rooms of the nation. The rapidly-advancing art of microphotography was sensibly utilized and computerized, with the result that every learning resources center could provide instantaneously any printed material that a learner required. So Johnny does have the printed word available to him in 1998, but not simply through the meager collection of books that a single library can offer him. Rather he can secure on his micro-reader screen the pages of almost any book in print anywhere in the world.[5]

In Johnny's educational world learning never stops. Gone are the artificial divisions between "home," "school," and "library." The whole universe provides the resources for the curriculum. Through the imaginative development of electronic media and other learning aids, and with the skillful guidance of master teachers, Johnny's educational horizons are limited only by the various abilities and aptitudes he possesses. There is no such thing as failure in school, since every learning experience is geared to the individual student's needs. Marks are unnecessary since the student is programmed for success before he proceeds to the next level.

[5]The art of microphotography is advancing with phenomenal speed, as several of the large photographic and electronic producers compete for the ultimate market. It is now technically possible to reproduce the entire Bible or the complete text of an encyclopedia on a piece of film that is barely visible to the naked eye.

Learning is a continuum in which each child progresses as far as he can. And of course the arbitrary use of "grade levels" belongs to a former era in history, when students were roughly classified by age and certain other untenable criteria. The keynote of education in this age is independent learning and study based on the values, goals, and aspirations of the student and of society.

BORN THIRTY YEARS TOO SOON?

Virtually every technique and resource described above has been developed in the laboratory and tested experimentally. It is widely agreed in progressive educational circles that the methods of discovery and inquiry must rapidly replace the rote learning still so prevalent in many schools. It is equally accepted that the greatest possible variety of learning resources should be used to enrich the learning process for each student.

However, a more profound understanding of communications media and their effect on human life is essential if education in the future is to be vitalized and strengthened in the manner described above. *The various forms of media are an integral part of life in the twentieth century.* Consequently they cannot be considered as a mere adjunct or aid to education, but must be understood as a major force in every learning process in the modern world. As Marshall McLuhan has so graphically stated, "Our conventional response to all media, namely that it is how they are used that counts, is the numb stance of the technological idiot."[6]

Computer-assisted instruction provides one of the clearest examples of the significant influence of media. Not only is the programmed content here of obvious importance, but the entire teacher-learner relationship is subject to drastic change.

Computers can substantially enhance the learning process. As the computer's potential for learning is realized, it has been claimed that the teacher's role in the educational process will become less important. Experience teaches us that this will not be the case. On the contrary, computer-based systems will strengthen the teacher-learner relationship. Teachers will operate as managers, with a complex network of learning resources available and the means for deploying them flexibly. They will have a ready record of each student's performance and a ready access to the information the student needs during each stage of his progress. Teachers will be able to devote more time to slow learners and will have the means for challenging fast learners to even greater accomplishments. Slow learners will see a merciful reduction, possibly the disappearance, of pressures from their peer groups. Tutorial and even dialogue systems employing computers will allow the fast student to explore subjects in greater depth, or the

[6]Marshall McLuhan, *Understanding Media: The Extensions of Man*, 2nd ed. (New York: McGraw-Hill Book Company, 1966), p. 32.

slow student to catch up with his peers through extra effort. Teachers will be developers of human beings—not mere dispensers of facts and keepers of records.[7]

In the advancing computer age, media will be truly a vital and integral component of every learning sequence. This is the real message for the educator, whether he be a teacher, curriculum worker, or learning resources specialist.

BUILDING THE BRIDGE

If one accepts the basic concepts inherent in this view of Johnny's educational world of 1998, a more practical and pressing matter looms on the immediate horizon. How do we get from here to there? And what about the multitudes of students we must educate along the way?

It is the main purpose of this handbook to assist the administrator, supervisor, coordinator, and teacher in planning effectively the role of media in the educational process. We are not concerned here with hair-splitting definitions, and so to prevent repetition the following common terms will be employed interchangeably throughout this handbook: learning resources, educational media, learning media, instructional materials, and instructional resources. These terms will encompass all kinds of learning media, including audio-visual and other aids.

It is the further purpose of this text to suggest methods of planning for and administering learning resources in flexible ways that will provide for the changes that are constantly occurring. We can no longer afford the 30-year gap between innovation and general adoption of sound ideas in schools. If we do not move in tempo with the times, our schools will rapidly become curios in the antique shop of society.

This handbook does not present detailed descriptions and applications of specific learning resources, such as educational television, programmed learning, computer-assisted instruction, films, and dial access systems. This task has been satisfactorily accomplished in other publications. Rather it is the authors' goal to discuss the role of media in the total educational spectrum, and to suggest criteria for the selection of appropriate learning resources for the whole curriculum. Finally, guidelines are established for the effective integration of media into the entire learning process, both for the present and for the future.

ORGANIZATION OF THE HANDBOOK

In Chapter 2 a basic rationale of educational administration is developed as the foundation for a sound media program. The dimensions of

[7]C. H. Springer, "The 'Systems' Approach," *Saturday Review*, L, No. 2 (1967), 58.

the administrative process are explored and changing concepts in educational administration are discussed in depth.

In Chapter 3 the relationship of media to a sound program of curriculum development and instruction is explored. Criteria are developed for the selection of learning resources to meet the objectives of the curriculum and the needs of the individual learners.

Chapter 4 discusses in detail the responsibilities of administrators, supervisors, coordinators and teachers in planning for the effective administration of a learning resources program. The roles of the superintendent, assistant superintendent in charge of instruction, assistant superintendent for business affairs, coordinators of elementary and secondary education, principals, subject area curriculum coordinators, and teachers are analyzed.

Chapter 5 deals with the relationship of learning resources personnel to the total learning process. The roles of key media staff members are outlined, including the coordinator or director of learning resources, the librarian, and the media coordinator in the individual school.

Chapter 6 presents suggestions for school plant design to make optimum use of learning resources currently and in the electronic future. Guidelines for new construction and for the adaptation of older buildings are given. Individual building and district-wide media centers are discussed.

Chapter 7 discusses the organization of cooperative media services at the regional level, and presents criteria for determining where various learning resources should be produced and disseminated.

Chapter 8 sets forth guidelines for financing media programs, and discusses various sources of funds, as well as typical budget considerations for learning resources.

In Chapter 9, procedures for evaluating the effectiveness of media programs are presented.

SUMMARY

From relative isolation in separate cultures, man has rapidly been thrust into involvement with other peoples and lands. One of the main factors in this transformation is the instantaneous electronic media of this technological age. According to Marshall McLuhan, man now lives in a global village. Such a concept has far-reaching implications for educators.

The curriculum of the past, geared as it was to the basic textbook, is totally inadequate to meet the learning needs of today's youth. Realizing this fact, many schools in the 1950s and 1960s recognized that students differed, and began to plan for individualization of instruction. Many learning aids were used by teachers to enrich and supplement the curriculum. New organizational patterns such as team teaching and non-grading were tried in an effort to meet more individual learning needs. However, it was the technological explosion of educational media in the late sixties that at last pointed the way toward real individualization of the learning process.

It is difficult to predict the future, but it seems fairly certain that the school of the future will be more of a learning center with no standard classrooms as we know them today. Most of the space in the center will house individual carrels equipped with the latest in learning aids. There will be full-time teachers in the center but only part-time students. Much learning will take place in the home learning center, and the pupil may spend a total of only two or three days a week in the community center with teachers supervising his work. The computer will be a major force in the educational system, both in the home and in community learning centers. Many lessons will involve independent interaction between the student and the computer, which will keep accurate records for the information of teachers, guidance counselors, and psychologists, as well as for the student himself. Other pupil learning activities might include symphony concerts, live television programs via communications satellites, individualized physical development, home research from a personal terminal, seminar discussions, reading books on a micro-reader, and many audio-visual experiences in the carrel. With such technical support, the teacher will be free to explore ideas with students, to promote inquiry, to counsel, discuss, and advise. He will do much more than merely dispense facts.

It is widely agreed today that the methods of inquiry and discovery must rapidly replace the rote learning still so prevalent in many schools. It is equally accepted that the greatest possible variety of learning resources should be used to enrich the learning process for each student. However, a more profound understanding of communications media and their effect on human life is essential if education in the future is to be truly individualized as described above. The various forms of media are an integral part of twentieth century life and cannot be considered a mere adjunct or aid to education. They must be understood as a major force in the learning process.

In the advancing computer age, media will be a vital component of every learning sequence. It is the purpose of this handbook to help educators plan effectively the role of media or learning resources in the educational programs of today and tomorrow.

SUGGESTED ACTIVITIES AND PROBLEMS

1. Read one of Marshall McLuhan's books and evaluate critically his major premises in terms of their educational implications.

2. Defend or refute George Bernard Shaw's claim that schools are prisons for children.
3. You are the administrator of the twenty-first century community learning center described in this chapter. What problems could you anticipate in the coordination of learning resources for the curriculum? How would you try to solve them?
4. In terms of research findings on the learning process, evaluate Johnny's 1998 educational program as it is highlighted in this chapter.

SELECTED READINGS

"Computerized Classrooms Are Almost Here," *Changing Times*, March, 1967, pp. 24–28.

EDP and the School Administrator, American Association of School Administrators. Washington, D.C., 1967.

Goodlad, John I., "Learning and Teaching in the Future," *NEA Journal*, LVII, No. 2 (February, 1968), 49–51.

"Libraries: Fact and Fancy," *The Shape of Education for 1966–67*, Vol. 8. Washington, D.C.: National School Public Relations Association, National Education Association, 1966.

McLuhan, Marshall, *Understanding Media: The Extensions of Man* (2nd ed.). New York: McGraw-Hill Book Company, 1966.

McLuhan, Marshall, and Quentin Fiore, *The Medium is the Message*. New York: Bantam Books, Inc., 1967.

Moore, Harold E., ed., *Planning for Education in Litchfield Park in 2000 A.D.*, Educational Services Bulletin No. 21. Tempe, Arizona: Bureau of Educational Research and Services, College of Education, Arizona State University, 1967.

Springer, C. H., "The 'Systems' Approach," *Saturday Review*, L, No. 2 (1967), 56–58.

Suppes, Patrick, "The Computer and Excellence," *Saturday Review*, L, No. 2 (1967), 46–50.

Technology in Education, an *Education U.S.A.* Special Report. Washington, D.C.: National School Public Relations Association, National Education Association, 1967.

Wiman, Raymond V., and Wesley C. Meierhenry, eds., *Educational Media: Theory into Practice*, chap. 11. Columbus: Charles E. Merrill Publishing Company, 1969.

2

Administration
and Learning
Resources

Throughout the brief history of administration, and educational administration in particular, a number of different meanings have been attached to the term "administration." Even today there is no general agreement among writers in the three fields of public administration, business administration, and educational administration, or, for that matter, within any of the above fields.

At various periods *administration* has been defined as: (1) management, (2) a taxonomy, (3) organization, (4) leadership, (5) decision-making, (6) a process, and (7) human engineering. The above list is neither chronologically arranged nor all-inclusive, and the terms are not mutually exclusive—democratic leadership and human engineering are certainly similar, if not equivalent definitions of administration.

At present, attempts are being made to adopt an adequate theory from other fields or to develop new theories of educational administration. The acceptance of the federal government as a partner in education, the demands made by teachers for a voice in decision making, and the growing use of the computer are making it difficult for the student of educational administration and the practicing school administrator to keep up to date.

Therefore in this chapter it seems desirable to review some aspects of educational administration and, where appropriate, to point out their relevancy to the administration of learning resources.

No attempt will be made here to give a comprehensive treatment of educational administration. There are many excellent books, several of which are included in the bibliography, to which the reader may refer for greater detail.

Topics discussed in this chapter include: (1) administration as leadership, (2) administration as a process, (3) the team concept in administration, (4) the application of theory to educational administration, (5) the systems approach in educational administration, and (6) ways of securing community support for learning resources. The first two topics, administration as leadership and administration as a process, are given the most complete treatment.

ADMINISTRATION AS LEADERSHIP

The leadership which is exerted directly by the school administrator or encouraged in other staff members is usually a dominant force in insuring success for the educational enterprise. It, therefore, would seem highly desirable to review briefly some aspects of the many faceted and often misunderstood term.

THE MEANING AND NATURE OF LEADERSHIP

Since the turn of the century there have been more than 600 different investigations of the nature of leadership. In a recent review of literature on the subject, one researcher found in excess of 130 different definitions.[1]

The authors of this handbook view leadership as a function that may be assumed by any individual at any time under particular conditions favorable to or requiring leadership. They agree with the conclusion of Jenson, *et al.*, that:

All meanings of the term leadership imply that to lead is to take some responsibility for getting a group or an organization from one place to another, one point of view to another, from one state of being to another, or one course of action to another. . . . leadership means having skill in assuming responsibility for getting a group to take some sort of purposeful action.[2]

The late Kimball Wiles, analyzing writings on leadership, reported that research does not support the early trait hypotheses of leadership which attempted to find relationships between traits and leadership.[3] This may come as a shock to the administrator who believes he is a born leader.

Wiles noted that since 1935 a "situational approach" has been taken in the study of leadership. He reported that the following conclusions seem to be supported by research:

1. Leadership is a group role.
2. Leadership, other things being equal, depends upon the frequency of interaction.

[1] Bernard H. Bass, *Leadership, Psychology, and Organizational Behavior* (New York: Harper & Row, Publishers, 1960), p. 87.

[2] Theodore J. Jenson, James B. Burr, William H. Coffield, and Ross L. Neagley, *Elementary School Administration*, 2nd ed. (Boston: Allyn & Bacon, Inc., 1967), p. 414.

[3] Kimball Wiles, *Supervision for Better Schools*, 3rd ed. (Englewood Cliffs, N.J.: Prentice-Hall, Inc., 1967), p. 32.

3. A status position does not give leadership. (It may actually interfere.)
4. Leadership in any organization is widespread and diffused.
5. The norms of a group determine the leader.
6. Leadership qualities and followship qualities are interchangeable.
7. Persons who try to persuade too much or who give evidence of a desire to control are rejected for leadership roles.
8. The feeling that people hold about a person determines whether they will use his behavior as leadership.
9. Leadership shifts from situation to situation.[4]

Perhaps the ever-widening schism between teachers and school administrators might not be occurring if administrators had a clearer understanding of the nature of leadership and an honest desire to exert a type of leadership that is consistent with the above conclusions.

CONCEPTS OF LEADERSHIP

The literature on this important topic is replete with concepts of leadership. The following concepts include those most frequently mentioned:

Central Figure Concept. Here the leader is the central figure in any given group—the individual who can gain and hold the focus of attention of those around him.

Group Goals Determiner Concept. This concept defines leadership in relation to group determination of goals. The leader is the person who leads the group in determining objectives.

Sociometric Choice Concept. This concept applies in cases where the leader is chosen by the group. It suggests that an individual is selected to be leader because he conforms to group stereotypes regarding leadership qualities.

Group Dimension Determiners Concept. This is a more sophisticated extension of the previously discussed group goals concept. Here the leader attempts to ascertain the dimensions along which groups vary. For example, cohesiveness, integration, morale, sociability, and the like. Leadership would be exerted by attempting to improve each dimension as the need arose.

Leadership Behavior Concept. Under this concept leadership is a behavioral phenomenon defined in terms of leadership behaviors. It might be said that the person who volunteered the most suggestions in a group discussing learning resources was assuming a leadership role in the group.

Role-Image Concept. In this concept of leadership, the behavior of the person is combined with the image of expectancy of his role by those in the group. There is some research indicating that individual and group satisfactions are positively influenced to the extent that role expectancy of the leader and role fulfillment coincide.[5]

This last leadership concept has important implications for the

[4]*Ibid.,* pp. 32–34.
[5]The six leadership concepts have been adapted from Jenson, Burr, Coffield, and Neagley, *Elementary School Administration,* pp. 416–18.

administration of learning resources. Unless the roles of all personnel are clearly defined and understood (see Chapter 4) and unless there is some procedure for feedback concerning the extent to which role expectancies are being met, considerable dissatisfaction may result.

LEADERSHIP STYLES

A definition of leadership quoted earlier in this chapter suggests that leadership implies taking some responsibility for accomplishing something—for getting things done—for directing the resources of an organization toward accomplishment of the institutional goals and standards. In practice this leadership force is exerted in the various and diverse ways which may be referred to as styles of leadership.

The student of leadership may prefer the triangle concept—autocracy, democracy and *laissez-faire* as advanced by Kurt Lewin. Styles of leadership, however, are more frequently thought of as falling along a simple line continuum. Although an administrator may believe he practices a particular style of leadership, he has probably used several styles in any one day without being aware of it. Some of these styles will be defined here and briefly discussed. Where appropriate, implications will be drawn for the administration of learning resources.

Autocratic style. The leader who uses this style habitually determines the goals, selects the course of action, and assigns tasks or roles to each group member. He also sees that group members give a creditable performance. As a consequence he alone must assume responsibility for the success or failure of the enterprise. Individuals using the autocratic or authoritarian leadership style in various types of enterprises exert their authority in the following different ways: (1) physical force, (2) dominance, or (3) manipulation. Fear is usually the underlying force that results in compliance on the part of the group members. Although the autocratic administrator is gradually disappearing from the educational scene, it might be that he is only giving way to the same type of autocratic power wielded by teachers. Autocratic leadership is undesirable regardless of who holds the big stick. If the director of learning resources is not discouraged from exercising this type of leadership, there is little hope that learning resources will be utilized to the fullest extent.

Manipulative or disappearing style. The leader who uses this style loses himself in the group. He tries to assume a peer relationship with group members. He manipulates the conditions so that all decisions are made by the group and allows group members to enjoy the successes and weep over the failures, for after all they made the decisions. This type of leader may eventually work himself out of a job and disappear altogether from the scene.

A less desirable variation of this style is practiced by the leader who pulls strings and snaps his fingers "behind the scenes" but attempts to play the role of a democratic leader when he is "on the stage." This is obviously a sham and cannot be tolerated.

Democratic style. In democratic leadership the leader works as a member of the group in setting goals, selecting the course of action, and distributing tasks. All policies are derived from actions taken by the group. The leader assumes, with the group, responsibility for the success or failure of the enterprise. The school administrator using this style knows, however, that in the final analysis his immediate superior, or the board of education in the case of the superintendent, holds him accountable for the results of the decision.

As intimated elsewhere in this handbook, the time is rapidly disappearing when an administrator can expect a full measure of success if his habitual style of leadership deviates too much from the democratic pattern. Teachers rightfully demand opportunities to participate in making decisions that affect them. The administrator who formerly captained the educational ship alone will either become increasingly more competent in using a leadership style that includes faculty members in decision making, or teachers will take over the helm and he will be relegated to swabbing the deck.

Certainly no decisions affect teachers, and ultimately boys and girls, more than those made about learning resources. It therefore seems appropriate to suggest that all staff members and even pupils should be involved in making these crucial decisions.

Laissez-faire or anarchic style. The individual who practices this style gives complete freedom to individuals and groups without the benefit of his own direction or participation. This type of leader provides the environment, materials, and opportunities for staff members to carry on the work of the organization, but he does not use his talents to interfere with or participate in the decisions made or actions taken by others.

Unfortunately, this leadership style is often mistaken for democratic leadership by both administrators and staff members. Under this type of leadership, or rather no leadership, the educational ship is not only without a captain—it has lost its rudder.

Sometimes school administrators who practice democratic leadership in the more familiar aspects of their job follow a hands-off policy when they are treading on strange ground. The motivating force that gave birth to this handbook was the hope that learning resources would become more familiar territory for those administrators or future administrators who knew and understood the basic ideas in this text. They would thus be better able to give much-needed dynamic democratic leadership in the area of learning resources.

Other names for leadership styles. Because of the strong feelings aroused by the terms generally used to describe leadership styles, there are those who recommend that other terms should be substituted. One suggestion has been that leadership styles be described as *nomothetic, idiographic,* and *transactional.*[6]

1. *Nomothetic leader.* This is a leader who places the welfare of the organization and conformity of role behavior to expectations above that of the individual and the satisfaction of individual needs.
2. *Idiographic leader.* This type of leader places the welfare of the individual above that of the organization. He views his authority and status as delegated to him.
3. *Transactional leader.* The transactional leader practices a style of leadership that is a compromise between the extremes of the above two styles. This type of leader sees the need to achieve organizational goals but he makes every effort to see that individual personalities are not sacrificed as they strive to attain these goals.[7]

LEADERSHIP, INNOVATION, AND CHANGE

The literature on leadership for innovation and change has placed a great deal of emphasis on the innovator and has been strangely silent on the setting. A student of organizational climate warns us that, "attention to organizational health ought to be a priority one for any administrator seriously concerned with innovativeness in today's educational environment."[8]

It would seem from the above statement that the administrator who is anxious to see widespread adoption and use of the newer more powerful and more complicated learning resources might take a hint from the agricultural expert, or for that matter, from the farmer. Any tiller of the soil knows that unless the ground is well prepared the best seed will not produce an abundant crop. Like the parable of the sower in the Bible, too much innovative seed in the past has fallen on barren ground.

In the exercise of leadership then the administrator should concern himself with the leadership style that is most likely to improve and maintain the health of the organization. The writers maintain that the use of a democratic leadership style with emphasis on the team concept is the best way to insure good organizational health: "the school system's ability not only to function effectively, but to develop and grow into a more fully-functioning system."[9]

[6]See J. W. Getzels and E. G. Guba, "Social Behavior and the Administrative Process," *School Review*, LXV, No. 2 (1957), 423.

[7]Adapted from Stephen J. Knezevich, *Administration of Public Education* (New York: Harper & Row, Publishers, 1962), pp. 100–101.

[8]Matthew B. Miles, "Planned Change and Organizational Health: Figure and Ground," in *Change Processes in the Public Schools* (Eugene, Oregon: The Center for Advanced Study of Educational Administration, University of Oregon, 1965), p. 13.

[9]*Ibid.*, p. 12.

As an illustration of the manner in which the educational administrator exerts leadership in innovation and change, the authors suggest a careful study of the following guidelines by Wigren for districts planning to introduce educational television into their instructional programs:

The value of analyzing the problems that television might help solve and making clear the school district's objectives for using the medium.

The importance of bringing the entire staff in on the initial planning for the change so that no one segment of the educational staff feels it is being operated on by another.

The necessity of maintaining teamwork and *esprit de corps*—a teamwork that grows from within rather than one that is imposed from without.

The need to experiment gradually in a few schools before launching ETV broadly in many, thus enabling the school district to iron out the major problems before universal application is made.

The value of using television in the in-service program for teachers first before starting its use at the in-school level with pupils.

The need to provide sufficient staff to undertake the television responsibility so that it is not added to an otherwise full teaching or administrative program of other staff members.

The importance of providing time for the staff to plan together; for television teachers to prepare, locate and run down resources; to prepare guides for teachers and to visit classrooms to see how pupils react and what follow-up is made by classroom teachers.

The urgency of conducting teacher in-service experiences on the utilization of television in the classroom: class organization, techniques of utilization and implementation.

The importance of building adequate evaluation procedures into the program from the beginning so that the experiment might be improved from year to year in a continuing fashion.

The need to emphasize quality rather than quantity in the programs which are produced: attempting to do a few programs well rather than attempting to do more than can be done adequately with available staff and resources.[10]

LEADERSHIP AND EDUCATIONAL ADMINISTRATION

The authors of this handbook support the position that leadership is a broader term than administration. As previously stated, leadership is a role that the administrator may share with other members in the organization. The administrator should not only be a strong, effective leader, but he should also be adept at developing and utilizing the leadership potential in others. Unfortunately, all administrators are not good leaders, but a skillful leader is usually a good administrator.

[10]Harold E. Wigren, "The Process of Change in Educational Television," in *Perspectives on Educational Change*, ed. Richard I. Miller (New York: Appleton-Century-Crofts, Division of Meredith Publishing Company, 1967), p. 182. Copyright © by Meredith Publishing Company. Reprinted by permission of Appleton-Century-Crofts.

The reader should not conclude from the discussion thus far in this chapter that just because the good leader exerts "power with" the group instead of "power over" it, he has surrendered his authority.

In accepting a position in educational administration an individual is assuming a leadership responsibility which carries with it a certain amount of authority. It is an axiom of good administration that the delegation of responsibility must be accompanied by commensurate authority to discharge that responsibility successfully. A good administrator knows how to use authority wisely without being authoritarian. He must never forget, however, that when he accepts authority he is obligated to exert leadership and to accept responsibility for the outcomes of the enterprise.

EDUCATIONAL ADMINISTRATION AS A PROCESS

A study of educational administration, and indeed of all administration, can be approached from at least three different points of view. An early and still-popular concept visualizes school administration in terms of a cluster of substantive problems to be solved. Chapter headings in textbooks on educational administration and titles of university courses frequently reflect this viewpoint. A second point of view describes administration in terms of the patterns of relationship among individuals in a social system—in this case the school system. The third approach to administration places emphasis on the process of dealing with the substantive problems that must be solved in furthering the goals of the social system.

In view of the fact that this entire handbook is devoted to substantive problems (learning resources) and that considerable space has already been devoted to the social system—earlier in this chapter in the leadership section and in other chapters dealing with organization—the administrative process will be discussed here at some length.

DESCRIBING THE ADMINISTRATIVE PROCESS

As far back as 1916 the French industrial scholar Henri Fayol identified the administrative process by listing a series of special terms to which he attached special meanings.[11] Since that time approximately eight other variations of the list have been suggested. In Table 1 can be found three of the nine lists of terms that have been used to describe administration as a process. These three lists were selected from the nine for inclusion in this text because they are representative of the evolution

[11]See Henri Fayol, "Administration Industrielle *et Generale,*" in *General and Industrial Management,* ed. Constance Starrs (London: Sir Isaac Pitman & Sons Ltd., 1949).

through which the lists have gone. Examination of all nine lists would reveal that they have all included either five or seven steps, except the last two which have six items. It also is interesting to note that *decision making* did not appear on any list until 1957.

Table 1. Evolution of Views of Administration as a Process: Viewer, Date, Reference, and Steps in the Administrative Process

Gulick and Urwick (1937)	Gregg (1957)	Jenson et al (1963)
Papers on The Science of Administration	*"The Administrative Process"*	*Elementary School Administration*
Planning	Decision-Making	Deliberating
Organizing	Planning	Decision Making
Staffing	Organizing	Programming
Directing	Communicating	Stimulating
Coordinating	Influencing	
Reporting	Coordinating	Coordinating
Budgeting	Evaluating	Appraising

The first list in Table 1 is probably one of the better known ones because it became a popular indoor memory sport for students of educational administration when the word POSDCORB was coined from the first letters of each word in the list.

Several writers in the field of educational administration have characterized these lists of classified activities as taxonomies. Griffith defines a taxonomy and classifies POSDCORB as one of the best known ones when he writes:

A taxonomy is a classification of data according to their natural relationships, or the principles governing such classifications. Taxonomies have served useful purposes in practically all the sciences. In fact, one could probably make a very good argument to support the contention that any science begins with a taxonomy. Possibly the most widely known administrative taxonomy is POSDCORB which, when developed, was thought to be the ultimate in administrative thought.[12]

As the basis for discussion of the administrative process in this handbook, the authors have selected the steps in the list suggested by Jenson, *et al.*

The authors want to make it clear that the following discussion of the administrative process does not mean that they subscribe to the belief that decision making is a mechanical process. The previous treatment of administration as leadership should dispel that notion.

[12]Daniel E. Griffiths, *Administrative Theory* (New York: Appleton-Century-Crofts, Inc., Division of Meredith Publishing Company, 1959), pp. 17–18.

Any attempt to turn the microscope on a behavioral process is very difficult because a process cannot actually be broken down into discrete steps. To study the administrative process, however, it has been necessary to postulate a series of steps. In analyzing these sequences of action it is helpful to imagine a motion picture that now and then breaks away from the chronological sequence of the story with a "flashback" to an earlier episode. At times these flashbacks are annoying, and yet they are necessary in order that the viewer may understand the story.

The reader, therefore, should understand that designating the steps in the administrative process as *deliberating, decision-making, programming, stimulating, coordinating,* and *appraising* is merely an attempt to focus attention on the general order or approximate sequence of events that a good administrator would follow.

To use another analogy, the steps in the administrative process are a route which the administrator will traverse. Just as in highway travel the tourist finds many detours and frequently does not know when he has crossed the border from one community to another, so also the administrator will not always have a smooth journey from one step to the next. There will be detours, roadblocks, blind alleys, and an absence of road signs.

DELIBERATING

Someone has suggested that the only exercise some persons get is jumping to conclusions. The individual who wishes to be a successful school administrator cannot afford to be in this category. Neither can he hope to be successful if he deliberates too long, drifting on the sea of procrastination and refusing to make a decision. As is true in so many walks of life, timing is important to success.

How then should the administrator approach a problem? In this first step he must take time to deliberate and plan a course of action. He must clarify his thinking about the problem. He must make certain that he understands the various facets of the problem and considers possible alternate courses of action. If he requires additional information he must search for it.

He consults with other members of his staff and with citizens in the community when appropriate. Finally, he is ready to make a decision.

As an illustration, let us assume that a school system is considering possible use of educational television. Here is a real challenge to the administrator. He would first deliberate and plan a course of action. He would try to determine whether or not the demonstrated values of ETV are applicable to his system's particular instructional requirements. He would clarify his thinking by reading about ETV, visiting schools that are making extensive use of it, and consulting with specialists in the field. He would consult with the members of his administrative team and involve them and other faculty members during the information gathering period. He doubtless would also sound out the board of education during the deliberating stage and keep them informed of his progress. He now must make a decision.

DECISION MAKING

It was indicated earlier in this chapter that some writers in the field of educational administration define the total field as *decision making*. When this thesis is examined in terms of the overall job—that of making decisions that will accomplish the goals of the institution—this definition of administration does make some sense. It also is true that an administrator spends a considerable amount of time making decisions and helping other individuals to make them. It is further true that collateral decisions must be made beginning during the first step of the administrative process and continuing after the *decision-making* step. However, there are many other actions that an administrator takes in addition to the *decision-making* step. The authors, therefore, are considering *decision making* as only part of the administrative action cycle and not the entire process. *Decision making* as defined here is choosing a course of action from among several well-defined and frequently competing alternatives after due deliberation and careful consideration of all recognizable facets of the problem.

Let us now return to the example of the administrator who is studying the feasibility of adopting ETV. He now has arrived at the *decision-making* step. After carefully weighing all factors, he decides that ETV has much to contribute to the educational program. He therefore decides to recommend to the board that an extensive program of instruction by television be inaugurated in his school system. He recognizes this as a major decision, but he realizes that there will be numerous other decisions that must be made in the implementation of the major decision. He also is aware that the other steps in the administrative process must now be sequentially followed.

PROGRAMMING

The AASA list uses the term "allocating resources" for this step and considers organizing, staffing, budgeting, and supply management as included in this category.[13] After a decision has been made, the administrator must organize for action—the resources of the institution must be programmed in order that the necessary steps can be taken to carry out the decision. Just as the accuracy and quality of the work of a com-

[13]American Association of School Administrators, *Staff Relations in School Administration*, Thirty-third Yearbook (Washington, D.C.: National Educational Association, 1955), pp. 17–22.

puter depends upon the skill of the programmer, so the solution of an administrative problem depends upon the quality of the decision made by the administrator and the skill used in *programming* the execution of the decision.

Programming, then, in a nutshell, is choosing the necessary human and material resources of the institution and organizing them in the best possible way to implement the decision made in step two above.

Again using for illustration the adoption of ETV by a school district, once the decision has been made, how should it be programmed? First, the staff requirements must be reviewed and the gaps filled in the organization. It may be necessary to change the administrative organizational pattern and to revamp the instructional schedules. Second, the buildings must be examined to find out if the various instructional areas are adequate for TV viewing, and to plan any necessary changes. Third, equipment and other materials necessary for TV instruction must be selected. While the above procedures are taking place, costs must be estimated and budgeted and other steps taken that are necessary when innovations are being made in the educational program. During this same period, planning and programming of the remaining steps in the administrative process also should be taking place.

STIMULATING

The first step of the administrative process involved deliberation on whether or not to adopt ETV. The second step was an affirmative decision. In the third step the necessary human and material resources were assembled and organized, and it will now become necessary to set the program in motion. This step in administration, which starts the action and keeps the institution moving toward the accomplishment of its goals, is the fourth step—*stimulating*.

At this point the administrator concerned with adopting ETV arouses all the interest he can in the innovation. As a leader who uses the democratic style, he believes in interaction among the staff. He solicits opinions, discusses issues involved in the change to ETV, and asks for suggestions for possible actions that should be taken. He answers questions asked by staff members and others and tries to drum up enthusiasm for the project. In this step the administrator is clarifying issues, arousing interest, motivating the staff, generating enthusiasm, and developing positive attitudes toward ETV because he knows that this fourth step—*stimulating*—is a crucial one.

COORDINATING

The staff members now understand the issues, and they are greatly interested in ETV. Many of them are highly motivated to begin working with instructional TV and they are enthusiastic about its potential. The administrator now is concerned with the fifth step in the administrative process, namely, *coordinating.* This is the phase in which teamwork is developed. It is necessary in an organization to have a division of labor in order that its objectives may be realized. Good timing is essential. Knowledge of conditions outside the organization is also of the utmost importance. In *coordinating,* answers to questions of the following type must be found. What part, if any, will the local TV station play? What will be the respective roles of the librarian and other personnel in the learning resource centers in respect to ETV? What new patterns of communication need to be developed within the staff? What will be the nature of the supervisory program? What types of in-service education programs need to be planned? *Coordinating,* then, is insuring that conditions are favorable and the climate is right for action—it makes certain that the "time is ripe."

APPRAISING

This is the final and culminating action in the administrative process. In respect to ETV, the steps *deliberating, decision making, programming, stimulating,* and *coordinating* have all been followed. It is now time to appraise what has been accomplished. Has ETV become an important part of the instructional program? Is it getting results with regard to the objectives of the curriculum? Do the teachers and children enjoy this medium of instruction? Are the costs within the budget? If ETV is not succeeding as well as anticipated, what may be some of the reasons? What should have been done that was overlooked? The *appraising* phase of the administrative process attempts to discover reasons for the failure or success of an educational enterprise. It is at this stage that a critical evaluation is made to determine the effectiveness of the plan of action followed in the previous five steps.

Unfortunately, this final and very important step is frequently neglected or inadequately taken. For the individual who would become increasingly skillful in the use of the administrative process, an appraisal of previous decisions is a necessary prelude to beginning a new cycle in the process.

SPECIFIC LEADERSHIP TASKS

Any move toward systematizing procedures for solving administrative problems is a move in the right direction. Administrators, therefore, should:

1. Become familiar with the steps in the administrative process.
2. Apply these steps in the solution of educational problems.
3. Rigidly appraise all decisions in light of the consequences.

4. Be willing to admit it when a poor solution to a problem has been made.
5. Constantly be on the alert for ways of improving procedures used in the solution of educational problems.

THE TEAM CONCEPT

In the section on *coordinating*, the importance of teamwork was stressed. The successful school administrator has learned the value of teamwork in furthering the goals of the institution. The day of the one man show is over, and some would say it really never existed. Fensch and Wilson make a strong case for the team concept when they state:

The term "superintendent" is gradually taking on a new connotation. Historically the term brought to mind the image of a person; now it is beginning to symbolize a process. It is becoming a function rather than an individual, a collective noun instead of a title. The new meaning is confirming the prediction that the management of a school system as a one-man operation is rapidly fading except in the very small school district; and the very small district is fading, too. The word "superintendency" describes the aggregate overseeing and leading of a school system's operations.[14]

INGREDIENTS OF TEAMWORK

The school official who would be successful in the administration of learning resources must know how to build a strong team. He is aware of the following essential elements that contribute to a closely knit organization:

First, the team must have a goal, purpose, cause, or objective identified, accepted, understood, and desired by all members of the team.
Second, the team must have spirit, morale, and the desire to win even at considerable individual sacrifice.
Third, the lines of authority and responsibility must be both clearly defined and understood.
Fourth, channels of communication must be established.
Fifth, leadership must discover and utilize to the fullest extent the creative abilities of each of the individuals and weld them into a smooth working team.[15]

The administrator who is seriously concerned with updating and/or expanding learning resources must become aware of the fact that the coordination and management of the new hardware adds many dimensions to the scope of educational administration. He should not, however, become so engrossed with and entranced by the mechanical aspects

[14]Edwin A. Fensch and Robert E. Wilson, *The Superintendency Team* (Columbus, Ohio: Charles E. Merrill Books, Inc., 1964), p. 3.
[15]Jenson, Burr, Coffield, and Neagley, *Elementary School Administration*, p. 433.

of these new media that he loses sight of the human dimensions of these more powerful and costly tools of learning. Brown and Norberg empha-size the human aspects when they state:

. . . we must realize that the fundamental problem in the administration of educational media is not the care and operation of elaborate technical systems, but the reorganization and reorientation of instructional procedures and human tasks that are involved. The aim is to help people assert more powerful, more creative, and more humane roles in teaching—through technology.[16]

SPECIFIC LEADERSHIP TASK

Expansion of learning resources requires additional personnel with new skills. These new personnel must be chosen with care and welded into a dynamic, smoothly-functioning team. Here is the challenge to real leadership.

ADMINISTRATIVE THEORY

This section and, in fact, this entire chapter may seem a bit incon-gruous with the handbook concept which implies practice of the "how-to-do-it" variety. The position of the authors in this respect is stated very succinctly by Hanlon when he writes:

. . . practice always implies theory, because practice is rational activity which involves knowledge of nature, purpose, structure, and function of the work involved therein. In other words, theory can exist without practice, but practice cannot exist without theory.[17]

The above viewpoint is the justification for a brief discussion of theory in this handbook.

Since the early 1950s, a search has been underway for a more scientific approach to educational administration. One of the most fruitful attempts has been the movement toward the development of an adequate theory of educational administration. The vast resources of the natural sciences, social sciences, and the humanities have been tapped; cues have been taken from public and business administration, and, to date, several theories of educational administration have been suggested and discussed.

In a brief work of this nature no attempt has been made to include a comprehensive treatment of administrative theory. The intent of the authors is to point out that there is an increasing concern over the absence of an adequate theory of educational administration, and that

[16]James W. Brown and Kenneth D. Norberg, *Administering Educational Media* (New York: McGraw-Hill Book Company, 1965), p. 14.

[17]James M. Hanlon, *Administration and Education* (Belmont, Calif.: Wadsworth Publishing Company, Inc., 1968), p. 12.

there is a growing body of literature on the subject of administrative theory. The authors believe that administrators should become more knowledgeable about this subject and should assist in developing and testing hypotheses based on the administrative theories. This, in turn, could lead to more adequate theories.

DEFINING ADMINISTRATIVE THEORY

In order that theory can be applied to educational administration it is necessary to assume that administration is in part a science. In his pioneer work on administrative theory, Griffiths makes the above assumption and lists the following characteristics of a science:

1. *Objectivity*. It must be free from prejudice or personal bias and capable of being tested by any individual who has the intelligence and the technical equipment to make the necessary observations.
2. *Reliability*. This is the degree to which knowledge can be verified by confirmation from other researchers studying the same problem.
3. *Operational definitions*. Concepts to be used must be defined in terms of the operations by which the data is obtained.
4. *Coherence or systematic structure*. The data dealt with must not be a mere collection of unrelated items of information, but a well-organized, systematic account of the facts.
5. *Comprehensiveness*. The magnitude of its scope is an important characteristic of scientific knowledge that differentiates it from common-sense knowledge.[18]

In the same work Griffiths suggests the following additional criteria for a theory of administration, in view of the fact that administration is an applied science. He discusses theory as: (1) a guide to action, (2) a guide to the collection of facts, (3) a guide to new knowledge, and (4) an explanation of the nature of administration.[19]

A number of definitions of theory have been suggested, two of which are included below. Van Miller defines it as follows:

A theory is a rational explanation of how something is put together, of how it works, and of why it works that way. A theory may never really be tested, but a theory provides a basis for generating testable principles or procedures or hypotheses, and the results of such tests yield presumptive evidence as to the validity of the theory.[20]

In their very significant work on educational leadership theory Saunders *et al.* propose the definition following:

Theory is a set of assumptions or generalizations supported by related philosophical assumptions and scientific principles. These assumptions or generaliza-

18Griffiths, *Administrative Theory*, pp. 22–23.
19*Ibid.*, pp. 25–27.
20Van Miller, *The Public Administration of American School Systems* (New York: The Macmillan Company, 1965), p. 567.

tions serve as a basis for projecting hypotheses which suggest a course of action. The hypotheses are then subjected to scientific investigation. The findings of this scientific investigation are evaluated in order to validate new scientific principles and philosophical assumptions.[21]

It would seem that the above definitions are quite similar and that their implication for educational administration is clear, namely, that school administrators must find scientific bases for their actions.

The administrator who is concerned with improving learning resources must realize that when his past experiences have encouraged him to conclude that a certain action will bring about certain other acts or events, he is using theory. If he is not fully aware of the theoretical bases for his action, he may make poor decisions. For example, suppose a superintendent has noted that learning and instruction have improved greatly in a neighboring district after overhead projectors were made standard equipment in all classrooms. The next year he orders overhead projectors for all classrooms in his district and expects immediate improvement in the educational program.

NEED FOR THEORY IN ADMINISTRATION

It is not likely that adequate theories of educational administration will be developed and used intelligently unless administrators become aware of what might be achieved through the use of theory. Thompson presents the following as possible advantages of an adequate theory of administration:

1. It would go a long way toward preparing students of educational administration for change.
2. It might offer a system of thinking which would enable the administrator to incorporate knowledge produced by the several disciplines.
3. It would direct the students' attention to processes and relationships rather than to techniques.[22]

Although eight or ten (depending on the definition) theories of administration are now being discussed in the literature on educational administration, it seems inappropriate to select one to discuss here. Instead, the reader is referred to the several excellent references in the bibliography and to others like them.

SPECIFIC LEADERSHIP TASK

Administrators should become familiar with the literature in the field of administrative theory and do some theorizing on their own.

[21]Robert L. Saunders, Ray C. Phillips, and Harold T. Johnson, *A Theory of Educational Leadership* (Columbus, Ohio: Charles E. Merrill Books, Inc., 1966), p. 5.

[22]James D. Thompson, "Modern Approaches to Theory in Administration," in *Administrative Theory in Education*, ed. Andrew W. Halpin (Chicago: The University of Chicago, Midwest Administration Center, 1958), pp. 22–24.

THE SYSTEMS APPROACH AND EDUCATIONAL ADMINISTRATION

In recent years some exciting developments have taken place in our way of examining and improving the structure and operation of organizations. This new perspective includes some highly complex man-machine systems, and is referred to as the *systems approach*. One aspect of the systems approach receiving much attention at present is *systems analysis*. This may be defined as "the comparison of alternative means of carrying out some function, when those means are rather complicated and comprise a number of interrelated elements."[23]

Although still in its infancy, this approach seems to hold considerable promise for improving educational administration in general and the administration of learning resources in particular. In discussing the computer and educational administration, Ramseyer cautions us as follows:

> The greatest single factor in the changing role of an administrator in a computerized system is the manner in which he relates himself and his staff to the beneficial and productive aspects of the computer. The inability to effectively capitalize on the potentials will result in intolerable waste and a breakdown in the administrative process.[24]

Although the above statement does not apply to the *systems approach per se*, it certainly is quite apropos.

PLANNING SYSTEMS FOR SCHOOLS

It would seem that the systems approach in general and, in some instances, systems analysis in particular could prove quite useful to the administration of learning resources. The systems approach seems applicable in the following areas, among others:

1. The analysis and solution of instructional problems.
2. Decision making in respect to learning resources.
3. Research on effectiveness of various learning resources.
4. Procedures for the distribution of learning resources.
5. The planning of facilities for learning resources.
6. Budgeting and cost studies related to learning resources.

If the administrator is to take advantage of the systems approach, he should become thoroughly familiar with the literature dealing with its

---

[23] J. A. Kershaw and R. N. McKean, *Systems Analysis and Education* (Santa Monica, Calif.: The Rand Corporation, Memorandum RM-2473-FF, October, 1959), p. 1.

[24] John A. Ramseyer, "The Computer and Educational Administration: Some Notions and Implications," in *Computer Concepts and Educational Administration*, eds. Robert W. Marker, Peter P. McGraw, and Franklin D. Stone (Iowa City, Iowa: The Iowa Information Center, College of Education, The University of Iowa, *in cooperation with* The University Council for Educational Administration, 1966), p. 135.

various aspects, including the use of the computer in educational administration. He also should obtain some experience in designing systems. The following steps have been suggested in planning "systems for schools." (They also are shown in Figure 2 in diagrammatic form.)

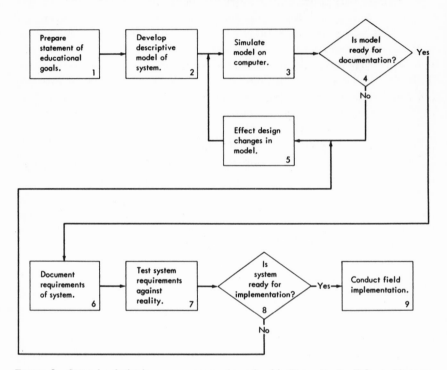

FIGURE 2. Steps in designing new systems for schools. (From R. L. Egbert, "Systems Designs for Schools," in Don D. Bushnell, ed., *The Automation of School Information Systems,* Department of Audiovisual Instruction, NEA, 1964.)

1. As a first step to guide the development of systems for schools, operational goals must be stated. Furthermore, priorities must be attached to these goals to enable the system designers to plan effectively.

2. The second step is to produce a descriptive model of the system. The system thus stated must be so designed as to permit achieving the stated goals. Thus, the initial description must be "ideal" oriented and must be divorced from restrictions imposed by reality. To ensure internal consistency and to permit close analysis of the plan, logical flow diagrams must be constructed.

3. Step three involves computer simulation of the model. This simulation should include representation of students, school personnel, curriculum, space, and equipment, and should examine various operating rules. Computer simulation will enable manipulation of the model and will give additional information about its characteristics and requirements.

4. Based on experience in simulating the model, a decision must be made

whether the model is ready for initial documentation. The making of this decision is indicated as step four.

5. If the model requires changes before documentation is accomplished, the designer moves to step five which calls for making necessary modifications in the model. He then proceeds through another simulation phase.

6. If the simulation study demonstrates that the model is theoretically sound, a document should be prepared detailing personnel and material requirements of the system as represented in this model.

7. With the requirements of an ideal system specified, the next step is to test these requirements against reality—both as to availability of personnel and material and feasibility of applying the program. (By feasibility, we refer to such problems as cost and relationships with school patrons.)

8. The reality test described as step seven provides the basis for another decision—whether the system is ready for implementation. If the system is not ready for implementation, the designer must return again to step five, make modifications to the model, and move again through steps three, simulation; documenting; and reality testing.

9. If the system proves to be ready for field testing, the system designer should attempt tests in schools representing as wide a range of designs and requirements as possible.[25]

PROGRAM EVALUATION REVIEW TECHNIQUE

This special adaptation of the systems approach, (known as PERT), enables the administrator to plan and follow efficiently an educational project in which it is necessary to achieve certain specific objectives in a scheduled period of time. A graphic approach is used in PERT, and it is characterized by a linear network of arrows, circles with numbers, time and cost estimates, and dates for the execution and completion of each phase of the project.

According to Justus, PERT has the following basic steps:

1. Identify and organize objectives.
2. Plan your project.
3. Schedule the project.
4. Get regular reports, once the project is underway, and evaluate the project continuously.
5. Recycle as necessary.

Under basic step 2 above, the following procedures are outlined:

1. Arrange activities in logical sequence.
2. Number the events.
3. Secure time estimates for activities.
4. Determine cost estimates.

[25]R. L. Egbert, "Systems Designs for Schools," in *The Automation of School Information Systems*, ed. Don D. Bushnell (Washington, D.C.: Department of Audiovisual Instruction, National Education Association, 1964), pp. 130–31.

5. Develop a project plan.
6. Identify the critical path (there could be several of them).
7. Transfer all elements of project to diagrammed network.[26]

Since it is merely a specific adaptation of the systems approach, the uses previously mentioned also would apply to PERT.

ADVANTAGES OF THE SYSTEMS ANALYSIS APPROACH

So many changes are taking place in the field of education that it is almost impossible for the administrator to separate the wheat from the chaff. He must be on the alert for techniques that will assist him to make better decisions in a shorter period of time. It would seem that systems analysis offers this promise. Coulson and Cogswell indicate its advantages when they state:

The systems analysis is no magic formula for the solution of educational problems, but it does offer two distinct advantages over more conventional survey or "common sense" analysis procedures. First, the formal structure of the flow charts provides a relatively systematic framework for examining interactions among the various components of a complex system. A person who applies systems analysis procedures is less likely to overlook major weaknesses in the communication network or in the decision structure of the system.

A second advantage is that the school design variables with which a systems analysis is primarily concerned (e.g., communication and decision procedures) are variables that can be manipulated. And this is the ultimate purpose of the systems analysis, to identify operations and procedures that can be modified so as to produce a more effective system. The variables that are often examined in conventional analyses, such as the number of square feet of floor space per student or the socio/economic status of students, are much less amenable to direct manipulation.[27]

SPECIFIC LEADERSHIP TASKS

The administrator can improve his leadership by:

1. Keeping up to date on the latest trends in the use of the systems approach in educational administration.
2. Applying the systems approach to appropriate aspects of the administration of learning resources.

COMMUNITY SUPPORT FOR LEARNING RESOURCES

The public is no longer the silent partner in the educational process. Parents and other lay individuals in all socio-economic groups are vitally

[26]John E. Justus, "PERT," *School Management*, XI, No. 12 (1967), 25.
[27]John E. Coulson and John F. Cogswell, "Systems Analysis in Education." Paper presented at the Conference on the Development and Use of Data Banks for Educational Research (Boston, December 4, 1964), p. 10.

concerned about education today. They not only place in education their hopes for the future, but many believe it is the last hope for mankind as well. Some individuals may be concerned for different reasons. Although they may acknowledge the importance of education, they are greatly concerned over its rising cost. The tax burden for many is becoming intolerable.

Good school-community relations have been one of the prime objectives of informed and enlightened school districts for years. The obligation of the school to keep the community informed is emphasized in a recent text on school public relations:

> Because public schools are owned and operated by the people of the state and of the local community, there is an obligation on the part of boards of education, administrative officers, and other school employees to take the public into their confidence and to provide them with the information they need in order that they understand the total educational program. The public must be made aware of the opportunities that are available for their participation in the total social task of making good schools even better.[28]

The newer learning resources and the facilities to house them are expensive. In the initial stages of the rapid expansion of newer instructional media—both hardware and software—the federal government has contributed funds generously. Whether or not this federal financing will increase, remain at the same level, or decrease is uncertain. It seems safe, however, to predict that in any event the administrator who desires the best possible learning resources will need to have the support of the community solidly behind him.

SECURING COMMUNITY SUPPORT

What is unique about securing community support for learning resources? Do not the same principles used for developing good school-community relations in general also apply here? The authors believe they do apply, but caution the administrator to be aware of certain differences in their application. It would seem essential that the following characteristics of the newer learning resources be kept in mind in seeking community support for them:

1. Because much of the new hardware and software is of recent origin and constantly changing, the lay public has had little or no experience with it.
2. The hardware is expensive and some of the most expensive equipment quickly becomes obsolescent.
3. It is not easy to produce tangible evidence that will convince taxpayers that the additional cost is justifiable.
4. Additional specialized personnel are required, which increases appreciably the administrative staff.

[28]James J. Jones, *School Public Relations* (New York: The Center for Applied Research in Education, Inc., 1966), p. v.

5. Infrequent use of expensive equipment and facilities is looked upon as an uneconomical accountability of public funds.
6. Teachers may not be sympathetic toward the increased mechanization of instruction and thus may adversely influence the attitude of the community.

The above must be kept in mind by school administrators desiring to secure community support for learning as they apply the following principles of public relations reported by Jones:

1. Public relations should be based upon a clear understanding of the objectives and functions of education.
2. Public relations should recognize the legal responsibility of the state and local educational authorities.
3. The public relations program should reach the whole community.
4. There should be well thought-out long and short term objectives.
5. The board of education should adopt a policy based upon the recommendations of the superintendent for a public relations program.
6. The effectiveness of any public school is conditioned by the degree of public confidence the school enjoys.
7. A citizen's interest and wholesome attitude in respect to public education are conditioned by correct information.
8. A sound program of public relations requires high staff morale.
9. The public relations program should cover all aspects of school activities, with proportionate attention given to each according to its relative merit.
10. The financial support for all the various agencies should come from the regular school budget.[29]

Applying the principles. It would be quite easy to take each of the above ten principles and make a special case of their application to the administration of learning resources. Instead, the writer will select several and elaborate on them with the hope that the reader will make a similar application of the remaining principles.

Principle 3 is one that should be followed scrupulously. Too frequently, when support is being sought for an innovation only the more privileged segments of the community are informed and involved. It is important to emphasize that all pupils can benefit from expanded learning resources. Taxpayers whose children no longer attend public school, or never did, should not be neglected either.

The need for high staff morale as suggested in principle 8 is of serious concern here. In the first place, in order to keep staff morale high, teachers must participate in making decisions concerning the improvement of learning resources. In the second place, they must understand and believe in the many changes taking place in learning and instruction as a consequence of expanded learning resources. Finally, teachers must feel competent and comfortable in using the new media.

[29]*Ibid.*, p. 16.

In the instance of principle 9, learning resources as the backbone of the instructional program must receive top priority in the public relations program. In order to do so, it may be necessary to give less emphasis to some of the timeworn more spectacular aspects of the program, for example, athletics.

In planning a program to keep the public informed, the administrator can benefit from the following objectives in telling the school story. Kindred and associates suggest:

First, people should understand the purposes of education in a democracy.

Second, the story should seek to develop a broader and deeper understanding of the instructional program.

Third, reports should be made periodically on the accomplishments of pupils.

Fourth, changes in the nature and number of the pupil population should be emphasized and repeated often.

Fifth, it is highly important that explanations be made of financial management of schools in the district.

Sixth, citizens should become acquainted with problems facing the local school system.

Seventh, popular confidence in the worth and value of the educational system should be increased.

Eighth, citizens should understand more fully the duties and responsibilities of those who direct and carry on the work of the school system.

Ninth, the special services that play a vital part in the education of children should be explained.

Tenth, citizens should be induced to assume greater responsibility for the quality of education provided by the local district.

Eleventh, the final objective should be that of establishing a strong partnership between the school and community.[30]

SUMMARY

The administrator who wishes to be successful in the administration of learning resources must be familiar with the various concepts of leadership and must become adept in performing desirable leadership roles. He also should strive to perfect a democratic leadership style.

Knowledge of the administrative process is of importance to the administrator. Skill in using the steps of *deliberating, decision making, programming, stimulating, coordinating,* and *appraising* can be of great assistance to him in problem solving.

An understanding of the team concept in school administration and the ability to organize and work with an effective team can contribute much to the improvement of learning resources.

[30]Leslie W. Kindred and associates, *How to Tell the School Story* (Englewood Cliffs, N.J.: Prentice-Hall, Inc., 1960), pp. 12–14.

Although they are in their early stages of development, the application of theory and the systems approach to the solution of educational problems is a fertile field for the school administrator.

Finally, the successful administration of learning resources requires community support. Without this, many instructional innovations will never begin their growth, let alone bear fruit.

SUGGESTED ACTIVITIES AND PROBLEMS

1. Using Griffith's characteristics of a science as a basis, take a position that administration is either an art or a science and present arguments for the position you take.
2. From your experience, give several examples of leadership shown by an administrator in the improvement of some aspect of the learning resources program.
3. Select a problem related to the learning resources program and demonstrate how each step in the administrative process would be applied in its solution.
4. Select a school or school system that you believe is doing an excellent job in the use of learning resources. Arrange to interview several key persons for the purpose of finding out how the innovations were introduced and adopted.
5. Outline and discuss the procedures you would use to gain community support for educational TV.

SELECTED READINGS

Abbott, Max G., and John T. Lowell, eds., *Change Perspectives in Educational Administration*. Auburn, Ala.: The School of Education, Auburn University, 1965.

EDP and the Administrator. Washington, D.C.: American Association of School Administrators, 1967.

Erickson, Carlton W. H., *Administering Instructional Media Programs*. New York: The Macmillan Company, 1968.

Fensch, Edwin A., and Robert E. Wilson. *The Superintendency Team*. Columbus, Ohio: Charles E. Merrill Books, Inc., 1964.

Frey, Sherman H., and Keith R. Getschman, eds., *School Administration: Selected Readings*. New York: Thomas Y. Crowell Company, 1968.

Griffiths, Daniel E., *Administrative Theory*. New York: Appleton-Century-Crofts, Inc., 1959.

Halpin, Andrew W., *Theory and Research in Administration*. New York: The Macmillan Company, 1966.

Hanlon, James M., *Administration and Education*. Belmont, Calif.: Wadsworth Publishing Co., Inc., 1968.

"How to Get Your Staff to Accept Change," *School Management*, XI, No. 3 (1967), 117.

Jones, James J., *School Public Relations.* New York: The Center for Applied Research in Education, Inc., 1966.

Kimbrough, Ralph B., *Administering Elementary Schools—Concepts and Practices.* New York: The Macmillan Company, 1968.

Lane, Willard R., Ronald G. Corwin, and William G. Monahan, *Foundations of Educational Administration—A Behavioral Analysis.* New York: The Macmillan Company, 1967.

Miller, Richard I., ed., *Perspectives on Educational Change.* New York: Appleton-Century-Crofts, 1967.

Miller, Van, *The Public Administration of American School Systems.* New York: The Macmillan Company, 1965.

"PERT: A Management Tool You Can Use," *School Management,* XI, No. 12 (1967), 24.

Trow, William Clark, *Teacher and Technology—New Designs for Learning.* New York: Appleton-Century-Crofts, 1963.

Wiles, Kimball, *Supervision for Better Schools* (3rd ed.). Englewood Cliffs, N.J.: Prentice-Hall, Inc., 1967.

3

An Integral View
of Curriculum Development,
Learning Resources, and
Instruction

It is easy to become enamored with the fascinating world of color television, random dial access, computer-assisted instruction, and other captivating media. Indeed many schools throughout the land have introduced various learning resources into the instructional program in recent years. Eight-year-olds take beginning French via TV; high school seniors in study carrels dial sequences in chemistry; and seventh graders visit the city museum of natural history. Twelve-year-olds view a color film on human reproduction; kindergartners visit a farm; and junior high students slide single-concept science films into their own projectors.

"Isn't it marvelous?" the casual observer is likely to exclaim. "The days of the dull single textbook are gone; the learning environment is so much richer today!" *Or is it?* The mere introduction of a variety of educational media and experiences is no guarantee of a sound instructional program. Learning resources do not have intrinsic value in themselves. A school administrator who builds a TV studio, a dial access system, and a film library into his new high school may not be contributing anything significant to the learning processes of his students. Far too many schools are leaping into the new media without considering where they are going or how they propose to get there. We dare not adopt the new gadgetry simply because it is on the market and in the educational literature.

THE RELATIONSHIP OF LEARNING RESOURCES TO INSTRUCTION IN THE LOCAL SCHOOL DISTRICT

In the view of the authors, learning resources should be considered only within the total process of curriculum development and instruction. Therefore decisions regarding media are best made only after extensive progress in curriculum design.

A growing problem of curriculum development lies in the matching of curriculum content to instructional technology and organization. Too many of the new teaching aids and organizational patterns are used without reference to their unique fit to particular curriculum goals and sequences. The recent movement of major industries into the "knowledge industry" reenforces the question of what and how curriculum content is to be programed into the communications systems available. Undoubtedly each of our . . . local school systems will not be able to do all of its own programing, but each should at least be able to make intelligent selections by its own criteria, among those programs to become available. . . . Each district, perhaps in concert with its neighbors, must as a minimum, it is believed, draw up its own design of the curriculum, including overall goals and expected areas of content, and some specifications for its pupil population of the alternative scopes and sequences of content needed and the instructional resources thereby required.[1]

There are those who believe that local curriculum development is impossible, and that the job should be turned over to (1) the federal government; (2) a national curriculum commission; or (3) the giant "learning" corporations which have organized to design and market both hardware and software. The arguments for and against local district responsibility for curriculum development have been cogently expressed elsewhere.[2] *The authors here simply state their firm belief that curriculum determination and/or design is the legitimate and necessary function of a strong, well-staffed local school district.* We agree with the following statement prepared for the United States Senate Subcommittee on Education in April, 1967, by William M. Alexander:

Strengthening of local curriculum development—Any fundamental efforts at improvement of the curriculum of . . . school districts in the United States must place high priority on improvement of the leadership and the processes of curriculum development in these districts. The alternative is to abandon local responsibility, turning over curriculum development to State and National agencies, and this is not considered a satisfactory alternative. Improve State leadership, utilize National resources better—yes. But eliminate the opportunity for local school people to make decisions regarding the programs they must direct—no. The need is to enable local leadership to make intelligent decisions based on full knowledge of available curriculum possibilities.[3]

[1]William M. Alexander, "Curriculum Development," *Notes and Working Papers Concerning the Administration of Programs Authorized under Title III of Public Law 89–10, E.S.E.A. of 1965,* as amended by Public Law 89–750. Prepared for the Subcommittee on Education of the Committee on Labor and Public Welfare, United States Senate (Washington, D.C.: Government Printing Office, April, 1967), pp. 103–4.

[2]Ross L. Neagley and N. Dean Evans, *Handbook for Effective Curriculum Development* (Englewood Cliffs, N.J.: Prentice-Hall, Inc., 1967), Chaps. 2, 3.

[3]Alexander, "Curriculum Development," *Notes and Working Papers Concerning the Administration of Programs Authorized under Title III of Public Law 89–10, E.S.E.A. of 1965,* p. 104.

MEDIA AND THE PROCESS OF CURRICULUM DESIGN

If the reader accepts the previous conclusions that learning resources are an integral part of the process of curriculum development and instruction, and that this total process can best be carried out in the strong local school district, what then is the next consideration?

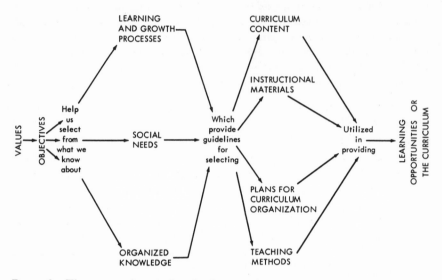

FIGURE 3.   The process of curriculum development.[4]

Figure 3 depicts the logical sequence of curriculum development, culminating in the instructional program or the learning opportunities offered to students. Moving from identification of values to actual instruction is a complex and scientific procedure, requiring proper staff organization followed by definite sequential steps. Let us examine a workable structure for curriculum development in a school district and then refer back to Figure 3 to trace the process of curriculum design.

ORGANIZING FOR EFFECTIVE CURRICULUM DEVELOPMENT

The basic administrative unit should be the district curriculum council or steering committee. All administrators with some responsibility for supervision of instruction are logically members, including the assistant superintendent in charge of instruction, the subject area curriculum coordinators, the coordinator of learning resources, and principals. In very

[4]Robert S. Fox, "Curriculum Development with a Purpose," *Theory Into Practice*, I, No. 4 (1962), 204.

large districts not all administrators and supervisory personnel will be able to serve on the curriculum council. However, each group should be adequately represented. The chief school administrator will meet with the council on occasion. Also, it is imperative that teachers representing all levels of instruction are members of the district curriculum council. (See Chapter 4 for a detailed description of the responsibilities of the various professional personnel listed above.) In addition, a school psychologist, the director of guidance services, and the librarian in charge of the professional collection can be valuable members of this council.

The district curriculum council's main responsibility is to coordinate all curriculum and instructional programs in the district, and to recommend basic policy changes to the chief school administrator. The council also organizes, under direction of the assistant superintendent in charge of instruction, the various subject area committees which carry out the continuing work in curriculum evaluation and change.

District-wide subject area curriculum committees are the key to effective curriculum development. They should be chaired by the subject area

FIGURE 4. Curriculum Advisory Committee at work. (Radnor Township Schools, Wayne, Pa.)

curriculum coordinator (see Chapter 4 for job description) and should include in their membership teachers from all levels, a principal, the coordinator of learning resources, and the assistant superintendent in charge of instruction. If they are really expected to function in a meaningful way, these committees need time during the school day and year to work. Key personnel need to be employed for continuing curriculum work during the summer, and adequate professional resource materials must be available. For example, a subject area committee studying newer objectives and courses in mathematics cannot proceed very far unless the dozen or so major programs currently used in the field are available for analysis. Finally, expert resource consultant help is required at key points throughout the process of curriculum evaluation and design. The math committee needs to have available the services of a top-level consultant to help analyze, for example, the common elements of content found in the major math programs on the market. Then the committee will be in a position to adopt, adapt, or re-write a curriculum.

THE PROCESS OF CURRICULUM DESIGN

It is the responsibility of the district curriculum council under the leadership of the assistant superintendent in charge of instruction to initiate or maintain action on the broad front of curricular change. Only this group can keep in focus the various forces that tend to affect the curriculum in a school district. The curriculum council is charged, therefore, with the task of maintaining balance in the instructional program, through constant review of priorities.

As depicted in Figure 3, the initial concern is identification of values, which are basic determinants of the remainder of the process. The curriculum council, the administrative staff, and ultimately the board of education, need to agree on those individual and societal values that the school feels committed to uphold through the learning experiences made available to the students. Such value determination will then lead to a statement or re-statement of the philosophy of the school district—the fundamental concerns that should occupy the attention of the teaching and administrative staff and the learners.

The specific goals which the school aims to attain are then derived from the statement of philosophy, and these become the objectives. At this point many schools publish the philosophy and objectives in the faculty handbook, file them mentally away, and get on with the "real business" of curriculum making. This is a fatal step, and if taken, can doom the entire project. To be meaningful, objectives must be refined further until they can be stated as *learning or behavioral outcomes*. Only when the curriculum worker indicates how the behavior of a learner will be changed in the accomplishment of a certain objective does the process of goal identification take on real meaning.

REQUIRED READING

Robert F. Mager, *Preparing Instructional Objectives* (Palo Alto, Calif.: Fearon Publishers, 1962).
Taxonomy of Educational Objectives, The Classification of Educational Goals (New York: David McKay Co., Inc., 1956–1964), Handbook I: *Cognitive Domain*, and Handbook II: *Affective Domain*.

Careful specification of the general educational objectives for the school system in terms of learning outcomes will lead the curriculum council (see Figure 3) to three major sources of curriculum content: learning and growth processes, and the resulting needs of each learner; social needs, or the demands of society on the school; and the sum total of man's organized knowledge. At this point the curriculum council should be able to identify the major categories or organizing points around which the curriculum can be built. Historically, we have organized by discipline: history, mathematics, physics, theology, and music, for example. But what about cybernetics, sex education, and biochemistry? Do they deserve a place in the already cluttered elementary and secondary school curriculum? The district curriculum council is the logical group to consider these fundamental questions and to identify or revise the basic sets of learning experiences to be offered by the school. By referring again to Figure 3 the reader will see that the process outlined above leads to *plans for curriculum organization,* or subject areas to be taught in the school system. These become the basic groupings of curriculum content.

The subject area curriculum committee now picks up the process of curriculum development, and begins to consider objectives for the subject field. In its first few meetings the science committee, for example, identifies goals for the total curriculum, elementary and secondary. This process leads to the organization of content for the various levels of instruction. The result at the upper secondary level may be a decision to organize an interdisciplinary seminar and laboratory course to enable advanced students to explore the interrelationships that are being discovered among the traditional disciplines of chemistry, physics, and biology.

Considerable work then is necessary to specify instructional objectives in behavioral or performance terms. According to Robert F. Mager,

> An objective is an *intent* communicated by a statement describing a proposed change in a learner—a statement of what the learner is to be like when he has successfully completed a learning experience. It is a description of a pattern of behavior (performance) we want the learner to be able to demonstrate.
>
> When clearly defined goals are lacking, it is impossible to evaluate a course or program efficiently, and there is no sound basis for selecting appropriate materials, content, or instructional methods.[5]

In his book, which should be in the hands of all curriculum workers, Mager describes how to write objectives that will explain the desired terminal behavior of the learner:

> *First,* identify the terminal behavior by name; you can specify the kind of

---

[5]Robert F. Mager, *Preparing Instructional Objectives* (Palo Alto, Calif.: Fearon Publishers, 1962), p. 3.

behavior that will be accepted as evidence that the learner has achieved the objective.

Second, try to define the desired behavior further by describing the important conditions under which the behavior will be expected to occur.

Third, specify the criteria of acceptable performance by describing how well the learner must perform to be considered acceptable.[6]

As the subject area curriculum committee develops the behavioral objectives and subsequent learning sequences for the various units of content to be taught, the members must certainly be aware of the voluminous research in learning[7] which points to one significant conclusion: *True learning involves much more than the simple acquisition of factual knowledge.* In fact the modern curriculum worker who would adopt such a narrow definition of learning is lost before he starts. He would be immediately inundated with the exploding mass of new facts in any subject area, which could not possibly be taught even if the entire school day were devoted to the single discipline in question.

Real learning involves the processes of inquiry and discovery, where the student is led to explore, to experiment, to question, to debate. In building any curriculum sequence, it is imperative to include opportunities for observation, reflection, and problem solving. Learners become more self-motivated as they discover opportunities to form their own concepts, generalizations and insights; and as they are led to relate new ideas to old ones in the constant search for meaningful identity as human beings. This is the stuff that real learning is made of—not the dull routine of recitation, memorization, and repetition that so often marked the drive for excellence in American schools of the 1950s and 1960s. Thousands of students never tasted the thrill of learning for its own sake, and dropped out along the way. Countless other thousands discovered how to "beat the system" and stuck it out until graduation. No such sterile curriculum will suffice for the 1970s and 1980s. In an age of space exploration, color television, and globe-girdling jets, the curriculum must be as exciting as the world of the learner.

THE ROLE OF MEDIA AND METHOD

It is important to emphasize again that *only at this point in the process of curriculum development are we prepared to consider instructional*

---

[6]*Ibid.,* p. 12.

[7]Ronald C. Doll, *Curriculum Improvement: Decision-Making and Process* (Boston: Allyn and Bacon, Inc., 1964), Chap. 2.

John D. McNeil, *Curriculum Administration, Principles and Techniques of Curriculum Development* (New York: The Macmillan Company, 1965), Chap. 1.

Percival M. Symonds, *What Education Has to Learn from Psychology* (New York: Teachers College Press, Teachers College, Columbia University, 1964).

Goodwin Watson, *What Psychology Can We Trust?* (New York: Teachers College Press, Teachers College, Columbia University, 1961).

materials and teaching methods. It is imperative that learning resources and techniques of instruction be designed to aid in accomplishing the objectives of the learning sequence. For instance, even the best documentary film on Adolf Hitler and the Third Reich must be related to the behavioral outcomes and content of the appropriate unit in modern world history before the film becomes relevant as a learning resource.

Also, modern concepts of the nature of the learning process, which were capsulated in the preceding discussion, require considerable imagination and flexibility in the use of instructional materials and methods (1) For example, if students are really to have the opportunity to inquire, to exchange ideas with their teacher and with each other, and to debate various issues, there must be ample opportunity for confrontation in small groups of ten to fifteen. Perhaps the only learning aid required here would be a chalkboard. The method obviously is group discussion. (2) To meet other learning objectives students can study on their own in carrels, using materials previously prepared and stored electronically. In this way true individualization of the learning process can be achieved. (3) The two preceding methods can often be supplemented by large-group instruction, where major concepts introducing a unit of instruction can be presented to several hundred learners at one time. Through the selective use of overhead transparencies, 16mm film clips, closed circuit television, and various student response systems, a skilled lecturer can effectively teach 200 students instead of the 40 he might have in a regular classroom.

IDENTIFYING SOURCES OF MEDIA FOR INSTRUCTION

Keeping pace with the knowledge explosion is the fantastic proliferation of educational media, which at the same time widens and complicates the choices available to educators concerned with relating media to curriculum and instruction.

As Carlson and Tillman have stated:

The teacher is challenged constantly to choose materials that will
*provide open rather than closed experiences
*encourage rather than stifle creativity
*stimulate original rather than uniform responses
*provide variety and balance rather than excessive use of a single material
*establish personal rather than impersonal relationships.[8]

The district coordinator of learning resources is the local expert in identifying and cataloging various sources of media. The subject area

[8] Mildred A. Carlson and Rodney Tillman, "Selection and Evaluation of Learning Materials," *Childhood Education*, XLIII, No. 5 (1967), 270.

curriculum coordinators (Chapter 4) are quite knowledgeable in their own fields, and will always work cooperatively with the learning resources specialist to make sure that all possible choices of instructional media are available for study or preview. Decisions on the selection, production, and use of learning resources are the joint concern of the subject area curriculum committees, the assistant superintendent in charge of instruction, the coordinator of learning resources, the subject area curriculum coordinators, and the teachers.

Usually, basic decisions on appropriate learning resources are made as part of the total process of curriculum development, which is briefly described earlier in this chapter. Therefore it is imperative that an up-to-date inventory of the sources of media be readily available. Furthermore, since the final determination of day-to-day media use is ideally made by the teacher, such complete sources must be accessible to each classroom or learning center. For example, the secondary social sciences teacher needs to know the content and availability of pertinent videotapes and motion picture films about the United Nations, if the world organization is a part of his curriculum.

Following is a list of major sources of learning resource information.

*Educational Products Information Exchange (EPIE), 527 Lexington Avenue, New York, N.Y. 10017. An independent, non-governmental, non-industry source of information regarding the availability and performance of instructional materials and equipment. The EPIE Institute publishes *The EPIE Forum,* a product information service which is issued nine times yearly from September through May.

*National Information Center for Educational Media, McGraw-Hill Films, 330 West 42nd Street, New York, N.Y. 10036. Center established in 1967 at the University of Southern California to research new methods of automated cataloging and to compile information about instructional materials, to be stored in a master computer file.

Two publications available, $29.50 each: *Index to 16mm Educational Films,* and *Index to 35mm Educational Filmstrips.* Order from McGraw-Hill Films.

*Educators' Progress Service, Randolph, Wisconsin. Annually revised guides to a variety of instructional materials: *Educators' Guide to Free Films,* $9.50; *Educators' Guide to Free Film Strips,* $7.00; *Educators' Guide to Free Tapes, Scripts, and Transcriptions,* $6.75.

**New Educational Materials,* Citation Press, Scholastic Magazines, Inc., 904 Sylvan Ave., Englewood Cliffs, N.J. 07632, $2.75. A book which evaluates approximately 300 instructional aids and over 300 books in all major curriculum areas. Evaluations by teachers, librarians, administrators, and curriculum specialists.

**Free and Inexpensive Learning Materials,* Division of Surveys and Field Services, George Peabody College for Teachers, Nashville, Tennessee 37203, $3.00. Comprehensive listing of 3,500 different media items, arranged under 120 categories. Completely revised every two years. All entries evaluated by staff of Division of Surveys and Field Services. Indexed and cross-referenced.

Textbooks in Print, published annually by R. R. Bowker Co., New York, N.Y., $3.00. Listing of elementary and secondary textbooks, supplementary books, and professional texts, classified by subject. Other Bowker publications on encyclopedias and other reference works may be additional valuable sources.

Sources of Information on Educational Media, U.S. Department of Health, Education and Welfare, Office of Education. Available from Superintendent of Documents, U.S. Government Printing Office, Washington, D.C. 20402, $.20. A comprehensive little booklet listing many sources of motion pictures, film-strips, records, tapes, transcriptions, and audio-visual equipment. Also included are listings of selected catalogs of elementary and secondary school books; a selected list of journals concerned with educational media; a selected list of periodicals concerned with new educational media; sources of information re-garding the planning of facilities for use of new media; and selected summaries of research studies including new educational media. Somewhat dated but a good 20¢ worth!

The district coordinator of learning resources will usually have available the major learning resources periodicals and the catalogs of the publishers and producers of instructional materials. He will also have available the numerous specialized publications such as the *Source Directory of Prepared Transparencies*, by Graflex, Inc. and the DAVI *National Audio Tape Catalog*.

Teachers, coordinators, and supervisors should be encouraged to attend appropriate educational conferences where new media and learning aids are displayed. Visiting days are needed to provide opportunities for trips to outstanding learning resources centers in other school districts.

In summary, every effort should be expended to expose teachers, administrators, and subject area curriculum committees to all the pertinent learning resources that are available in the curriculum areas under study. Only then can intelligent decisions be made with regard to the most appropriate media for a particular learning sequence.

LEARNING RESOURCES AND THE INSTRUCTIONAL PROGRAM—SELECTION, USE, ADAPTATION, AND PRODUCTION

Employing the most effective learning resources and teaching methods to achieve the objectives of instruction is a real challenge to the educator. If one approaches the task in a businesslike manner, however, there is every reason to expect a successful venture. The basic question to be raised is a simple one: Which learning resources and accompanying teaching techniques will best enable the learner to attain the prescribed behavioral objectives?

CRITERIA FOR SELECTION, USE, ADAPTATION, AND PRODUCTION OF
INSTRUCTIONAL MEDIA

Integrating learning resources effectively into the instructional program requires a well-developed set of criteria. With the flood of materials on the market, it is essential to develop a careful plan for consideration of appropriate media. For example, there are many free "learning aids" that are pressed on school administrators by certain industrial and commercial interests; extremist groups; and many well-meaning, but partial, individuals and organizations. When definite policies have been adopted regarding the introduction of learning resources into the instructional program, then any requests for consideration of materials or media can be handled properly.

General statements of some school board policies may be found in *Instructional Materials, Selection Policies and Procedures*, California Association of School Librarians, Box 3231, Daly City, Calif. 94015, $1.50.

Suggested criteria for the integration of learning resources into the curriculum and instruction are as follows.

1. All media in any subject field should be reviewed by the subject area curriculum coordinator and his curriculum committee, as well as by the coordinator of learning resources. Thus any request from an individual or group to consider learning aids for the school program would be referred immediately to the appropriate subject area committee for study.

2. Learning experiences should be as real as possible. Students living in or near Philadelphia, for instance, should have opportunities to visit Independence Hall rather than merely reading about the events which happened there. Visits to a museum or planetarium, if there is one within reasonable distance, might be preferable to the use of more abstract learning modes back at school. Resource persons from the community can be employed very effectively in some learning situations. If there is no comprehensive list of community resources and persons, several schools can combine efforts to create one. It will be a most valuable aid in achieving some of the learning objectives.

3. What learning resources are actually available, given the realities of the budget, available staff, time for completion of the course of study, and other pertinent factors? By this stage, the various sources of media information listed earlier will have yielded their bounty, and the curriculum committee should have on hand for study various textbooks, supplementary books, academic games, films, tapes, and other possible resources to be considered.

4. Evaluation methods must be devised to enable the curriculum committee to compare available materials. An excellent guide for evaluation

and selection of instructional materials was developed by the Montgomery County Public Schools, Rockville, Maryland. Several of the basic principles from this manual are worth quoting:

*The most important objective in all evaluation procedures is to locate and make available for teachers and pupils the most suitable materials that can be found in the various subject areas.

*Materials should be evaluated by those who are to use them. Group evaluations are generally preferable to individual evaluations. Evaluations are best when they are based upon the actual experience of using the materials in a teaching-learning situation.

*Instructional materials should be considered in terms of the total curriculum and should be closely coordinated with curriculum revision to assure current and suitable materials.[9]

The Montgomery County guide includes separate criteria for the evaluation of books; films, filmstrips, slides and transparencies; tape and phonograph recordings; flat pictures; maps; charts; globes; workbooks; programmed materials and various items of instructional equipment.

Each of the evaluation guides lists questions in six basic categories:

  I. Is the material authentic?
 II. Is the material appropriate?
III. Will the material catch and hold the interest of the users?
 IV. Is the content of this material well organized and well balanced?
  V. Is the technical quality of this material acceptable?
 VI. Is the cost of this material justified?[10]

For the specific criteria that are listed under each of these major headings, the reader is directed to Appendix 1, where several of the Montgomery County criteria are presented in their entirety. Appendix 2 lists an elementary school textbook evaluation score card.

It is essential to successful selection and use of instructional materials that appropriate criteria for evaluation be available. Curriculum committees may prepare their own or take advantage of the work already accomplished by others. The process is highly subjective, and criteria lists serve only as guides, not "final examinations." Remember, careful study of the media, preferably involving student use, should always precede adoption.

An example in the economics field will serve to demonstrate the importance of careful evaluation. Several widely-used guides to free and inexpensive materials list publications of the Foundation for Economic Education, without much explanatory comment. In their book, *Overcharge,*

---

[9] *Review and Evaluation Procedures for Textbooks and Instructional Materials* (Rockville, Maryland: Montgomery County Public Schools, 1968), p. 1.
[10] *Ibid.,* pp. 16–17.

Montana Senator Lee Metcalf and his co-author, Vic Reinemer, make this statement about articles in the *Freeman*, the monthly magazine of the Foundation for Economic Education: "Recent *Freeman* articles call for repeal of the income tax, U.S. withdrawal from the United Nations, abolition of public post offices, public education, public roads and public power, and getting the government out of all business, even its own."[11]

"The teacher who orders literature from FEE is likely to receive material which has the blessings of the John Birch Society. More than half of the 80 books on FEE's literature list, 47 to be exact, are also on the John Birch Society's 'approved' list."[12]

5. Often it is necessary to adapt certain instructional materials for use. A portion of a book, filmstrip, or tape may be extracted, subject to copyright regulations, if the entire content is not deemed applicable to the instructional program. The same criteria for evaluation would apply. Indeed only after preview and study of the entire learning aid would it become apparent that only a part of the material might be sufficient to achieve one of the behavioral objectives.

6. How does the curriculum committee decide whether to *buy* or *lease* certain items of instructional equipment? This is a very pertinent question, considering the proliferation of expensive and sophisticated learning resources. To complicate matters further, many companies offer sales, lease, and lease-to-own contracts. To arrive at a sensible answer, the evaluators might consider the following criteria:

A. Estimate the useable life of the equipment, and figure repair and maintenance costs for each type of contract—sales, lease, or lease-to-own.
B. Try to estimate how fast the instructional area under question is changing. Will this particular learning aid be in use long enough to justify the initial cost? Is there a comparable resource that may achieve the instructional objective more economically?

   For example, a number of 8mm cartridge films, sound and silent, plugging into small rear screen projectors, might provide the same program that is also available on a much more expensive dial access system.
C. In the case of very expensive equipment in rapidly-changing fields—i.e. computers—the best decision usually is to lease. Otherwise vast sums of capital money can be tied up in obsolete gear.

7. When does it pay to produce instructional resources? The answer to this question depends on the availability of first-rate materials in the commercial and educational markets. For example, a great variety of beautiful color transparencies, with intricate overlays, can be purchased

---

[11]Lee Metcalf and Vic Reinemer, *Overcharge* (New York: David McKay Co., Inc., 1967), p. 182.
[12]*Ibid.*, p. 187.

from a number of sources. If the science committee can locate a set which meets the needs of a biology sequence, then it would be desirable to acquire the necessary transparencies. On some occasions, however, no suitable materials may be on the market. In this case, the only satisfactory solution lies in production at the local or regional level. (See Chapters 5 and 7 for additional discussion on production of learning resources.)

The importance of appropriate learning resources in successfully implementing the instructional program cannot be overestimated. Curriculum development, media, and instruction are inextricably related.

SUMMARY

In this fascinating world of new media, it is easy to conclude that the learning environment must be so much richer. However, the mere introduction of a variety of educational media is no guarantee of a sound instructional program. In the view of the authors, learning resources should be considered only within the total process of curriculum development and instruction. Consequently decisions regarding media are best made only after extensive progress in curriculum design.

We firmly believe that curriculum determination and/or design is the legitimate and necessary function of a strong, well-staffed local school district, using all available resources from the national, state, and regional levels. In organizing for effective curriculum development, the basic administrative unit should be the district curriculum council or steering committee. All administrators with some responsibility for supervision of instruction are logically members, except in very large districts. It is imperative that teachers are included in the membership of this council. The district curriculum council's main responsibility is to coordinate all curriculum and instructional programs in the district, and to recommend basic policy changes to the chief school administrator. The council also organizes, under direction of the assistant superintendent in charge of instruction, the various subject area committees which carry out the continuous work in curriculum evaluation and change.

In the process of curriculum design, the initial concern is identification of values, which are basic determinants of the remainder of the process. Next will come a statement or re-statement of the philosophy of the school district followed by specification of goals which the school aims to attain. These objectives must be refined further until they can be stated as learning or behavioral outcomes. Only when the curriculum worker indicates how the behavior of a learner will be changed in the accomplishment of a certain objective does the process of goal identification take on real meaning.

The curriculum council is now ready for consideration of three major sources of curriculum content: learning and growth processes, social needs, and the sum total of man's organized knowledge. The basic groupings of curriculum content, or the subject areas to be taught, are identified, revised, or refined.

At this point the subject area curriculum committee picks up the process of curriculum development by considering objectives for the subject field. This is followed by specification of instructional objectives in behavioral or performance terms. As the various learning sequences are then developed, the curriculum committee members become increasingly aware that modern learning must involve much more than the simple acquisition of factual knowledge. The processes of inquiry and discovery are vital, and opportunities to observe, reflect, and solve problems are needed in every curriculum sequence. Learners become more self-motivated as they begin to form their own concepts, generalizations, and insights, as they are taught to relate new ideas to old ones in the continuing search for meaningful identity as human beings. This is what real learning is made of—not the dull, monotonous routine of recitation and memorization which has characterized so many classrooms.

Only at this point in the process of curriculum development is the subject area committee ready to consider instructional materials and teaching methods. It is imperative that learning resources and techniques of instruction be designed to aid in accomplishing the objectives of the learning sequence. The district coordinator of learning resources works cooperatively with the subject area curriculum coordinators and the curriculum committees to insure effective selection, production, and use of appropriate instructional media for each developing learning sequence. Decisions regarding learning resources are then made as an integral part of the total process of curriculum development.

The district coordinator of learning resources is the local expert in identifying and cataloging various sources of media. He needs to expend every effort to see that teachers, administrators, and all other curriculum workers have available the choices among all pertinent learning resources. This requires an extensive program of acquiring source materials, specialized publications, and models for study and trial use. Also, professional personnel should be encouraged to attend conferences where new media and learning aids are displayed, and to visit outstanding learning resources centers.

Integrating learning resources effectively into the instructional program requires a well-developed set of criteria. For example, the subject area curriculum coordinator and his curriculum committee should be responsible for reviewing and evaluating all media in the specific subject field. Visits to historic places, museums, and other community resources must be evaluated against the less concrete learning modes employed in the school. Methods must be devised to enable the curriculum committee to compare available materials and experiences. The Montgomery County Public Schools, Rockville, Maryland, have developed an excellent guide for evaluation and selection of instructional materials. Curriculum committees may prepare their own criteria or use guides already prepared by other districts. The process is highly subjective, and criteria lists serve only as guides. Careful study of the media and other resources and experiences, preferably involving student participation, should always precede adoption. Special criteria have been developed to help educators decide whether to buy, lease, or produce certain items of instructional equipment and materials.

SUGGESTED ACTIVITIES AND PROBLEMS

1. Defend or refute the position that curriculum design is the legitimate and necessary function of the local school district.
2. Read *Preparing Instructional Objectives* by Robert F. Mager. (See *Selected Readings*.) Select a subject area and write a set of objectives for a learning sequence in that field.
3. Interview a school district coordinator of learning resources to determine how he keeps abreast of the new educational media. Write up your findings.
4. Develop an evaluation guide for a specific learning resource, such as a textbook, filmstrip, or audio tape.

SELECTED READINGS

Bloom, Benjamin S., ed., *Taxonomy of Educational Objectives*, Handbook I: *Cognitive Domain*. New York: David McKay Company, Inc., 1956.

Carlson, Mildred A., and Rodney Tillman, "Selection and Evaluation of Learning Materials," *Childhood Education*, XLIII, No. 5 (1967), 266–70.

Krathwohl, David R., Benjamin S. Bloom, and Bertram B. Masia, *Taxonomy of Educational Objectives*, Handbook II: *Affective Domain*. New York: David McKay Company, Inc., 1964.

Mager, Robert F., *Preparing Instructional Objectives*. Palo Alto, Calif.: Fearon Publishers, Inc., 1962.

Neagley, Ross L., and N. Dean Evans, *Handbook for Effective Curriculum Development*, Chaps. 6, 7, and 8. Englewood Cliffs, New Jersey: Prentice-Hall, Inc., 1967.

Saylor, J. Galen, and William M. Alexander, *Curriculum Planning for Modern Schools*. New York: Holt, Rinehart & Winston, Inc., 1966.

4

Organizing
the Staff for
Effective Administration
of Learning Resources

To meet the increasingly complex and varied learning needs of its students, a modern school system has to be well organized. This is particularly true of the learning resources program, which is such an integral part of the total process of curriculum development and instruction. Teachers and administrators who have a clear conception of their function in the whole educational program are better able to work toward the goal of providing the best learning experiences for each individual.

It is the purpose of this chapter to describe the roles of various professional personnel in organizing and administering an effective learning resources program for a school district. A total pupil enrollment of at least 6,000 is assumed, since it is doubtful that smaller systems can afford the administrative personnel and material resources necessary for a first-rate effort in curriculum development and instructional media.[1]

THE CHIEF SCHOOL ADMINISTRATOR

A dynamic, alert, intelligent superintendent of schools is the key to a successful learning resources program. Although he will have little time to participate directly in media selection, production, or use, his attitudes and actions in the top administrative post profoundly influence teaching methods and resources. The superintendent's obvious interest in the latest instructional innovation involving computers, for example, is bound to carry over to the other members of the administrative team. In all respects he sets the tone for district philosophy and practice.

SPECIFIC LEADERSHIP TASKS

The chief school administrator can direct the development of a sound learning resources program by demonstrating positive, democratic leadership in the following ways.

[1]C. O. Fitzwater, *School District Reorganization, Policies and Procedures*, U.S. Office of Education (Washington, D.C.: Government Printing Office, 1958), pp. 84, 87.

1. Analyze the budget to determine total funds expended for various instructional media in the several subject areas. Such a study should show differences in expenditures between elementary and secondary education, and between schools in the district. The superintendnt will then know exactly what his media dollars are buying.

2. Read as much as possible in the field and route pertinent articles and books to other members of the administrative staff. Keep up-to-date on new developments.

3. See that the agendas of the district administrative council or curriculum council provide for periodic discussions on learning resources.

4. Support budget requirements for various media recommended by the assistant superintendent in charge of instruction, and growing out of current curriculum studies in the district.

5. Work with other chief administrators and the local intermediate unit staff to provide or expand needed cooperative services in learning resources. All but the very largest districts will find it too expensive and impractical to purchase and distribute certain instructional materials at the school system level. (See Chapter 7.)

6. Visit innovative schools and learning resource centers at least two or three times a year. It is easy to get into a rut, and getting out of the office for such field trips is a healthy experience for any superintendent.

7. Spend considerable time in the schools, classrooms, and other learning centers of the district to observe the role of media in many teaching-learning situations. Confer with teachers, coordinators, and principals.

8. See that the board of education gets periodic reports on the learning resources program and its contribution to the fulfillment of curriculum objectives. Invite key personnel such as the coordinator of learning resources to make visual presentations to the board on occasion.

9. Make sure that professional contracts provide released time for participation of all staff members in the program of curriculum development, including selection of appropriate instructional media.

In summary, the chief administrator's main task is to provide top-level support for the learning resources program. This is evidenced by his enthusiasm, his expanding knowledge of the field, and by his coordination of all curriculum activities in the school district. His most important personnel decision concerns the administrator to whom he delegates the responsibility and authority for the development of the curriculum and supporting media.

THE ASSISTANT SUPERINTENDENT IN CHARGE OF INSTRUCTION

As shown in Figure 5, the assistant superintendent in charge of instruction is a key figure in the administration of the learning resources program. Indeed, his responsibilities encompass supervision and coordina-

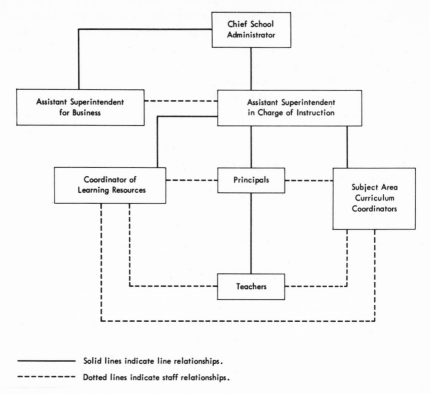

Solid lines indicate line relationships.

- - - - - - - - Dotted lines indicate staff relationships.

FIGURE 5.   Organization for administration of learning resources.

tion of the entire instructional process in the school system, including curriculum development. He is a line officer to whom the principals, curriculum coordinators, and the coordinator of learning resources report. In every sense this assistant superintendent is the team leader for instruction. The comprehensive job analysis for this position has been detailed in other works.[2] The following discussion will concentrate on the principal responsibilities of this administrator in the field of learning resources.

SPECIFIC LEADERSHIP TASKS

The assistant superintendent in charge of instruction directs the development of the instructional media program in the following ways:

1. He keeps up-to-date on the latest research and technical develop-

2Ross L. Neagley and N. Dean Evans, *Handbook for Effective Supervision of Instruction* (Englewood Cliffs, N.J.: Prentice-Hall, Inc., 1964), pp. 76–80; and *Handbook for Effective Curriculum Development* (Englewood Cliffs, N.J.: Prentice-Hall, Inc., 1967), pp. 133–34.

ments in the field of learning resources. The assistant superintendent will rely primarily on the coordinator of learning resources and the curriculum coordinators to discuss with him new trends and experiments in such fields as dial access retrieval and programmed instruction by computer. But he must include in his professional reading enough articles and books in the media field so that he is conversant with current streams of thought and action. This will require the scheduling of certain definite working hours for reading, study, and personal "hands-on" testing of new learning aids.

2. As the leader of the instructional team, the assistant superintendent in charge of instruction meets regularly with all of those administrators who report directly to him: the coordinator of learning resources, the principals, and the subject area curriculum coordinators. (See Figure 5.) This group forms the nucleus of the district curriculum council, which makes all major decisions regarding the instructional program and its supporting media. Such a council should meet weekly or biweekly depending on the stage of curriculum development in the district. It is suggested that an entire morning be set aside for in-depth discussion on such matters as the proposed experimental introduction of computer-assisted instruction, or the development of an interdisciplinary high school science course. Normally, the subject area coordinators will present recommendations from their committees for consideration by the curriculum council, but the floor should always be open for free-wheeling, brainstorming discussions on the state of the learning resources program in the district, and its obvious relationship to the developing curriculum and the instructional program.

The assistant superintendent may be the catalytic agent in this council of key instructional leaders. Indeed, to be successful in his major leadership role, he must rise to the challenge of coordinating the dynamic, democratic group action that will emerge from such a group.

3. The assistant superintendent in charge of instruction delegates considerable responsibility and authority to the coordinator of learning resources, and expects him to work cooperatively with the principals and subject area curriculum coordinators in exploring new thrusts or changes in instructional aids. In the media field, the coordinator of learning resources is obviously the right arm of the assistant superintendent, who relies heavily on him for guidance in making the ultimate decisions regarding introduction or modification of media systems and resources in the district. (See Chapter 5 for discussion of the roles of the coordinator of learning resources and other media personnel.)

Consequently there should be a close, almost daily contact between these two administrators, with many informal discussions on such topics as new library acquisitions, the place of filmstrips in instruction, and whether the district should join the new county or regional instructional materials center. (See Chapter 7.)

4. The assistant superintendent spends at least two days a week in the schools talking with principals, curriculum coordinators, and teachers, and participating in the instructional program as an observer and resource person. There is no substitute for active involvement in the learning experiences of students; an office-bound administrator soon loses touch with the realities of teacher-student interaction.

5. The subject area curriculum coordinators work closely with the assistant superintendent, keeping him informed of the evolving instructional program in their various fields. He sits as a participant, whenever possible, with the subject area committees, and knows the current status of each curriculum study. He also lends his own resource assistance to the deliberations.

6. The assistant superintendent in charge of instruction keeps the chief school administrator informed on all major instructional projects, especially possible changes or experiments being considered by the subject area committees or the curriculum council. This is particularly important if there are budget considerations involved, for instance, in the introduction of new educational technology. The superintendent should never be surprised by a question like this after a rotary club speech: "Dr. Brown, what's this we hear about the school district contemplating the purchase of a computer to teach the kids to read?" If the assistant superintendent is doing his job in this respect, the chief administrator will always be fully informed.

7. After full deliberation by the subject area committees and the curriculum council, and after recommendations by the coordinator of learning resources, the assistant superintendent will need to make some final decisions regarding curriculum, instruction, and learning resources for the next budget year. For example, if there is a strong recommendation that comprehensive sex education course sequences be developed and supported by instructional materials, how much will all of this cost? And must this need be weighed against others of equal or greater importance? At this point, after due consultation with his subordinates, the assistant superintendent prepares his budget recommendations for the superintendent.

8. Beyond the school district, the assistant superintendent in charge of instruction has a major responsibility, with the coordinator of learning resources, for determining the extent of district participation in county, regional, state, and federal programs for learning resources. While Chapters 7 and 8 discuss these areas in detail, it is important to note here that the assistant superintendent should have an excellent

working relationship with the county superintendent's office or intermediate unit, especially if a cooperative regional instructional materials
center is operating or planned.

In some larger school districts positions such as coordinator of elementary or secondary education are found. Usually these administrators
report directly to the assistant superintendent in charge of instruction,
serving as his assistant administrators for elementary or secondary education. They are therefore delegated certain responsibilities in the learning
resources program by him.

THE ASSISTANT SUPERINTENDENT FOR BUSINESS

As seen in Figure 5, the business office is subordinate to the chief school
administrator, and the assistant superintendent for business works in a
staff relationship with the assistant superintendent in charge of instruction on matters pertaining to budgeting, purchasing, and other items
involving finance. Optimum administrative organization suggests a superintendent's cabinet or administrative council which would include all
second echelon personnel. The developing school district budget is the
joint concern of these administrators.

With regard to learning resources, the assistant superintendent for
business participates in major budget conferences. He meets regularly
with the other top administrators, both in cabinet and individually. He
keeps himself informed on the changing learning resources field, mainly
through his contacts with the assistant superintendent in charge of
instruction.

Since the media budget is inextricably tied to the developing curriculum and the objectives of the entire instructional program, the major
decisions regarding proposed expenditures should be based on curricular
needs. The business administrator, therefore, should not oppose a budget
item simply because of its cost. The financial requirements for media
naturally grow out of the professional decisions made in the curriculum
council, and in the offices of the assistant superintendent in charge of
instruction. The assistant superintendent for business can play a valuable
role in citing figures and percentages from the current budget, in presenting cost analyses, and in summarizing other financial data that may
be required. In no district, however, should he have sole decision-making
power over line items, especially in the instructional areas. In summary,
his function in the budget-making process for curriculum and learning
resources is supportive and advisory.

Once the district budget is adopted, the business administrator has the
important job of purchasing materials and services. Here again he relies
on the professional judgment of those competent in instruction to pre-

pare the specifications for filmstrip projectors, dial access equipment, or new library books. He then orders the recommended learning resources, within the various budget categories.

The assistant superintendent for business then supplies each administrator and coordinator with a monthly budget analysis, showing expenditures in each category to date. It is his job at this point to inform individuals and departments of their spending rate. For example, assume that the high school library is allocated a budget of $80,000 for new acquisitions, and spends $74,000 in the first seven months of the budget year. It is the responsibility of the business administrator to inform the librarian that there is a $6,000 balance in that category for the remaining five months.

There should always be a contingency item in the learning resources budget to allow for unanticipated needs by teachers, librarians, and media personnel. Even with careful budget preparation, the rapidly-changing media field demands some flexibility in budgeting. Teachers and learning resources personnel are unable to completely assess the learning needs of next year's pupils when they participate in the budget-making process. Decisions regarding the re-allocation of contingency funds will be made mainly by the assistant superintendent in charge of instruction, the coordinator of learning resources, and other concerned coordinators and teachers. After formal action by the school board authorizing such transfers, the assistant superintendent for business will then increase the appropriate account accordingly, and administer expenditures in the prescribed manner. (See Chapter 8.)

THE SUBJECT AREA CURRICULUM COORDINATOR

Filling a relatively new position in many school districts, and still unheard of in others, the subject area coordinator is rapidly becoming a key figure in the organizational structure of school districts that really believe in sound curriculum development. With the explosion of research studies, national and regional curriculum projects, and the almost daily increase of available learning resources in every subject field, it is impossible for generalists like the assistant superintendent in charge of instruction or the coordinator of elementary education to keep fully abreast of the progress in every discipline or subject area. Consequently the position of subject area curriculum coordinator is emerging. The following paragraphs examine the nature and responsibilities of this position, and then focus on the implications for learning resources.[3]

As can be noted in Figure 5, the subject area coordinator reports

[3]Neagley and Evans, *Handbook for Effective Curriculum Development*, pp. 137–41.

directly to the assistant superintendent in charge of instruction. He works cooperatively in a staff relationship with principals, teachers, and the coordinator of learning resources. Basically, the subject area curriculum coordinator is the local expert in his field. He usually will be an experienced master teacher with an advanced degree in his major. He is expected to possess up-to-date and increasing knowledge of the latest research and experimentation in his subject field, and to be fully informed on the various pertinent national, state, and regional studies.

This curriculum coordinator's role has grown from that of the old high school department head, and in advancing districts is now a full-time position, with responsibilities for the elementary and secondary curriculum. In smaller school systems and in those just inaugurating the concept, the newly-appointed coordinator is often released half-time from teaching.

SPECIFIC LEADERSHIP TASKS

The main functions of the typical subject area curriculum coordinator which pertain to learning resources can be described as follows:

1. He serves as chairman of the district-wide curriculum committee in his field. This group, composed of teachers, a principal, the coordinator of learning resources, and the assistant superintendent in charge of instruction, continually evaluates and revises the curriculum. For example, the science committee would be responsible for examining the philosophy, objectives, content, teaching methods, and learning resources for the elementary-secondary science curriculum. Articulation, individualization of instruction, consideration of a new film series—all of these would be likely topics for discussion and action. This committee would ultimately decide on the instructional resources to be recommended for a particular learning sequence, but only after many other preceding steps in the process of curriculum development. (See Chapter 3.)

2. The subject area coordinator meets often with the coordinator of learning resources to make sure that he is up-to-date on the latest media in his field. For example, the language arts coordinator would want to know about the new filmstrips in linguistics, the latest video-tape series on great English poets, and the experimental computer program in beginning reading. One of these might ultimately be considered by the language arts committee, and the coordinator must be completely knowledgeable about all of them and others that continually come down the pike.

3. He regularly visits schools and classrooms to observe, participate, and confer. By knowing teachers and principals well, the subject coordinator is in a better position to evaluate cooperatively the learning resources now in use.

4. The subject area curriculum coordinator keeps his superior, the assistant superintendent in charge of instruction, fully informed on the latest curricular trends in his particular field and is a constant resource regarding the feasibility of using various instructional media. The assistant superintendent, for example, may call on the mathematics coordinator to give him an up-to-date review of the major nationally-known math projects and the learning resources developed for each.

THE PRINCIPAL

The best instructional program is only as good as the schools in which it is implemented. And, by many measures, a school is only as good as its principal. As the educational leader of his faculty, the principal sets the tone for the entire educational process. His enthusiasm for excellence in teaching and learning is infectious. As he visits the classrooms and other learning centers of his school, he observes the curriculum and learning resources in action. He works with individual teachers, and he works with the entire staff, helping them to become a team. If the principal is really sincere and concerned about good instruction, most of the faculty will join him in the effort to provide it.

In many ways the principal has one of the most difficult and demanding jobs in the school district. He is called to be a first-rate administrator and supervisor of instruction. Among other things, he must be talented in plant management, public relations, cafeteria operation, psychology, curriculum theory, and personnel administration. As a phase of his leadership in improving instruction, he has an important role in the development of effective learning resources.

SPECIFIC LEADERSHIP TASKS

The principal assists in the administration of the learning resources program in several significant ways.

1. Within the framework of cooperatively-developed district curriculum guides, he encourages his staff members to experiment with new media that show promise in realizing the stated goals of instruction. If a teacher discovers through her professional reading a promising single concept 8mm film presentation on cell growth, the wise principal, after conferring with the science curriculum coordinator, will encourage use of the film in the teacher's biology unit. If the experimental use is successful, the teacher may be asked to discuss the film with the science curriculum committee, with a view toward further use in the district and possible addition to the particular unit's resource list.

2. The principal serves as a member of the district curriculum council

and is able to present his own views on learning resources, as well as reflecting the ideas of his staff. From his classroom visits and other supervisory activities, the principal brings a wealth of helpful data to any problem on the council agenda.

3. He confers on a regular basis with the coordinator of learning resources and the subject area curriculum coordinators to deepen his own understanding of instructional media and their relationship to the evolving curriculum.

4. While his desk is usually piled higher with unread periodicals than those of other administrators, the principal tries to keep himself generally abreast of new developments in learning resources through his professional reading.

5. At the request of the assistant superintendent in charge of instruction and the subject area curriculum coordinators, the principal recommends master teachers to serve on various curriculum committees and to participate in extra-contractual summer work. The principal is best qualified to know the strengths of his own staff members.

6. The principal plans faculty meetings around curricular themes that seem to grow out of the deep concerns of his staff. He handles many of the routine items by bulletin so that faculty time may be devoted to the discussion of such topics as: "The computer and instruction"; "What happened to programmed learning?"; "Can instructional television help us do a better job?"; "Anyone for wet carrels in the classroom?" While not guaranteed to keep a tired teacher alert after 4:00 P.M., such topics will provide livelier discussion than "Improving playground supervision." The principal, of course, invites his fellow coordinators and administrators to certain meetings as resource persons.

7. Principals should visit each other's schools often and have lunch with one another occasionally, just to explore common goals, aspirations, and problems, without emphasizing the latter. They should also visit exemplary schools to get ideas for improving their own curriculum and learning resources.

THE TEACHER

The role of the teacher is changing rapidly from that of dispenser of information to that of learning guide. Some of the newer technology is bringing closer the day when the one-to-one relationship between teacher and learner can be realized for at least part of the school day. In many places the classroom itself is disappearing in favor of a number of smaller learning spaces, housing from one to fifteen students at a time for various purposes. There is no doubt that the media revolution is having its most profound effect on the crucible of the curriculum—the classroom, or learning center. And the teacher, of course, stands at the forge.

The ways in which teachers perceive the learning process and the relationship of the new media to it will have profound effects on tomorrow's pupils—what they learn and how well they learn it. By and large the teaching profession seems to have survived the first shock waves of instructional television, programmed learning, and other electronic threats. It is clear by now that technology will not replace the teacher but enable him to do a much better job of teaching than he has ever been able to do in the past. This is true in part because many of the routine information-giving aspects of the teaching-learning process can be presented via programmed texts, computers, and video tapes that can be retrieved on call by dial access equipment. All of this technology, and much more, frees the teacher for the person-to-person confrontation that is the essence of the learning process. Teachers and students can interact, question one another, debate, and exchange ideas as they never could before with a one to thirty teacher-pupil ratio.

And so the teacher of today and tomorrow is very much involved in the whole spectrum of learning resources. Participating as he should in the entire process of curriculum development, he has an opportunity to select from an ever-growing inventory of instructional media to help him achieve the goals of a unit or course of study. And he has a further opportunity to participate in the production of certain learning aids, working in cooperation with media specialists, programmers, and other technicians.

By forming a working relationship with the administrators and coordinators whose roles were outlined earlier in this chapter, the teacher has a unique opportunity to participate in that most exciting of enterprises —the development of curricula and supporting media for the better education of the student.

SUMMARY

A school district must be well organized to administer effectively a program of learning resources. Teachers, coordinators, and administrators need to have a clear conception of their function in the entire educational process, including curriculum development.

A dynamic, alert *superintendent of schools* is the key to a successful learning resources program. While he will have little time to participate in the actual media selection, production, or use, his attitudes and actions profoundly influence the other members of the staff.

The *assistant superintendent in charge of instruction* is also an important figure in the administration of the learning resources program. He is a line officer, to whom the principals, the curriculum coordinators, and the coordinator of learning resources report. He is the team leader for instruction and therefore sets the tone for curriculum development. He coordinates the whole instructional media program through cooperative action with other administrators and coordinators.

The *assistant superintendent for business* participates in major budget conferences involving instruction. Decisions on proposed expenditures for learning resources are based on curricular needs. This administrator serves as an advisor on the instructional budget. His main function, after budget approval, is control of expenditures within limits adopted.

The *subject area curriculum coordinator*, while new in many school districts, is rapidly becoming an important person in the organizational structure of districts that believe in sound curriculum development. The subject area coordinator is the local expert in one particular discipline or field of study. He works cooperatively with principals, teachers, and the coordinator of learning resources and reports to the assistant superintendent in charge of instruction. The subject area coordinator works at the elementary and secondary school levels and chairs the district-wide curriculum committee in his field.

The *principal* has one of the most difficult and demanding jobs in the school district. He is expected to be a first-rate administrator and supervisor of instruction. In the field of learning resources, he encourages his teachers to experiment with new media, to participate in the work of district-wide curriculum committees, and to help plan faculty meetings on topics pertaining to the curriculum and learning resources. The principal serves on the district curriculum council and works in a staff relationship with his fellow principals, the coordinator of learning resources, and the subject area curriculum coordinators.

The role of the *teacher* is changing rapidly. Technology and other media will enable the teacher to do a much better job in guiding the learning process. Many of the routine information-giving aspects of the teaching-learning process can be presented via programmed texts, computers, and video-tapes. This frees the teacher for the person-to-person confrontation that is the essence of the learning process. The modern teacher is very much involved in curriculum development, and in the selection and production of varied learning resources.

SUGGESTED ACTIVITIES AND PROBLEMS

1. Interview an assistant superintendent in charge of instruction to ascertain his leadership role in the learning resources program. Write an analysis of the position, including his relationships to other staff members.

2. Discuss the authors' point of view regarding the assistant superintendent for business with an administrator currently employed in this position in a school district. How does he view his role in the media program? Evaluate both the authors' and the assistant superintendent's conclusions.
3. Locate a full-time subject area curriculum coordinator in a school system enrolling at least 6,000 pupils. Interview him to determine his conception of the job. What are his major responsibilities? With whom does he work, and in what capacity? In your written summary be specific regarding his contributions to the learning resources program.
4. Interview a principal and one of his teachers. Get their individual points of view regarding the involvement of teachers in the media program. Do all staff members participate in curriculum development and selection of learning resources? Compare the results of both conferences.

SELECTED READINGS

Conner, Forrest E., and William J. Ellena, eds., *Curriculum Handbook for School Administrators*, Chap. 15. Washington, D.C.: American Association of School Administrators, 1967.

Jenson, Theodore J., James B. Burr, William H. Coffield, and Ross L. Neagley, *Elementary School Administration* (2nd ed.), Chaps. 1, 4, and 5. Boston: Allyn and Bacon, Inc., 1967.

Joyce, Bruce R., *The Teacher and His Staff: Man, Media, and Machines*. Washington, D.C.: National Commission on Teacher Education and Professional Standards and Center for the Study of Instruction, National Education Association of the United States, 1967.

Neagley, Ross L., and N. Dean Evans, *Handbook for Effective Curriculum Development*, Chaps. 5 and 8. Englewood Cliffs, N.J.: Prentice-Hall, Inc., 1967.

——, *Handbook for Effective Supervision of Instruction*, Chaps. 5, 6, and 11. Englewood Cliffs, N.J.: Prentice-Hall, Inc., 1964.

5

Learning Resources and

the Educational Process

As a school administrator you will be constantly bombarded with requests from your faculty for new films, tapes, programmed instruction materials, textbooks, and transparencies. Your library will need more books, periodicals, micro-films, seating, stacks, and personnel. The audio-visual department will ask for more 16mm projectors, screens, 8mm single concept projectors, programmed instruction devices, tape recorders, record players, and darkening facilities for the classrooms. Then there are the myriad salesmen beating down your door, trying to explain how their product or equipment can make learning more vital, or solve the problems of teacher shortages and curriculum development. You will sometimes ask yourself, "Whatever happened to the good old days when the teacher ordered a textbook, some paper and chalk, and that was all she needed to teach?" Just what has happened to the field of education?

Like the society around it, education is faced with a rapidly expanding technological explosion. Business and industry have surrounded themselves with automated storage and retrieval systems, developed individualized manpower training programs, and rapid communications systems.

With the passage of the National Defense Education Act (NDEA), the Elementary Secondary Education Act (ESEA), and other legislative programs supporting education by the Federal and State Governments, the various curriculum groups across the country began to organize and develop their own teaching-learning programs. Soon schools began to get new programs in physics, mathematics, chemistry, history, English, reading, biology—each with related instructional materials as a necessary part of the curriculum.

As the various curriculums became standardized across the country, the leaders in the communications industry, particularly those in the area of information storage and retrieval, began to realize (at almost the same time, incidentally, as educators) that the traditional methods of teaching would no longer be adequate in meeting the rapidly enlarging needs of society. Thus the "education-business" partnership was born, and with it the technological revolution in the schools. Suddenly schools were confronted with computers, dial access systems, computer assisted instruction, television programming, programmed instruction, and complete courses on film.

Obviously, all the furor over technology and education did not occur overnight. Industry and the military spent years in research to determine the role technology could play in instructional programs (manpower training), management, and communications. But the schools, caught between the need for additional facilities to meet the tremendous increase in the number of pupils and the "knowledge explosion" created by a rapidly advancing technology, decided that the two problems were not interrelated and began to build. Large sums of money were allocated for construction, while little or no funds were appropriated to keep abreast of constantly changing curriculums and teaching methods.

One of the outcomes of this decision has been the creation of a "technological gap." The school of tomorrow must overcome this gap, but in order to do so the school administrator must first be willing to admit that:

*Present instructional programs are inadequate to meet certain obvious needs of students who will grow up and work in the world of the . . . [future].

*A new technology for instruction has been developed and proved through basic research and practice. This development has now reached a level that will permit rapid expansion of application and of further innovation.

*The new educational technology is capable of meeting and solving certain of the schools' major problems in instruction, organization, and administration.

*Application of the new technology will result in major changes affecting the administration, organization, and physical facilities of the public schools.

*Methods of instruction will be modified to a major degree, particularly in the presentation of information.

*Teachers and learners will have new roles and changed activities as a result of this technological change.

*A new kind of professional will be required to provide leadership in design, implementation, and evaluation of programs of education which make the fullest use of new media. The functions performed by this leader and the resources he brings will be among the essential determinants of success or failure in tomorrow's schools.[1]

TEACHING, LEARNING, AND LEARNING RESOURCES

If present methods of instruction which have been used for many years are inadequate to meet the needs of students, how will the introduction

[1] Barry Morris, ed., "The Function of Media in the Public Schools" (A Task Force Position Paper), *Audiovisual Instruction*, VIII, No. 1 (1963), p. 11.

of new methods, technology, and learning resources into the program overcome this inadequacy? In order to determine the answer to this question, it will be necessary to examine both present and future methods of instruction.

With present methods of instruction the teacher meets with five or six groups of 30 to 40 students each day, presenting the same material to each group. This is a very inefficient utilization of the teacher's and the student's time, not to mention the fact that different groups of students may or may not receive the same instruction. Certainly the good teacher will be using a variety of instructional materials and methods during any one presentation, which will offer some modicum of uniformity. However, you are well aware that as the day grows longer the teacher and the student begin to take on different attitudes toward teaching and learning. At this time materials which may be very important to learning are glossed over lightly by the teacher, and thus simply become irrelevant to the student.

But even more important than this is the fact that in an era when a student can hear and see in his living room what is happening on the other side of the world, schools can no longer afford to have that same student listen to a teacher trying to describe verbally the same event.

The student of the future will be confronted with learning in a variety of places. As suggested in Chapter 3, learning at school will take place in large group assemblies, small group confrontations (seminars), and individual study carrels.

During the large group assembly the teacher will present a carefully prepared and rehearsed program based on one or more objectives of the unit being studied. The teacher will utilize a variety of materials including video-tapes, selected slides, recordings, transparencies, and films. At selected points during the program, the students will be required to respond to questions flashed on the screen. A computer will tabulate these responses and present the instructor with a list of students who answered correctly and a list of those who gave the wrong answer, and why. At this point the instructor can continue with his presentation or, if he feels that the class is not ready to continue, he can now branch to an alternate path presenting the material in a different format.

At the end of the large group assembly, the two hundred or more students will be given specific assignments relating to the presentation, which they will now study as individuals. These assignments may consist of a series of articles culled from various magazines, a chapter from a book, or a session in the individual study center where the student will dial a prepared program from his carrel.

After the student has completed these assignments, he will meet in a group of ten to fifteen with the teacher in a seminar room to discuss,

FIGURE 6. (*Above*) Dial access audio-visual student carrel, (*below*) dial access audio tape banks. (Courtesy RCA.)

inquire about, and debate the issues brought forth during the large group and individual study sessions. Once the teacher is satisfied that all pupils understand all issues and have met the established objectives, he will move on to the next unit of study.

The learning process thus becomes a program in which technology, resources, and the teacher are brought together, each functioning in what it can do best—technology taking over the chores of teaching, continuously evaluating individual students, and providing quick access to knowledge; learning resources bringing the world into the classroom, taking verbal abstractions and making them concrete; and the teacher leading and guiding students on an individual basis into hidden areas of knowledge.

Since all or most of the teachers in the school system will be utilizing the above methods in a variety of patterns, it becomes apparent that a vast number of instructional materials, some rather sophisticated hardware, and a new type of service organization will be required.

THE TOTAL LEARNING RESOURCES CENTER

Have you looked at a learning resources center lately? In many schools the learning resources center is two separate operations. First there is the library. Just what is happening in the school library? The books are stored neatly on its shelves; some students seem to be milling around looking for books; others are seated at tables writing reports. The librarian is cataloging some new acquisitions, or perhaps preparing a bibliography for a teacher.

Next, there is the audio-visual department. What is happening here? The films, filmstrips, and tapes are all stored neatly on the shelves; some students are looking at a filmstrip over there in a corner. The AV director is cataloging some new films, or perhaps preparing a transparency for a teacher.

In order to determine the true nature of a total learning resources center, let us examine more closely the activities occurring in each of the above areas.

Students seem to be coming to these areas to study.

Some are reading books; others are viewing films, filmstrips, or listening to tapes.

Instructional materials are being stored in each area—books and other printed matter in one—projected materials and audio devices in the other.

Materials are being acquired, produced, and cataloged, and professional consultations are being offered to faculty and students.

It seems that what we now have are two separate organizations within the same school, each performing identical operations, the only apparent difference being the medium upon which the operation is being performed. How this dichotomy of function came into being will not be discussed here. However, the school of tomorrow will not be able to tolerate this division, since it perpetuates the following:

1. A teaching process which depends upon verbalism in a world in which the student (outside the school) has been learning through a rather sophisticated media system.

2. A dependence by the teacher and learner upon the printed page, primarily because of the emphasis placed upon the traditional library and the single textbook in the school program.

3. Lip service to other forms of communications systems simply because it is in vogue to have them.

Needless to say, this has proven to be very inefficient and highly uneconomical.

The learning resources center for the school district looking to the future must become an instructional support organization responsible for the development, implementation, dissemination, and evaluation of information transmission systems. These systems must be developed around: (1) the stated philosophy, objectives, and goals of the school, and (2) the objectives and goals of the students and faculty of the school system in terms of the curriculum.

If the student himself is to be responsible for more and more of his learning, where in the present and future schools is there a place where he can accomplish this? If there is any single facility in the school today that is designed for independent study and searching for information and that also provides the necessary professional personnel to assist and guide the student in his quest for knowledge, it has to be the library. The authors firmly believe that the school library must be the focal point of the individual student's learning. It must therefore be designed around the needs and activities of the student who will use it.

How will the student of tomorrow use the library? According to a report from the Educational Facilities Laboratories, the student will come to the library to:

*Find answers to specific questions that arise either from the teaching process or from ordinary curiosity.

*Go alone or as a member of a committee sent to get information.

*Carry out study hall assignments, that is, spend a specific amount of time studying in the library.

*Find material for projects such as a written report, a book review, a debate brief, or a research paper.

*Learn how to use the keys of a library—card catalogs, bibliographies, reference books, periodical indexes, etc.

*Look at motion-picture films, filmstrips,· or other audio-visual materials. Study with a teaching machine, listen to phonograph records or tapes, listen and record voice for language study.

*Locate quotations, excerpts, or data for speeches or projects.
*Read just for the fun of reading—one book or a hundred.
*Browse through current magazines and newspapers or look at the new book shelf.
*Talk with other students.[2]

The library portion of the learning resources center must also make provisions for the utilization of its services by the faculty of the school. While faculty will use the library for many of the same activities mentioned for students, faculty will also:

*Confer with the library staff on relevant materials to use for class work: those appropriate for general presentation in the classroom, those most suitable for students working in small groups, and those appropriate for use on an individualized basis.
*Preview films and filmstrips; confer on the purchase or rental of audiovisual materials, and on local production of same.
*Consult with librarians on book purchases, on the handling of special materials (pamphlets, sample magazines, government documents, etc.), on classification and cataloging problems, and on reader's problems and difficulties that the students may be having.[3]

If the library is to provide the services mentioned above to faculty and students, increased facilities and additional materials and equipment will be necessary.

For example, space must be provided for a large number of students to study independently. This will require study carrels to be placed unobstrusively throughout the library. Small group meeting rooms should be provided. Areas will be needed where students can view films and other projected materials, or listen to tapes and watch programs through the audio-video dial access system.

No longer can the library be thought of as a room with book stacks along the walls and a few tables and chairs provided for study purposes. Rather, the library must be a *large and comfortable* area where the student will want to come to learn. The floor should be carpeted and comfortable chairs provided in pleasant surroundings. "Floating" book stacks should divide the collection into various reading areas. The library, in fact, must become the student's home away from home.

The library, however, is only a part of the total learning resources center. As was mentioned earlier, the center is also responsible for the development and evaluation of information transmission systems. Therefore, space must be allocated for such services as the acquisition, production, and testing of instructional materials. (See also Chapter 6.)

[2]Ralph E. Ellsworth and Hobart D. Wagener, *The School Library: Facilities for Independent Study in the Secondary School* (New York: Educational Facilities Laboratories, 1963), p. 25.
[3]*Ibid.*, p. 25.

While facilities and services can only be determined by the total educational program of the school, if a total communications system is planned, then the following services with related facilities will be needed.

PRODUCTION SERVICES

The local production of materials developed to achieve the specific objectives and goals of the curriculum cannot be overlooked. In many instances commercial materials will be available to meet these objectives. However, the school district must be prepared to produce its own materials, particularly where they will be utilized in independent study.

Facilities should be anticipated for:

*Printing and duplicating: offset presses, spirit duplicator, copiers, plate making, stapling, collating, binding, storage.

*Photographic: film studio, darkrooms, drying rooms, film loading room, micro-film production, photographic reproduction area, and storage.

*Graphics: production room, layout room, copying area, model shop, storage.

ELECTRONIC COMMUNICATIONS SERVICE

The use of television, audio recordings, dial access, and radio for the transmission of educational programs is becoming more prevalent in the schools. Careful planning and proper design of these facilities is of great importance. Provisions must be made for the following:

*Television: studio, control room, video-tape room, distribution center, set construction dock, maintenance, and storage.

*Radio and Audio Recording: recording booth, control room, audio-dubbing and duplication room, transmission center, storage.

*Dial Access: area for tape banks (audio and video), maintenance, and storage.

CENTRAL STORAGE AND DISTRIBUTION

While many programs will be distributed throughout the district electronically, a centralized area will still be required for the storage and distribution of:

*Equipment: projectors, recorders, micro-readers, cameras, etc.

*Materials: maps, globes, films, filmstrips, books, periodicals, records, and many others.

LIBRARY TECHNICAL SERVICES

In this area all learning resources are processed for distribution to the school buildings within the district. Facilities will be needed for:

*Acquisitions
*Cataloging
*Maintenance and binding
*Storage

While the above services and facilities may appear formidable to many administrators, the process of curriculum development and learning envisioned in the future will be seriously curtailed if they are not provided. In some cases, several school districts (particularly those with less than 6,000 pupils) should begin developing a cooperative approach to many of these services. (See Chapter 7.)

CENTRALIZATION VS. DECENTRALIZATION

There is no single, universal solution to the problems arising from the controversy on centralization-decentralization of services. In general those services which will be of direct benefit to the students should be located where they are easily available to the students. The library is an excellent example.

Each building in the district will need a well-staffed, well-equipped library. However, the technical services portion of the library should be centralized in order to capitalize on volume purchasing and the savings in staff necessary to do the work.

The major production services (described above) should be centralized, since they require a considerable capital outlay and personnel with specialized skills. Limited facilities should be available in the individual schools to take care of the routine, day-to-day activities which normally occur there: e.g. the duplicating of reports, bulletins, preparation of simple visuals, storage of equipment.

With the establishment of a rapid, dependable district-wide distribution system, most major learning resource services, with the exception of the library, can and should be centralized.

STAFFING THE LEARNING RESOURCES CENTER

With the establishment of any instructional support program, whether it be computer services, curriculum consultants, counseling services, or a learning resources program, the provision of specially trained and qualified professional, technical, and clerical personnel is essential.

Since the services to be offered by the center are somewhat complex and require a number of personnel with varied training and ability, careful consideration must be given to the activities in which the staff will be involved. While these activities will be determined by the program to be offered in the district, the authors agree with Brown and Norberg that the staff of the learning resources center will be:

*Participating in the planning of instructional programs with respect to printed and audio-visual material, instructional devices, media, and systems

*Coordinating the selection and organization of collections of instructional materials for students and professional library resources for teachers

*Circulating instructional materials

*Coordinating the selection, processing, and distribution of textbooks

*Planning and producing instructional television and radio broadcasts and closed-circuit television programs in cooperation with appropriate curriculum or other committees

*Coordinating the use of instructional television and radio services

*Planning, designing, and preparing instructional materials, such as graphics, photographs, slides, filmstrips, motion pictures, recordings, and programmed materials, in cooperation with teachers

*Circulating appropriate printed, broadcast, and other information to schools and the lay public to acquaint them with the services, facilities, and materials of the educational media program

*Consulting with teachers and school administrators to identify instructional problems or opportunities related to the use of media and materials and to assist in solving problems or exploiting opportunities

*Planning and coordinating a variety of in-service training activities to assist teachers in the effective use of instructional media and materials

*Participating in the planning and design of school buildings and facilities to ensure the most effective and efficient use of technological resources in teaching

*Promoting and coordinating appropriate experimentation and research to ascertain the values of various instructional materials, techniques, and media and to develop better ways of using them.[4]

From the above it becomes apparent that the professional staff of the learning resources center will be a team of specialists concerned with the communications program—relative to the learning process—of the school system. As such, they are responsible for the efficient design and utilization of all carriers of information, and the effect of these carriers upon the learner.

Organization of the learning resources center staff. While the staff needed by the district will be determined by the number of services to be provided, the authors firmly believe that a learning resources center organized and staffed as presented here will enable the district to provide all of the services discussed in this chapter.

The coordinator of learning resources is responsible for the administration and supervision of the entire learning resources program of the school district. Reporting to the assistant superintendent in charge of instruction, he is expected to maintain close contact with all district

[4]James W. Brown and Kenneth D. Norberg, *Administering Educational Media* (New York: McGraw-Hill Book Company, 1965), pp. 285–86.

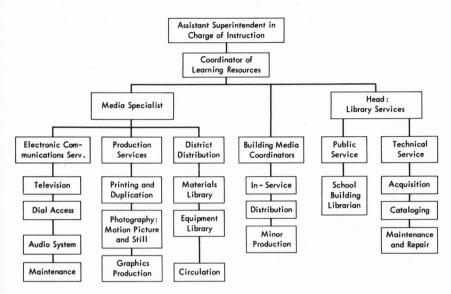

FIGURE 7.   Staff organization chart, Learning Resources Center.

administrators, curriculum coordinators, and teachers. As a member of the subject area curriculum committees, he will take the initiative in developing a sound philosophy regarding the role of learning resources in the instructional program.

Along with other members of the center's staff, he is responsible for:

*An in-service training program to bring about an effective utilization of all types of learning resources.

*The development of effective procedures for the evaluation and selection of learning resources and equipment.

*The preparation of the learning resources budget to be submitted to the assistant superintendent in charge of instruction, as part of the total instructional budget.

*Developing a program to train technicians, clerks, and students in the production of certain learning resources and the operation of instructional equipment.

*The continuous evaluation of the learning resources program based on the philosophy and objectives of the district.

The qualifications for this position include training in audio-visual communications, a background in curriculum development, successful teaching experience, training in research, skills in the areas of production, and successful experience in learning resource administration.

The head of library services will administer and supervise the library program of the school district. Reporting to the coordinator of learning resources, he also is expected to maintain close contact with school administrators, curriculum coordinators, and teachers. As a member of the learning resources team, he will meet with the subject area curriculum committee and take the initiative in developing a sound philosophy of the role of the library in the school's instructional program. With other members of the library staff, he is responsible for:

*Assisting with the learning resource center's in-service program relative to library services.

*The preparation of the library budget to be submitted to the coordinator, as part of the total learning resources budget.

*The development of effective procedures for the evaluation and selection of printed materials.

*Developing procedures for the acquisition, cataloging and maintenance of all learning resources.

*Developing a program to train technicians, clerks, and students to assist in the library technical service area.

*Assisting in the preparation of bibliographies of book and non-book materials for distribution to faculty and students.

*The continuous evaluation of the library program based on the philosophy and objectives of the school district.

The qualifications for this position include training in library science, successful teaching experience, a background in curriculum development, and successful experience in library administration.

The media specialist will administer and supervise the district's media program. He, too, is expected to maintain close contact with school administrators, curriculum coordinators, and teachers. As the third member of the learning resources team he will meet with the subject area curriculum committees and take the initiative in developing a sound philosophy for the role of media in the school's instructional program.

With other members of the media staff he is responsible for:

*Assisting with the learning resources center's in-service program dealing with the utilization and production of materials, and the electronic distribution of programs.

*The preparation of the media budget to be submitted to the coordinator as part of the total learning resources budget.

*Planning the production of television programs.

*Scheduling the distribution of television programs.

*Coordinating the production of all instructional materials.

*Supervising the district-wide distribution service.

*Developing a program to train technicians, clerks and students to assist in the production of instructional materials.

*Continuously evaluating the media program based on the philosophy and objectives of the school district.

Qualifications for this position include extensive knowledge of electronic communications, skills in the areas of production such as photography and graphics, a background in curriculum development, and successful experience in media administration.

The school building librarian will coordinate the district library program within his building. A key person in the total learning resources program, he will work closely with administrators, faculty, and students within the building.

The building librarian's major responsibilities are to:

*Work closely with faculty members, keeping them abreast of developments in their subject area, through the use of up-to-date bibliographies and in-service programs.

*Work closely with students, guiding or leading them into the "gold mines of knowledge."

*Assist with the evaluation and selection of library materials.

Qualifications for this position include training in library science and a background in curriculum development.

The building media coordinator will, as his title implies, coordinate the district's media program within the school building. He, too, will work closely with the school's administrators, faculty and students.

The building coordinator's major responsibilities are to:

*Assist with the district learning resource in-service programs at the building level.

*Establish procedures for the distribution of material and equipment within the building, with the assistance of clerical and student help.

*Within the framework of procedures established at the district level, coordinate the evaluation and selection of learning resources within the building.

Qualifications for this position include training in audio-visual communications, skills in the production of materials, and a background in curriculum development.

In addition to the professional personnel discussed above, the school district must also provide adequate support personnel.

Technicians should be expected to:

*Maintain and repair audio-visual equipment owned by the district.

*Make periodic inventories of equipment and materials.

*Clean and repair instructional materials.

*Assist in the scheduling of materials and equipment.

*Check and process new materials for circulation.

*Assist in the production of instructional materials.

Clerical personnel will:

*Assist in the procurement of materials for preview purposes.

*Type letters, reports, and other items.

*Maintain the files and records of the learning resources center.
*Schedule all equipment and materials.

Graphics personnel will design and produce the artwork for instructional materials used in the classroom and for television and photography.

SPECIFIC LEADERSHIP TASKS

The chief school administrator should encourage the proper utilization of learning resources by his faculty in the following ways:

*Determine learning resources services needed in his district.
*Provide meaningful in-service programs in the area of learning resources.
*Provide the necessary personnel, facilities, equipment, and materials to implement a learning resources program.

SUMMARY

Education, like the society around it, is faced with a tremendous knowledge explosion created by the technological revolution. With the introduction of new curriculum programs, educators soon found themselves confronted with computers, dial access systems, computer assisted instruction, television, and complete courses on film.

Faced with a tremendous increase in pupils, large sums of money were expended in school construction, while little or no funds were appropriated for keeping abreast of the technological advances proven to be successful in business and industry. In order to overcome the technological gap which resulted from this, the school administrator must take steps to introduce a balanced program of teaching, technology, and learning resources—each functioning in what it can do best.

With the introduction of a balanced teaching, technological, and learning resources program, the old concept of separate library and audiovisual departments will no longer be adequate. They will be replaced by an instructional support organization responsible for the development, implementation, dissemination, and evaluation of information transmission systems—the learning resources center.

The public service portion of the center will offer students and faculty areas where they can study independently and view and listen to a variety of instructional materials.

The center will also offer services for the production of materials used in the teaching and learning process.

In order to accomplish these services a team of learning resources specialists will be required.

The coordinator of learning resources, dynamic and industrious, will be instrumental in developing a sound philosophy regarding the role of learning resources in the instructional program and in developing a variety of in-service programs to meet the needs of the teachers. Through his leadership, effective procedures for the evaluation and selection of materials will be developed.

The head of library services will be instrumental in developing a sound philosophy of the role of the library in the instructional program. He will be responsible for introducing procedures for the acquisition, cataloging, and maintenance of all learning resources.

The media specialist will take the initiative in developing a sound philosophy for the role of media in the school's instructional program. Under his supervision the development of procedures for the production and distribution of materials, including television and dial access, will be established.

The building librarian will work closely with administrators, faculty, and students, coordinating the center's library program at the building level.

The building media coordinator will work closely with administrators, faculty, and students, assisting in the production and distribution of materials and equipment at the building level.

With the professional learning resources team concerned primarily with the instructional and learning process, additional learning resources support personnel—technical and clerical—will be required.

The staff of the learning resources center, working as a team and with teachers and students, will help in creating a teaching-learning process which is dynamic and meaningful to the student.

SUGGESTED ACTIVITIES AND PROBLEMS

1. Interview an assistant superintendent in charge of instruction and a faculty member in the same school district on the role of learning resources in their present instructional program. In your written report be specific as to how they are chosen as part of a learning sequence.
2. Discuss the authors' conception of the total learning resources center with a librarian and a director of audio-visual services. Critically evaluate both the authors' and their conclusions.
3. Read two articles on the use of technology and learning resources in a specific subject area. Present a written synopsis to the class.

SELECTED READINGS

Brown, James W., and Kenneth D. Norberg, *Administering Educational Media,* Chaps. 1, 2, and 12. New York: McGraw-Hill Book Company, 1965.

Coulson, John E., ed., *Programmed Learning and Computer-Based Instruction.* New York: John Wiley and Sons, Inc., 1962.

Deterline, William A., *Introduction to Programmed Instruction.* Englewood Cliffs, N.J.: Prentice-Hall, Inc., 1962.

Diamond, Robert M., ed., *Guide to Instructional Television.* New York: McGraw-Hill Book Company, 1964.

Ellsworth, Ralph E., and Hobart D. Wagener, *The School Library: Facilities for Independent Study in the Secondary School.* New York: Educational Facilities Laboratories, Inc., 1963.

The Impact of Technology on the Library Building. New York: Educational Facilities Laboratories, n.d.

Ofiesh, Gabriel D., principal investigator, *Dial Access Information Retrieval Systems: Guidelines Handbook for Educators,* Project No. BR-1042. Washington, D.C.: U.S. Department of Health, Education, and Welfare, 1968.

Orr, William D., ed., *Conversational Computers,* Chap. 7, 8, and 9. New York: John Wiley and Sons, Inc., 1968.

Silberman, Harry F., and John E. Coulson, "Automated Teaching," in *Computer Applications in the Behavioral Sciences,* ed. Harold Borko, Chap. 14. Englewood Cliffs, N.J.: Prentice-Hall, Inc., 1962.

Weisgerber, Robert A., ed., *Instructional Process and Media Innovation.* Chicago: Rand McNally & Co., 1968.

6

Planning the School Plant
for Optimum Use
of Learning Resources

The growth in educational technology is taking place so rapidly and the cost becoming so reasonable, that the "hardware" and its corresponding speed of acceptance in the public school has outstripped the know-how to provide adequate school plant facilities in which it is possible to make optimum use of these new learning resources. New school plants must be built and old ones modernized to take full advantage of the most advanced teaching and learning technology known today and, to the extent possible, dreamed of for tomorrow. Particular attention must be directed to the many past errors made in respect to such critical factors as viewing angles and distances; visual, sonic, and thermal environments; and storage and distribution systems. A new look must also be taken at the design of facilities for other supporting functions including origination, production, video-taping, and recording.

The planning of educational facilities is such a broad subject, and trends in school plant design are changing so rapidly, that it would not be sensible to attempt to give more than a brief treatment to this topic in a work of these limited dimensions. This chapter, therefore, will discuss briefly the tasks involved in planning and modernizing facilities for the optimum use of learning resources. Attention will be given to space requirements, locations and affinities of spaces, proper electrical and electronic facilities, adequate visual, sonic, and thermal environments, adequate display and storage facilities, and any unusual features necessary for this electronic age.

Throughout this chapter the terms "instructional materials center," "educational media center," and "learning resources center" will be used interchangeably.

COOPERATIVE PLANNING OF FACILITIES FOR LEARNING RESOURCES

Some of the mistakes that have been made in preparing educational facilities for learning resources may have been due to lack of know-how, but many of these errors have been due to inadequate planning. A variety of circumstances has contributed to this inadequate planning. Among others the following are worthy of note: (1) insufficient planning time, (2) little or no involvement of staff members in planning, (3) lack of consultant help in the field of learning resources, (4) inadequate educational specifications, and (5) inability to keep pace with technological changes.

TECHNICAL CONSULTANT HELP

It is assumed that representatives of all groups that will use the school plant will be involved at some stage in the planning. This would include administration, faculty, non-certificated personnel, students, and citizens of the community. Individuals in charge of curriculum and instruction must assume a heavy burden in the planning stages. If, however, the plant is to provide the proper environment and facilities for learning resources, the technical aspects of planning must be done by individuals who are well versed in technical fields. Within the school district the coordinator of learning resources, librarians, and building media coordinators should be deeply involved in the development of educational specifications and in working with the architect and experts in visual, sonic, and thermal environmental control. Free consultant help is usually available from the manufacturers of audio-visual equipment and other electronic devices, study carrels, and school furniture. It might be a wise investment to contract for outside expert consultant help in an area that is changing as rapidly as the one under discussion.

THE IMPORTANCE OF EDUCATIONAL SPECIFICATIONS

The preparing of educational specifications for any building project is the important first step after a decision has been made to construct a new facility or modernize an old one. In respect to the planning of areas for the use of learning resources, the educational specifications can be critical.

For the purpose of this discussion "educational specifications" are defined as *the document containing the educational requirements for the new facility or one to be modernized prepared for the design team of architects and engineers.*

What guidelines are needed for writing educational specifications? In a companion work the authors recommend the following basic information for inclusion in educational specifications:

1. The educational philosophy and objectives of the school.
2. The educational aspirations of the community.
3. Data concerning the number and ages of the students to be housed.
4. A brief explanation of the type of curriculum and the instructional procedures to be used.

5. A list of the number and kinds of facilities that are required, including future expansion.
6. Suggestions concerning the qualitative aspects of each space and area.
7. Affinities and relationships of the various facilities.
8. Activities that will take place in each area.
9. A list of the furniture and equipment for each space.
10. Special requirements of instructional and supervisory personnel.
11. Type and amount of tackboard, chalkboard, storage, and similar needs.[1]

Educational specifications are usually written by one person after many individuals have contributed the information to be included in them. During the collection of this information and the writing of the document, frequent consultation with the architect will insure better educational specifications. At all stages of the development of the educational requirements, the help of specialists in the various aspects of learning resources—both those inside and those outside the district—should be sought. Table 2 is a facsimile of a section of the educational specifications for the instructional materials center in a middle school. Note that this facility is located in the Commons Area.

Although all of the eleven items listed above are important as an aid in planning educational facilities for instructional media, certain items are particularly appropriate to the topic under discussion. For example, under item 4 instructional and learning procedures requiring special environments and facilities must be spelled out in sufficient detail so that the architect clearly understands the specific requirements.

Item 6 provides the opportunity for the learning resource specialists to tell the architect about the desired qualitative aspects of each space and area. It is in this section of the educational specifications that the desired visual, sonic, thermal, and aesthetic environments are described in some detail.

Affinities and relationships of the various facilities are a very important consideration in planning facilities for learning resources. Many schools are placing the building learning resource center in the center of the school, and all the academic learning areas are then grouped around it. Relationships of this kind would be mentioned under item 7 in the educational requirements.

Item 8 in the communication to the architect describes the activities that will take place in each area of the new facilities being planned. One important element that should be included under this item is the need for proper electrical outlets, wiring, and conduits.

The list of furniture and equipment for each space and area to be recommended under item 9 also has many implications for learning re-

[1]Ross L. Neagley and N. Dean Evans, *Handbook for Effective Curriculum Development* (Englewood Cliffs, N.J.: Prentice-Hall, Inc., 1967), pp. 254–55.

sources. One important decision that must be made concerns whether or not the furniture and equipment are to be purchased by the architect or by the district. Depending upon legal aspects, source of funds, and other contingencies, many schools prefer to contract for all movable furniture and equipment separately. It will, however, be necessary for the architect to know the type and amount of furniture and equipment that will eventually be used in each space and area.

One complaint of professionals interested in providing the best possible facilities for learning resources has to do with the amount of display and storage spaces. Item 11 in the educational specifications should make these specific needs known to the architect.

SPECIFIC LEADERSHIP TASKS

The administrator is advised to do the following:

1. Do involve staff members in developing educational specifications.
2. Do engage expert consultant help.
3. Do pay particular attention to the aspects of planning that affect the use of teaching-learning media.

DESIGNING SCHOOL BUILDINGS FOR OPTIMUM USE OF LEARNING RESOURCES

The effectiveness of any learning resource, be it the simple slate and copybook of yesteryear or the most modern electronic teaching device available today, is influenced by the physical conditions under which it is used. Environmental conditions as near ideal as possible should be provided in the various learning areas and spaces. Ways of providing ideal visual, sonic, thermal, and aesthetic environments should be studied carefully before final decisions are made in planning or modernizing school facilities.

Maximum use of learning resources may also be hindered by an insufficient number and/or poorly located power receptacles. Electrical circuits must be planned to carry any anticipated future load safely, as well as the initial demand. In anticipation of the many new technological devices to be installed in the future, ample open conduits should be provided throughout new buildings so that electrical wires may be pulled through at a later date to serve these devices.

Adequate sized, built-in screens should be provided in each area where projection will take place. Ample bulletin board and other display facilities should be carefully planned, and the potential of chalkboards must not be overlooked as teaching aids.

Special attention must be paid to facilities for individual, small-group, and large-group instruction and learning. Accommodations for teachers to carry on independent study and to plan with each other must receive serious consideration in initial planning.

Table 2. Section of Educational Specifications, from Michael P. Marcase, *Educational Specifications for Austin Meehan Middle School* (Philadelphia, Pa.: School District of Philadelphia, 1967), pp. 43–46.

COMMONS AREA

Space	Unit Cap	Number Units	Total Area	Description of Functions and Special Considerations
A. Instructional Materials Center				
1. Individual Study/Reference Area	100	1	3,000	Main area of the IMC that provides books and periodicals for investigation, study, and leisure reading; individual study carrels, small group study tables, checkout area, card catalog, and indices. Single entry/egress area that serves as a control device and relates to charging desk. Entrance leads into a more informal area that changes into a study area with accompanying quietness.
				Furniture types should be mixed and include study carrels, lounge furniture and small group study/reference tables, to accommodate 4 to 6 pupils.
				Provide maximum height perimeter wall, shelving and scattered 42 inch free-standing shelving. Maximum capacity of shelving 12,000 books.
				Floor should be completely carpeted with wireless loop underneath carpet to carry audio programs to students using wireless inductance-type earphones.
2. Individual Electronic Study Area	15	1	880	This area should flow into and be a portion of the Individual Study/Reference Area by means of a movable partition. Relate to Communication Center.
				Provide individual "wet" carrels with connections for television, audio receival, and usage of portable A-V equipment. Zone area for several computer aided instruction stations, with acoustical partitions.

COMMONS AREA

Space	Unit Cap	Number Units	Total Area	Description of Functions and Special Considerations
3. Conference/Group Instruction Area (divisible into 3 areas)	30	1	600	Space can be used as a classroom for library-use instruction and also be used as study area. Area should contain perimeter shelving for reference materials. Direct access that opens into Individual Study/Reference Area by means of movable partitions. Relate to Communications Center.
				Conference area to be divisible by movable partitions into three separate conference rooms; each conference area to open into the Individual Study/Reference Area.
				Provide area for use of overhead projectors, movie projectors, video-tape recorders, and TV reception.
4. Communication Center	—	—	600	Provide for: television receival, storage and distribution; A-V recording, storage and transmission; and capability to deliver audio-visual program to carrels or classrooms via dial request.
				Provisions to produce or reproduce graphic instructional materials using diazo process and/or photographic process. Storage and circulation of A-V equipment to instructional staff.
				Relate to Language Electronic Lab, Individual Electronic Study Area and Conference/Group Instruction Area.
5. Staff Area			400	Direct access to Individual Study/Reference Area. Relate to Communication Center.
a. Work Room	2	1	(250)	Space for two clerical non-professional people for unpacking and readying books for the Study/Reference Area.
b. Office	2	1	(150)	Space for person in charge of IMC. This "Curriculum Media Coordinator" supervises library and communication functions.

COMMONS AREA

Space	Unit Cap	Number Units	Total Area	Description of Functions and Special Considerations
6. Electronic Laboratory	30	1	(1,000)	Direct access to Language Classrooms, IMC, and student circulation.
				Each student station equipped with Level II (Listen-Respond) equipment. Five student stations equipped with Level III equipment.
				Student stations tiered and oriented toward teacher console for maximum teacher-pupil eye contact. These stations should have free front vision and movable partitions for control of lateral visions; also should be convertible to flat surface desk with provisions for storing mike-earphones.
				Teacher/instructor console should provide tape program sources, record program sources, individual and full student response system, as well as "all call" button and teacher monitoring facilities.
7. Student Store	10	1	300	Storage, display and sale of school supplies, paperback books, school banners, etc. Provide separate entrance and exit to aid circulation.

PROVIDING AN OPTIMUM VISUAL ENVIRONMENT

The new approach to providing an optimum visual environment in the various areas and spaces in school facilities has progressed far beyond the footcandle and light meter stages. They are, however, still in the picture to a certain extent. Providing an optimum visual environment is now becoming an increasingly more complicated matter. The advent of large open flexible spaces to be subdivided manually or by the flip of a switch, the accelerated pace in the adoption and use of many new electronic teaching-learning devices, and the new knowledge about conditions that determine the effectiveness of the seeing process all point to the need for a visual engineering approach in school plant planning.

As a prelude to a discussion of the visual environment, the following points are worth noting:

1. . . . the ability to see comfortably and efficiently does not increase in direct ratio to the quantity of light available.

2. *Illumination* is a product of light. Its adequacy is determined by degrees of intelligence used in the application of light for a specific task and the task's relationship to the total visual environment.

3. The *footcandle* is the unit by which we measure the lighting level of illumination at a given point. . . . This unit of light quantity is measured with a footcandle meter. The level of illumination is one of the basic factors in conditioning the environment for comfortable and efficient seeing, but it must be evaluated in its relationships with other basic factors.

4. Levels of illumination must be determined on the basis of *effective footcandles*. The art of determining levels of illumination for various seeing tasks has become more accurate because of the development of the Visual Task Evaluator (VTE) through research sponsored by the Illuminating Engineering Research Institute. Due to the fact that effective visibility of a task basically is a function of contrast within the task, the quantity of illumination cannot be determined intelligently apart from considerations of the kind of lighting system producing the light.

5. *Brightness* is defined as the luminous intensity of any surface. It may be created by either reflection or direct transmission of light. Brightness is measured in terms of candles per square inch and footlamberts. As mentioned in No. 3 above, the first unit is usually employed in measuring the brightness of a source of light. The footlambert is the unit adopted for measuring the brightness of other surfaces. In practice, the average brightness of any diffusive reflecting surface in footlamberts is computed by taking the product of the illumination in footcandles and the reflection factor of the surface (Footlamberts = Footcandles x Reflection factor). It is the footlambert that must be given prime consideration in providing the best environment for visual comfort and efficiency.

6. *Glare* is excessively high brightness due to the great differences in brightness within the total visual field. It is a somewhat general term, which can be understood more precisely in terms of direct glare and reflected glare.

7. *Brightness balance* is the key to visual comfort and efficiency. It is determined by the brightness differences maintained within the total visual field. The following suggestions in respect to *brightness balance* in the classroom are worthy of note:

a. The brightness of any surface viewed from any normal standing or sitting position should not be excessively higher or lower than that of the visual task.

b. The brightness of surfaces immediately adjacent to the visual task is of greater consequence in terms of visual efficiency and comfort than the brightness of more distant surfaces in the visual field.

c. The brightness-difference between adjacent surfaces in the total visual field should be kept at an acceptable minimum.

d. Regardless of the sources of light, both direct and reflected glare must be kept to a minimum.

e. Daylight and electric light systems should conform to the same set of recommendations for brightness and brightness-difference standards and should be coordinated in design to provide a balanced visual environment.

f. Any system of lighting should be planned so that it will make a maximum contribution to the provision of a cheerful, friendly, and aesthetically pleasing learning environment.[2]

LIGHTING FLEXIBLE LEARNING SPACES

The present trend toward more and more flexible learning spaces has created new problems in school lighting. When a large area is subdivided into several smaller learning areas, or several small areas expanded into a large one, the entire lighting scheme is changed. What may be an excellent visual environment under one condition may be unsatisfactory under the other. The problem, therefore, is to design a lighting system that approaches optimum conditions both in the total space and in the various-sized spaces into which the flexible facility is capable of being subdivided. The following ideas from an article by Gibson may help solve this problem:

1. Under today's recommended lighting levels of 70 to 100 maintained footcandles, the ratio of the brightness of the luminaire to that of the task should not exceed 5 to 1 and lower ratios are even more desirable.

2. To provide a good visual environment, the low brightness of any significant sized area should not be less than one-third task brightness. With a brightness ratio of 5 to 1 between luminaire and task, the brightness difference between high and low would be 15 to 1. This permits reasonable limits within which the architect should be able to provide desirable contrasts and color centers of interest in the space decor.

3. If a large divisible space is adequately lighted and then subdivided, light-

[2]Adapted from *NCSC Guide for Planning School Plants* (Columbus: Council of Educational Facility Planners, 1964), pp. 122–30.

ing levels on the task will vary relative to the area of space enclosed. It, therefore, is important that lighting systems planned for flexible spaces provide for the addition of lamps while maintaining the same pattern of luminaires.

4. As a result of recognition of the extreme importance of reflected glare or veiling reflections in the task, more attention must be given to better illumination on vertical planes. One solution has been the development of perimeter lighting systems using single lamp high output suspended indirect units—surface mounted or recessed troffer luminaires. The results have been very successful.

5. In order to design a flexible lighting system adequate switching patterns must be installed to accommodate the reorganization of space. New methods for switching are being experimented with but much work still remains to be done.

6. As individualized scheduling and instruction increases in popularity, new methods of localized lighting for individual work stations will be required.[3]

Another lighting problem peculiar to large spaces has to do with providing supplementary local lighting on chalkboards, display surfaces, demonstration areas, and even the instructor, if necessary.

SPECIAL PROBLEMS RELATED TO IMAGE VIEWING

Most of the readers can readily call to mind their feelings of frustration and discomfort as they presented or viewed a visual aid when the images on the screen were too dim or too bright, or the room was too dark for note-taking, or the light from the projection equipment was almost blinding, or other deterrents to good viewing were present.

Although much information has been accumulated concerning lighting for conventional learning tasks, there is still much to learn about adequate lighting systems for image viewing.

Visual environment and image viewing. In spite of the lack of knowledge in this area, progress is being made. The following suggestions include some of the most recent thinking concerning lighting during projection:

1. The surface on which the student is taking notes should be lighted to as nearly as possible the same brightness as the average brightness of the projected image.

2. There should be an absence of shadows on the writing surface, and there should be no light sources within the seated student's normal line of vision.

3. When in use, the brightness of other visual task surfaces, such as chalkboards and displays, should also about equal that of the projected image. When not in use, their surface brightness ought to be lower.

4. All other surfaces within the student's vision, including chalkboards and display areas not in use, should be less bright, but not less than 1/10 that of the average screen brightness.

[3]Adapted from Charles Dana Gibson, "How to Shed Light on Flexible Learning Space," *Nation's Schools*, LXXXI, No. 5 (1968), 68.

5. In large classrooms it is advisable to provide supplementary special "wash" lighting on the wall areas to bring their brightness up to the proper level in respect to the screen brightness.

6. Ambient light on the screen must be avoided at all costs. It tends to "wash out" the projected image.

7. To compensate for the fact that different media produce images of different brightness it is advisable to provide several levels of room lighting which are consistent with, and keyed to, the medium being used.

8. Pre-set levels of lighting should be controlled by the instructor or regulated by the projection equipment. There is no need to install elaborate and expensive devices if care is exercised in planning.[4]

The overhead projector can create some special problems in respect to brightness balance in the classroom if teachers insist on using it in a darkened room. The glare from the stage of the projector, particularly if the stage is below the eye level of the viewer, can prove quite annoying and even harmful.

In order to maintain the planned brightness balance in the classroom, projection screens that are not in use should not be visible. They should either disappear or be made inconspicuous in some way.

The control of natural light. Although there has been a trend away from excessive window space in classrooms today and numerous windowless classrooms have been built, control of natural light in schools still continues to be. of prime importance in many classrooms. Much of the ambient light that "washes out" images on the screen comes from the improper control of natural light. Streaks of light that sneak in because of inadequate window coverings can be particularly devastating.

If a school district can afford the higher installation cost and insure that they are properly maintained, a good grade of full-closure venetian blinds offer the greatest flexibility in the control of natural light.

A good grade of venetian blind is now available in which the slats run vertically instead of horizontally. They appear to work satisfactorily and are somewhat easier to maintain, as less dust collects on the slats. As every housewife who has had them knows, venetian blinds require frequent cleaning and regular maintenance to keep them operating smoothly.

A variation of the venetian blind is the externally-mounted louver which can be regulated from inside the classroom. Reports from a number of schools throughout the nation indicate that this system of daylight control performs quite satisfactorily.

[4]Adapted from A. Green, M. Gassman, W. Koppes, R. Caravaty, and D. Haviland, *Educational Facilities with New Media* (Washington, D.C.: Department of Audiovisual Instruction, National Education Association, 1966), pp. C–8–9.

Drapes are probably the second best choice for controlling natural light. If diffused daylight is desired for certain types of projection, two sets of drapes will be necessary—a translucent set and an inner opaque set. All drapes should be made of fire-resistant materials. They should be properly mounted and all cracks at the sides and top excluded.

The original standard type "blackout" window blinds used with or without other blinds are usually the least desirable. Although they do the job satisfactorily if hung correctly and channeled and stripped to produce a tight fit, they add little to the decor of the classroom. Roller blinds are subject to considerable wear and tear, and consequently require frequent maintenance.

Other procedures for controlling natural light such as tinted glass, large overhangs, fixed louvers, grids, and vision strips must be taken into consideration when attempting to provide the most satisfactory visual environment for image viewing and the use of other visual aids.

The time to plan for the control of natural light is during the planning stages of the school plant and not after it has been built. Decisions concerning the number and types of windows and their locations, skylights and clerestory lighting, borrowed light from peripheral corridors, transoms, glass doors to corridors or direct exits may seriously affect the ease with which natural light can be controlled.

PROVIDING AN OPTIMUM SONIC ENVIRONMENT

The trend in school plant planning toward large loft spaces and flexible learning areas has greatly mitigated against the provision of a good sonic environment. In respect to the use of electronic media in teaching, the blow has been an even more serious one. Open planning and the use of electronic teaching equipment are fundamentally incompatible with providing the most desirable acoustical conditions. It would seem, therefore, that school districts planning new facilities or modernizing older ones should insure that expert consultant services in sonic engineering are made available during the design stages of all teaching-learning spaces.

Explanation of terms. Before discussing the sonic environment, it seems desirable to explain the following basic terms:

Sound. Auditory sensations resulting from vibrations caused by variations in the atmospheric pressure. Sound is a highly individualistic matter.

Loudness. The degree of intensity of a sound. The degree of reduction in the intensity of sound is indicated in decibels.

Decibel. The unit used for measuring the intensity of sound. From a theoretical point of view, the decibel is a step in the measurement of the loudness of sound. The weakest sound that can be heard is rated at zero decibels.

Background noise. Sounds within the learning area or intruding from outside that may interfere with the teaching-learning situation. Certain background noises are being utilized to blanket sound transmission between groups working in spaces where flexible open planning exists.

Sound Reflections. Sound reflects from or bounces off surfaces it strikes in proportion to its wave length. The absorption qualities of the surface the sound strikes govern the intensity of the reflection.

Sound reverberations. Repeated reflections of a sound after the source has stopped producing it. The absorption qualities of the barriers, their location, and the size of the room determine the number of times sound impulses reflect before becoming inaudible.

Reverberation period. The length of time in seconds that it takes a 60-decibel sound to become inaudible.

Insulation against sound. A good sonic environment requires insulation against unwanted distracting external sounds.[5]

SUGGESTIONS FOR GOOD SONIC DESIGN

In general, good sonic design should guarantee that desired sounds within a teaching-learning space can be clearly and distinctly heard and unwanted sounds originating within or outside the space eliminated to the extent possible. Ability to hear well within a given space or area is determined by the size and shape of the space, the distribution and arrangement of sound-absorbing and sound reflecting surfaces within the space, and the location and intensity of the sound.

The following measures if adequately taken should contribute to good sonic design:

1. Provide effective sound insulation of each teaching-learning space or area.
2. Prevent or reduce the transference of sound between activities taking place simultaneously within a space or area.
3. Establish acoustical balance within the teaching-learning area by controlling inter-reflections and reverberation of sound and background noise within the room.
4. Reinforce, according to requirements, sound sources within the space or area.

Steps in planning. Insurance against sounds originating outside the building is the first step toward providing a good sonic environment in an educational facility. If a site is carefully selected in an area that has a relatively low ambient noise level, half the battle is won. However, there is always the threat that zoning might be changed in the area, new streets cut through, and flight patterns changed.

Play areas and playing fields should be planned so that distracting sounds of students at play do not interfere with teaching and learning taking place in the building. The distracting effects of some outside

[5]Adapted from *NCSC Guide for Planning School Plants*, pp. 105-7.

noises can be reduced by the orientation of the building on the site, reduction or elimination of windows, and the use of trees and shrubbery as sound baffles.

Zoning of the interior of the building is the second step in planning for a good sonic environment. Noisy areas such as shops, gymnasiums, and music rooms should be isolated from the areas reserved for independent work and study, group discussion, and listening and viewing. Traffic movement within the building is also a potential source of noise. It should be carefully planned to avoid as much distraction as possible.

The third step is to keep all operational noises of the building equipment to a minimum, for both the origination of sound and its transference. Air conditioning and ventilating systems, fans, blowers, and toilet flush systems are frequently responsible for producing unwanted noise.

Control of the transference of unwanted mechanical and other noises frequently is a difficult problem to solve. Corridors, climate control ducts, pipes, and conduits, if not properly treated, serve as channels through which unwanted noises flow.

Finally, within each teaching-learning station unwanted noises must be prevented from originating or at least must be minimized. In schools with individual room ventilators the noise level is frequently too high for good hearing. Therefore, this equipment should be selected for its absence of noise as well as for its other qualities.

Noisy projection equipment also can contribute unwanted noise during audio-visual or visual presentations. Even though they are serviced regularly, projector and fan motors can make wanted sounds indistinct and unintelligible. In some instances, it has been possible to diminish this interference by providing an insulated cover, shield, and acoustically treated stand for the equipment. However, the cover must be so constructed that sufficient ventilation is provided to cool the projector.

Sonic environment in various-sized spaces. Even with extensive use of the new electronic media, most learning depends at least in part on listening. Therefore, regardless of the size of the teaching-learning space, good hearing conditions are essential. Small areas require very little acoustical treatment, and average-sized classrooms up to approximately 1,000 square feet may be sound conditioned satisfactorily by providing acoustical materials around the perimeter of the room, with the exception of the area from which the voice of the instructor or other wanted sounds will emanate. Under this scheme, most of the ceiling area should present a hard reflective surface which will reinforce the sound source. If the floor is carpeted, it may be unnecessary to treat the room perimeter acoustically.

In larger teaching-learning stations the problem of insuring good hearing conditions is more difficult to solve. In fact, the complexity of the problem increases in relation to the size and shape of the space. The objective of providing a good sonic environment in a large teaching-learning area can be realized only if reflective and absorptive surfaces are so distributed within the space that students are not aware of any delayed repetitions of sound. If the room is too heavily blanketed with sound-absorbent material, it becomes "dead," and consequently not particularly good for listening.

A basic rule for acoustical treatment requires that surfaces in the area from which sound originates should be of the reflective type, and those opposite the sound source absorptive in quality. Contrary to some practice, all ceiling areas should be flat planes with reflective surfaces rather than acoustically treated. Domes and other curved surfaces should be avoided, because they focus rather than disperse sound. Pie shaped rooms (see Figure 12) result in better hearing because they facilitate sound dispersion and tend to shorten the reverberation period.

As the size of the teaching-learning station increases, the design of the floor area becomes of greater importance from an acoustical viewpoint, as well as for visual reasons. In larger rooms the floors should be sloped or stepped to improve the acoustical environment and thus enhance the general hearing conditions.

ACOUSTICAL PROBLEMS IN FLEXIBLE LEARNING SPACES

As previously stated, today's flexible learning spaces create many problems with respect to sound transmission from one space to another. Increased use of electronic teaching devices on the one hand and the desire for open flexible spaces on the other makes the search for the ideal sound barrier a serious one. The main problem to be dealt with, then, is the planning of a large, flexible, acoustically-satisfactory learning space that may be subdivided into two or more smaller learning areas, each of which has its own acceptable sonic environment.

The above specifications require sound barriers that are air-tight, have sufficient mass, and are not too rigid in structure. It has not been difficult to meet the above requirements in permanent or demountable partitions, but reasonably-priced, flexible or folding partitions that meet these requirements have just recently been made available on the market. Recently too, more has been learned about the use of low background noise to mask other unwanted noises as, for example, conversation.

A number of the newer schools are eliminating full partitions altogether. Schools favoring this type of open planning seem to be more concerned with sight lines than with the sonic environment. Although liberal use is made of carpeting, cabinet partitions, baffles, and acoustical materials on walls and ceilings, the sonic environment is not conducive to the use of audio-electronic teaching devices unless headsets or low volume speakers are available. Schools desiring to expand the use of electronic teaching devices must weigh carefully the psychological advantages and the greater flexibility of open spaces against their acoustical disadvantages.

SPECIFIC LEADERSHIP TASKS

Administrators concerned with providing the best possible sonic environment for the use of learning resources should:

1. See that competent consultant services in sonic engineering are available during the planning of new facilities or the modernization of older buildings.
2. Weigh carefully the relative merits of open planning in view of the difficulties involved in providing a good hearing environment.
3. Involve teachers in the planning so that they will become familiar with the conditions necessary for a good sonic environment.

PROVIDING ADEQUATE TOTAL CLIMATE CONTROL

Adequate total climate control is an important requirement in today's school facilities. It is as essential as good visual and sonic environments. The objective is to provide an environment that is conducive to learning. According to the NCSC Guide, the optimum thermal environment consists of:

Those thermal conditions which make possible dissipation of heat from the human body in the most effortless manner, thereby achieving maximum human efficiency. No two researches agree on exact combinations of radiant temperature, air temperature, relative humidity, and air movement that consitute the optimum. The general optimum ranges suggested are: balanced mean radiant temperatures; approximate air temperatures ranging from 69° to 70° F.; relative humidity between 40 percent and 60 percent; and air movement of 20 to 40 cubic feet per minute.[6]

The advent of air conditioning in schools has contributed greatly to providing adequate total climate control. Although air conditioning is not universally included in all new school plants, each year fewer and fewer schools are being built without it. It has long been recognized that cooling, rather than heating, is the real problem in providing climate control in occupied buildings, but schools have been slow in adopting what used to be considered a luxury item. Regular summer sessions, special summer activities, and twelve-month school terms have accelerated the rate of adoption of air conditioning. Less fenestration and more compact buildings have made it possible to include total climate control at a reasonable expenditure of funds. For a number of years, however,

[6]*NCSC Guide for Planning School Plants*, p. 113.

many administrators will be working in older buildings in which the installation of air conditioning might prove too costly to make it feasible.

Recently, some school districts throughout the nation have been utilizing the heat energy from their artificial lighting systems to both heat and cool their new school buildings. This offers considerable promise in total climate control.[7]

Electronic media and climate control. Individuals who are charged with the responsibility of planning for good climate control in areas in which electronic teaching aids will be used regularly must be aware of the following facts:

1. Schools with a commitment to extensive use of electronic teaching aids make greater use of large teaching-learning areas than other schools. It is more difficult to regulate climate control in these areas because of the larger number of occupants.
2. Reduced fenestration, or the absence of it, places most, or all, of the responsibility for ventilation on mechanical equipment.
3. Varying heat output from lighting levels and electronic equipment used in the various-sized spaces creates problems of temperature control.
4. Control of noises from ventilating and air conditioning equipment is very important because of the need for a good sonic environment in the use of electronic teaching aids.
5. Placement of mechanical ventilators, climate control ducts, exhaust systems, and thermostats is of prime importance in flexible learning spaces using airtight flexible or folding partitions if all spaces, large and small, are to have adequate total climate control.
6. Positioning and insulation of duct-work and the selection of fans, blowers, and other equipment require much thoughtful study if unwanted noises that may interfere with good hearing are to be eliminated.
7. Careful planning of climate control in the school television studio, projection rooms, and control centers is essential because of their special requirements and problems.

None of the above facts present insurmountable problems, but the administrator must remember that preventative planning is superior to, and less costly than, corrective measures taken after mistakes are made. Furthermore, in school plant planning, many errors cannot be rectified.

SPACE REQUIREMENTS, LOCATIONS, AND AFFINITIES

Some recommendations are being made by various individuals and groups concerning the space requirements for instructional materials

---

[7]See the *Barber-Colman Heat-of-Light System* (Rockford, Ill.: Barber-Colman Company, n.d.).

centers, learning resources centers, and instructional media centers—or whatever name you wish to call them. However, it would appear to the authors that, although experience may eventually make it possible to determine space requirements for the various-sized centers and their components, little accurate information is available at the present time. Many of the programs are so new and there are so many variables that facilities which seem ideal for a given district might be too large or too small for another, similar-sized district. When the elements of school size, age-group served, grade organization, presence of satellite centers in individual buildings, and the availability of a district or area learning resource center are introduced, the reader can see how complicated the matter really becomes. Add to the above a consideration of the zeal with which some schools promote wide use of learning resources as opposed to those schools whose storerooms are filled with equipment covered with dust or as yet unpacked, and the need for individualized specifications to fit the program of each particular school or district becomes apparent.

The authors also are aware of the fact that when space requirements are specified as *minimum* requirements, they soon become the standard or maximum requirements instead of a starting point. Even though the figures are given in ranges, the lower figure frequently is selected as the guide. The authors therefore wish to make it clear that any figures suggested for space requirements in this text are merely suggestions for each district to consider as a point from which to begin planning. It also needs to be clearly understood that the floor plans displayed in this chapter are illustrations rather than models.

The suggestions for the location of various facilities and their affinities to other parts of the building, however, may be considered as guidelines. On the topic of the location and affinities of learning resource centers, considerable rationale has been developed as a result of past experiences with school libraries and the recognition of practical considerations such as accessibility and the need for the best possible teaching-learning environment.

DETERMINING SPACE REQUIREMENTS

The position of the authors throughout this text has been that the school program is basic to all other planning. Decisions about personnel, organization and administration of learning resources, budget, and plant facilities and equipment must all be predicated on the instructional program. Therefore, before determining space requirements, a good hard look must be taken at the total teaching-learning process. This should be done prior to the time the educational specifications are developed. In following the guidelines for writing educational specifications found earlier in this chapter, it is important that under guideline 4 (a brief explanation of the type of curriculum and the instructional procedures to be used) the explanation of the instructional procedures is not too brief. It is at this point that crucial decisions must be made concerning the extent to which the school is willing to commit itself to the use of learning resources. During this period of deliberation, questions similar to the following might be raised:

1. How innovative have the members of the staff been in the past?
2. How extensively have learning resources been used in the past?
3. Will new facilities and equipment make it impossible for staff members to give the same old excuses for not using learning resources?
4. Is the district willing to institute a rigorous, continuing program of in-service education to bring and to keep staff members up-to-date in the use of learning resources?
5. How many additional personnel is the district willing to employ for staffing the expanded facilities for learning resources?
6. Will funds be made available to equip adequately the new facilities for learning resources, and to keep equipment and materials up-to-date?

The space requirements for learning resources in a particular school district should depend as much upon answers to questions of the above type as they do upon what media specialists suggest. Otherwise, much valuable and costly space will be idle or used for purposes for which it was not originally planned. A district must determine whether or not a minimum, average, or maximum program is desired, plan accordingly, and then see that it functions to the fullest extent. The authors are not intimating that districts should think only in terms of minimum programs. In fact, it is hoped that districts will "think big." The key is really a total commitment to the value of learning resources, the planning and equipping of excellent facilities, and a desire on the part of everyone to see that the facilities, equipment, and learning materials are used to the widest extent possible.

After a program has been decided upon and spelled out in the preliminary educational specifications, the next step in the determination of space requirements is to review plans of facilities for learning resources in schools that have decided upon a somewhat similar program. Examination of articles on school facility planning,[8] viewing American Association of School Administrators' filmstrips on recent architectural exhibits held at their annual conferences or a visit to the exhibits, and visits to recently built schools will provide many ideas concerning space requirements for the various special facilities for learning resources and their components. During this period, outside consultant services representing

[8]See current issues of *American School & University, Nation's Schools, School Management,* and *The American School Board Journal.*

the various educational media can be of great assistance. Caution, however, must be exercised that the school is not over-sold by the consultants. Their tasks are to make recommendations in their areas of competency with respect to facilities for a minimum, average, or maximum program for the use of learning resources, as previously determined by the school staff. As suggested earlier in this chapter, it is assumed that regular staff members who are specialists in learning resources have been involved in planning. Unless the school district has unlimited funds and a staff totally committed to the use of learning resources, the ardor and enthusiasm of the local specialists may have to be slightly checked, or the result will be maximum facilities when an average program had been decided upon. The reader is again reminded that the architect, representatives of the teaching staff, and other affected personnel should be involved during the entire planning process.

If copies are available, it is helpful to examine the educational specifications for schools to be visited prior to the actual visitations. In examining the educational specifications and during the visitations, the main focus of attention will be on the facilities for learning resources. However, it must be remembered that the entire building influences the teaching-learning process in various ways.

After this period of study and visitation, the final educational specifications should be prepared and submitted to the architect, who will begin his preliminary drawings. During this period, the planning committee should remain quite active and should not hesitate to criticize the preliminary drawings and to make recommendations for changes. When the architect has prepared final drawings, recommendations for changes should be kept to a minimum, as they can delay the project and even prove costly. Change orders after the construction contract has been let should be made only if a serious mistake in the planning has been discovered or if the contractor agrees to make the change at a minimal cost.

The district-wide educational media center. The authors have taken a strong position throughout this text that districts of sufficient size should have a district-wide educational media center. It will be necessary, of course, for smaller districts to combine their resources in order to have similar centralized services. (See Chapter 7.)

Two examples of district-wide or centralized media centers are included in this section. They are merely illustrative of what has been done in several areas of the nation. Figure 8 displays the floor plans and legend of the district-wide Instructional Service Center organized under the Elementary and Secondary Education Act of 1965 in McAllen School District in Texas. A unique feature is that the Center was developed by adapting three prefabricated buildings for this purpose. The library processing center is not shown in the floor plans. This district-wide media

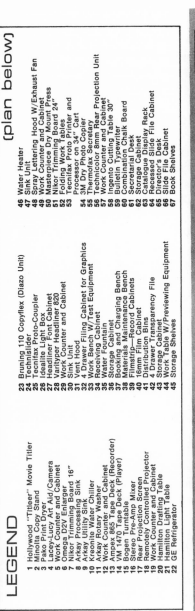

(plan below)

LEGEND

1 Hollywood "Titleer" Movie Titler
2 Minolta Copy Stand
3 Pako Print Dryer
4 Lacey-Lucy Art Aid/Camera
5 Work Counter and Cabinet
6 Omega D2V Enlarger
7 Nikor Trimming Board 16"
8 Arkay Processing Sink
9 Arkay Utility Sink
10 Kreonite Water Chiller
11 Arkay Rotary Washer
12 Work Counter and Cabinet
13 Ampex 865 Tape Deck (Recorder)
14 VM 1470 Tape Deck (Player)
15 Bogen Turntable
16 Stereo Pre-Amp Mixer
17 Rear Projection Screen
18 Remotely Controlled Projector
19 Work Counter and Cabinet
20 Hamilton Drafting Table
21 Hamilton Light Table
22 GE Refrigerator

23 Bruning 110 Copyflex (Diazo Unit)
24 Technislider
25 Tecnifax Proto-Coupler
26 Idealite Light Box
27 Headliner Font Cabinet
28 Varityper Headliner 820
29 Work Counter and Cabinet
30 Sink Unit
31 Vent Hood
32 4 Drawer Filing Cabinet for Graphics
33 Work Bench W/Test Equipment
34 Receiving Cabinet
35 Water Fountain
36 Storage Cabinet
37 Booking and Charging Bench
38 Materials Maintenance Bench
39 Filmstrip—Record Cabinets
40 16mm Film Cabinet
41 Distribution Bins
42 4 Drawer Transparency File
43 Storage Cabinet
44 Work Table W/Previewing Equipment
45 Storage Shelves

46 Water Heater
47 Sink Unit
48 Spray Lettering Hood W/Exhaust Fan
49 Work Counter and Cabinet
50 Masterpiece Dry Mount Press
51 Nikor Trimming Board 24"
52 Folding Work Tables
53 Tecnifax Proto Printer and Processor on 34" Cart
54 3M Dry Photo Copier
55 Thermofax Secretary
56 Technicolor 8mm Rear Projection Unit
57 Work Counter and Cabinet
58 Ingento Cutting Table 30"
59 Bulletin Typewriter
60 Combination Chalk Board
61 Secretarial Desk
62 Storage Cabinet
63 Catalogue Display Rack
64 Recessed Slide File Cabinet
65 Director's Desk
66 Slide File Cabinet
67 Book Shelves

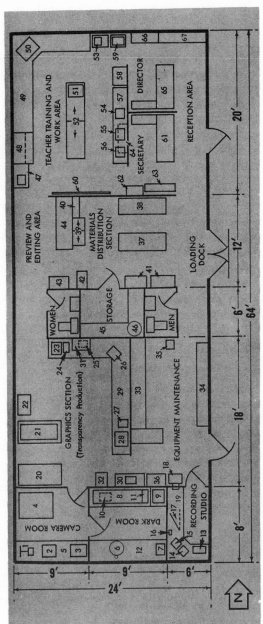

FIGURE 8. District-wide Instructional Service Center, McAllen School District, Texas. (From Dan Echols, "The Making of a Media Center," *Audiovisual Instruction*, XII, No. 8, 1967.)

center serves a school district of 10,000 students distributed among twelve elementary schools, two junior high schools, and a large senior high school. Examination of Figure 8 reveals that the Media Center is quite complete. It includes the following: (1) a work and training area for teachers, (2) a graphics section adequately equipped and staffed to produce various types of teaching materials specifically adapted to the instructional needs of the local curriculum, (3) a recording facility to make it possible to add auditory cues, as needed, to the visual materials produced by the graphic section—as well as to duplicate recordings on tape, (4) a materials distribution section to provide commercially available audiovisual materials to the schools from a central collection, plus providing (on a loan basis) the more sophisticated types of equipment as required for special uses, (5) an equipment maintenance section to keep the hardware fully operational, and (6) an administrative section for necessary direction and record keeping.[9]

Figure 9 is illustrative of a learning resources center that serves a wider area. This center, located at Red Oak, Iowa, also was funded under the ESEA. It services 79 separate buildings in a nine-county area. An interesting feature of this plan is the inclusion of a planetarium, which provides for the pupils in this large area learning experiences that were beyond the capabilities of the individual districts. A study of the plan reveals the following main areas in addition to the planetarium: (1) photography laboratory, (2) graphics section, (3) teacher production area, (4) study carrels, (5) viewing room with a rear-screen projection unit, (6) staff room, (7) materials room with check-out facilities, (8) conference room, and (9) secretarial and administrative spaces.[10]

The building educational media center. Building educational media centers are known by a variety of names in addition to the three used interchangeably in this chapter. Among the list of additional names are: knowledge resource center, instructional resources center, the school library—or any combination of the above terms and previously mentioned ones. These building educational media centers come in all sizes and shapes, depending upon philosophy and educational objectives of the school. In the more sophisticated versions many of the components found in the district-wide center are also duplicated in the building media center.

Illustrative of the various types of specialized facilities found in a 960-pupil elementary school instructional materials center are the following, together with their specified areas:

[9]Dan Echols, "The Making of a Media Center," *Audiovisual Instruction*, XII, No. 8 (1967), 798.

[10]W. Horner, R. Curtis, A. Nelson, P. Olive, and R. Williams, "Title III Serves Southwest Iowa," *Audiovisual Instruction*, XII, No. 8 (1967), 808.

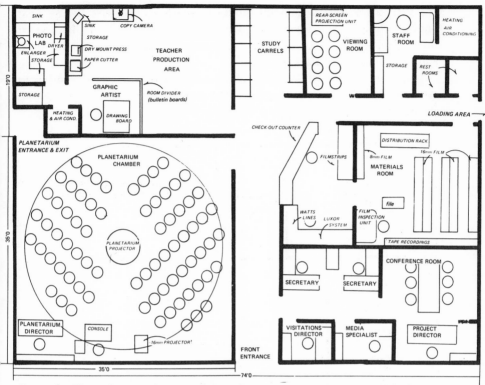

FIGURE 9. Floor plan: Southwest Iowa Learning Resources Center. (From W. Horner, R. Curtis, A. Nelson, P. Olive, and R. Williams, "Title III Serves Southwest Iowa," *Audiovisual Instruction*, XII, No. 8, 1967.)

Table 3. Facilities and their areas in an instructional materials center in a 960-pupil elementary school. Used by permission from Michael P. Marcase and Jack H. Neulight, *Educational Specifications McKinley School Replacement* (Philadelphia: School District of Philadelphia, 1967), pp. 33–36.

Facility		Area in square feet
Instructional Materials Center		4,060
1. Reading Room	2,200	
2. Study Carrel Area	250	
3. Workroom-Office	300	
4. A.V. Work Storage Room	430	
5. Closed Circuit TV Control Room	150	
6. Materials Production Area	500	
7. Storage Room	230	

Figure 10 displays the floor plan for a medium-sized secondary school instructional materials center. Accompanying the plan in its original source are words of caution to the effect that school districts should use the IMC areas only as general guides in planning, because in the final analysis the size of a given area depends on the activities to be carried on in that area. This, of course, supports what the authors have been stating throughout this text.

In planning, the educational media center should be made ample in size and flexible, so that it can be rearranged or expanded easily as new needs arise.

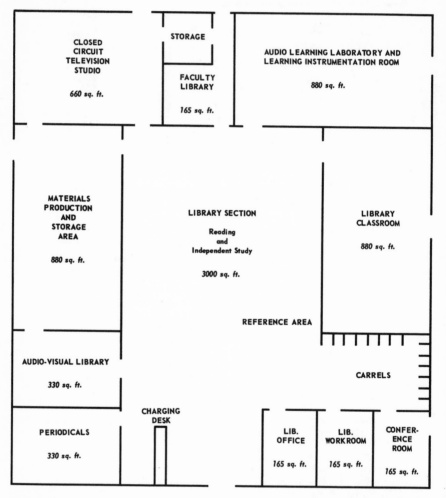

FIGURE 10. Suggested areas for a secondary school Instructional Materials Center. (Used with permission from *The School Instructional Materials Center and the Curriculum*, Curriculum Development Series No. 5, Harrisburg, Pa.: Department of Public Instruction, Commonwealth of Pennsylvania, 1962, p. 20.

Location and affinities. With regard to location, it is pretty well agreed that an educational media center should be the focal point of a school building's structural design and the heart of its educational program. Examination of a great many floor plans of recently-constructed elementary, secondary, and post-secondary school plants reveals that schools are literally being planned around their instructional materials centers. No longer is the gymnasium the show place in the school. At last, the spotlight is on the educational media center—it has become the central attraction.

Illustrative of this trend is the Fountain Valley School District in California which has recently completed the Harry Fulton School featuring five satellite classroom buildings grouped around a 10,000-square-foot Learning Center. Within the major center are found library facilities, audio-visual equipment, a television center, science and reading labs, study carrels, and cooperative teaching stations. This is the eleventh elementary school constructed in the district under this plan. All the schools have clusters of six or eight classrooms in each satellite, grouped around their own miniature Learning Center. Classrooms have sliding chalk boards in front of glass windows for better supervision of pupils.[11]

The above plan also suggests the practice of satellite educational media centers, which some schools that are organized around the "school-within-a-school" or the "little school" concept employ. Under this plan each subdivision of the total school has its own media center containing facilities for independent study, small group and project rooms, and various learning media. All centers are interconnected for call-up of material from each other, and in addition all media centers are connected with the district-wide educational media center which has electronic storage and retrieval capability.[12] In some instances a district-wide educational media center might actually be located in the school facilities occupied by a secondary school organized on the "school-within-a-school" concept.

The educational media center should be conveniently located at the heart of the school plant. It should be easily accessible to all other educational facilities surrounding it. A ground-floor location is most desirable, with easy access to a loading dock. In buildings of more than one floor it will be necessary to provide elevators or ramps to facilitate the movement of materials and equipment.

In planning the facility, noise-producing areas should be removed as far as possible from the center, and within the center itself noisy areas

[11]See E. Michael Brick, "Fountain Valley: Three Dimensional Teaching," *Educational Screen and Audiovisual Guide*, XXXXVII, No. 4 (1968), 16; and E. Michael Brick, "Learning Centers—The Key to Personalized Instruction," *Audiovisual Instruction*, II, No. 8 (1967), 796.

[12]See Green, *et al., Educational Facilities with New Media*, Sec. B, pp. 68–69.

should be isolated from quiet reading and study areas. Noise-producing areas in the media center should also be so located as not to interfere with nearby classrooms.

The reading area. No attempt will be made to describe the various components of the educational media center, with the exception of the facilities for readers. Since this is what now remains of the old school library, it seems worthy of some elaboration. Then too, there is danger that in some instances this area might be neglected in favor of facilities for the newer media.

In an authoritative publication of the Educational Facilities Laboratories, Ellsworth and Wagener suggest that schools should be thinking of facilities for readers that will seat 30 per cent of the enrollment. They suggest that during the transition from smaller to larger reading areas, the areas adjacent to the reading facilities could be occupied by classrooms or other similar spaces. As the school grows, the reading area could gradually expand into these spaces without exorbitant remodeling costs, providing the walls are non-bearing and no facilities with plumbing had to be included.

In a school of 2,000 students, to seat 30 per cent of the student body in the reading area would require 15,000 square feet, assuming a minimum of 25 square feet of floor space per reader. The same writers suggest the apportionment of reader space as follows: (1) study carrels—60 per cent, (2) group study rooms also serving as rooms for the use of audiovisual equipment—15 per cent, (3) space for flat-topped tables—8 per cent, and (4) space for lounge furniture—17 per cent.[13]

The total environment of the reading room is very important. Not only must the lighting and climate control be carefully planned, but the space should be both comfortable and attractive. It should be comfortably furnished, and carpeting is a must for the floor. A fireplace can contribute to producing a homelike atmosphere, particularly in the storytelling area of an elementary school reading room.

Ample display space should be provided, including areas for displaying works of art. Every attempt should be made to provide a good aesthetic environment.

Schools in the year 2000 may no longer need a reading room of the type previously described. Perhaps by then many written materials will be stored on tape in complete or abstracted form. The student, then, would be able to retrieve them in "print-offs" from the computer or on the monitor screen while seated at his carrel, which might be situated anywhere in the building. Until that time arrives, reading areas will be necessary.

[13]Adapted from Ralph E. Ellsworth and Hobart D. Wagener, *The School Library* (New York: The Educational Facilities Laboratories, Inc., 1963), pp. 50–51.

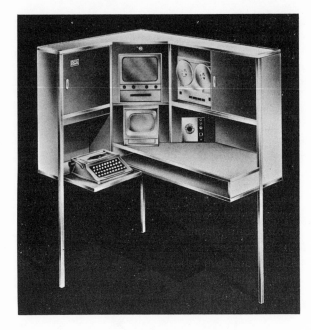

FIGURE 11. Student Carrel. (Courtesy RCA.)

Student carrels. It has been suggested that study carrels might be classified as dry, moist, and wet. The dry ones consist only of private study space, the moist ones include wiring and equipment for minimum audiovisual retrieval, and the wet carrels are fully equipped for all types of retrieval and response.

As previously mentioned, sixty per cent of the facilities for reading should be occupied by study carrels. They should be in groups not to exceed fifteen to twenty carrels distributed among the collections. Each student will require approximately 2′ x 3′ of work space as a minimum.

Since the recent emphasis on individualized instruction, the market has been flooded with many types of study carrels. They range from very simple visual dividers between desks made possible by raising a drop-leaf to a very sophisticated, fully-equipped carrel representing a pupil's "home base," including storage space.

The administrator faced with study carrel selection might consider the following criteria before making a decision:

1. The minimum working surface should be six square feet.
2. The visual "blinders" should be high enough to be slightly above the eye level of the seated student, which is approximately twenty inches above desk height. The side panels should be treated acoustically.
3. The bookshelves should be at least ten inches deep.
4. Two persons should be able to sit at one carrel when necessary—either a student and a teacher, or two students.

5. The basic carrel requirements consist of the desk top, visual barriers, and several 110 volt outlets for portable machines.

6. Additional optional fixtures include an open bookshelf, lockable book storage, under-desk storage, coat hook, coat locker, desk light, and control panel.

7. Carrels should be designed so that additional equipment may be installed later.

8. Carrels should be adaptable to either wall or floor wiring with plug-in type connections.

9. Carrels should be completely demountable so that they may be reassembled in different fashion and/or a new location, if educational changes so require.

10. Even though carrels have desk lights, the principal light source should be from the ceiling.[14]

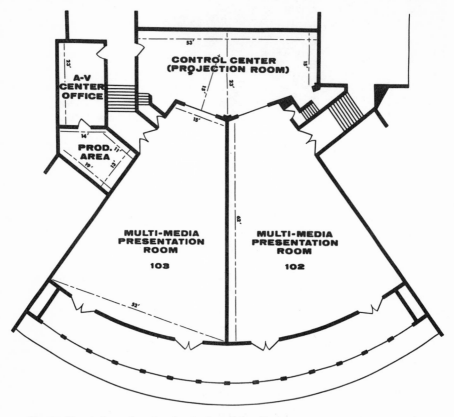

FIGURE 12. A floor plan showing both multimedia presentation rooms, a control room, and adjacent offices, Indiana State University, Terre Haute, Ind. (From Russell McDougal and James J. Thompson, "The Multimedia Classroom: Planning and Operation," *Audiovisual Instruction*, XII, No. 8, 1967.)

[14]Adapted from John Beynon, *Study Carrels: Designs for Independent Study Space* (Stanford, Calif.: Western Regional Center of Educational Facilities Laboratories, Inc., 1964), pp. 2–5.

LARGE-GROUP LEARNING FACILITIES

The multimedia classroom still has many problems to be solved. From a discussion of the new facility at Indiana State University shown above, the authors of this text have formulated the following suggestions for the design of large-group learning facilities:

1. The classrooms should be pie-shaped segments annexed to or components of larger educational complexes.
2. The seating capacity can conveniently be 255 students.
3. Slanting floors and theater-type seats are preferable.
4. An excellent-quality rear projection screen mounted at the front of the classroom is highly desirable. The dimensions of the screen should be at least 8' x 10' although 8' x 16' is more desirable.
5. Keep the lectern control panel simple. Arrange buttons and switches for the instructor's convenience, not the electrician's. Perhaps the buttons and switches could be of different shapes so the instructor knows by touch which machine he is about to activate.
6. Student-response systems, tele-lecture facilities, and other accessories should be planned from the beginning.
7. Bury the cable to the lectern.
8. Put rubber casters on equipment carts.
9. Install a system of work lights in the control room that do not interfere with projection when the screen is in use.
10. Make classrooms at least 18' wide in front to allow for display materials and to accommodate an overhead projector screen.[15]

In the same article the following cautions may be found:

1. Do not overcrowd multimedia classrooms.
2. When not in use the screen should be covered with a draw curtain on the classroom side. It should be remotely controlled from the instructor's lectern.
3. Doorways leading from the control room into the instructor's stage should have a glass panel to enable technicians to follow the progress of events on stage.
4. All entrances should be light trapped.
5. Teleprompter installations still leave much to be desired. Considerable experimentation still remains to be done before they are perfected.[16]

SPACES FOR COMPUTER-ASSISTED INSTRUCTION

A powerful new tool is now available for learning. If the past is any indication of the future, computer-assisted instruction will eventually be as commonplace as educational television. This means that new educational facilities must be planned with CAI in mind, and modernization programs also should be concerned about this new tool of learning.

15Adapted from Russell McDougal and James J. Thompson, "The Multimedia Classroom: Planning and Operation," *Audiovisual Instruction*, XII, No. 8 (1967), 826.
16*Ibid.*, p. 826.

FIGURE 13. General Electric Student Response System installed in Newhouse Communication Center, Syracuse University.

Laboratory for CAI. Specialized spaces for CAI must be provided if it is to function effectively. A number of experimental laboratories are now in operation, and others, doubtless, will be organized in various parts of the nation. School administrators and architects should examine and evaluate any existing models before one is designed for the local district.

In describing a CAI laboratory that provides space and instructional time for twenty-four elementary school pupils each period of the school day and space for experimentation and research, Featherstone and Bell suggested the following:

The laboratory should be located with direct access to the computer room, reception area, and other classrooms. Space should be provided for 24 carrels, front platform, lecterns, and projection booths.

Each of the 24 carrels must be large enough to contain a complete student console, which includes a cathode-ray tube display device, a tele-typewriter input-output device, an image projector, facilities for audio input and output, plus a writing surface of approximately four square feet, and storage for books and writing supplies.

Carrels must be soundproof and private (separated from others). Yet sight lines to screen and lectern are necessary. Six carrels should accommodate left-handed students. Tables and/or chairs should be adjustable for students from kindergarten to the sixth grade—chairs from 10 inches to 19 inches.[17]

In view of the fact that they have been elaborated upon in consider-

[17]Richard Featherstone and Norman Bell, "Space Design and Equipment for the CAI Laboratory," *American School & University*, XL, No. 8 (1968), 24–25.

able detail elsewhere in this chapter, the visual, sonic, and thermal environments necessary for CAI will not be discussed here. It is sufficient to remind the reader that those general principles of lighting, sound control, and climate control previously mentioned also apply in this case.

Carefully planned facilities for storage and display are essential for a superior educational media program. In addition to the types of facilities desired, their location is of paramount importance.

Storage spaces. The amount and location of storage spaces in an educational facility depend upon the extent to which educational media will be used and the degree of centralization desired. In a highly centralized system a minimum of classroom storage space is necessary. As a general policy, materials and equipment that are likely to receive almost daily use should be stored in or adjacent to the location in which they will be used. Other materials and equipment should be stored preferably in the learning resources center.

In planning storage areas, consideration should be given to protection of the equipment and materials from theft, fire, and dust. It also should be kept in mind that adjustable shelving and portable storage units provide greater flexibility in their use.

Display facilities. The modern school program requires ample display areas. The type of display facility and the amount of display space is determined by the grade level, purpose of the display, area of the curriculum, and specific teaching-learning activities. The following list of suggestions is worthy of consideration when planning display spaces:

1. Although there are many substitutes, light-colored, cork-faced tackboard makes the most satisfactory bulletin board.
2. The use of metal chalkboards for display purposes with magnets to hold up the display materials has not proved to be very satisfactory. One reason is that it is difficult to keep a supply of magnets on hand. They tend to disappear.
3. Make display areas as flexible as possible. Reversible tackboard-blackboard combinations have proved to be quite satisfactory.
4. Additional flexibility can be achieved by mounting chalkboards so they slide over bulletin boards either from the side or top.
5. Instead of the strips of cork that used to be standard equipment over chalkboards, install map rails with cork inserts in their place. These map rails with cork inserts also may be installed on corridor walls and in other parts of the building for display purposes.
6. Display boards in classrooms should be mounted so that their bottom edge is at the eye level of the seated pupils.
7. Adjustable shelves on which to display realia should be provided in classrooms and other areas.

8. Locked, glassed-in display cases should be provided in certain areas. Some schools have used them as part of the corridor wall, with the display unit opening into the classroom. Store-type display windows in which exhibits may be viewed from outside the school have proved quite useful from a public relations angle.
9. Installation of tracks or hooks in the ceiling across the front of the classroom makes it possible to suspend certain instructional aids.
10. As a space saver, use "swinging-leaf" type bulletin boards.

A unique variation of the "swinging-leaf" display board is found in the Edenvale elementary school in San Jose, California. Stanchions have been anchored in the floor throughout this completely open school, which has no interior walls, partitions, corridors, or doors. Display surfaces, chalkboards, and AV screens mounted on these stanchions, swivel to any desired position at any given time. These surfaces serve as partial partitions as well as for display.[18]

Screens for projection purposes should be standard equipment in all teaching-learning areas. The size, surface, and mounting are determined by the room size, shape, and type of projection. Expert advice should be sought during the selection process.

Wiring for the electronic age. No one doubts that the use of electronic teaching-learning devices in the schools will continue to increase. If we did not believe what we see happening, proof would be found in the fact that publishing firms, the original purveyors of printed materials (software), are now investing heavily in electronic teaching-learning aids (hardware).

Therefore, an important consideration faced by the school administrator in planning for electronic teaching-learning aids is the kind of wiring specifications required for buildings in the planning stages and those to be modernized. The following hints should prove to be helpful:

1. Plan the facility so that all wiring may be brought in through a central core. Cluster-type buildings similar to the ones mentioned earlier in this chapter lend themselves particularly well to this arrangement.
2. Plan the wiring system so that it can be readily adapted to future needs without costly alterations.
3. Depend upon the advice of a well-qualified electrical engineer in determining the amperage and voltage requirements. Provide him with all the necessary information concerning the electrical equipment to be used and its location. Keep in mind that it is better to provide too much electrical capacity rather than too little.
4. Designate 20 amperes at 110 volts AC as the minimum for receptacle circuits, except in rooms which have additional load requirements.

---

[18]"Solutions to Your Building Problems," *School Management*, X, No. 7 (1966), 111.

5. Provide sufficient circuits to allow the operation of equipment in any one area or all areas simultaneously without overloading circuits.

6. Install three double outlets on each classroom wall approximately 8 feet apart and 18 to 36 inches above the floor. Floor-installed receptacles must be recessed and protected. They are usually difficult to maintain.

7. Plan for additional outlets *above* work surfaces.

8. Provide for all safety precautions by the grounding of all outlets and appliances and by the use of fuses and circuit breakers.

9. Install oversized electrical power conduits to allow for additions and alterations, and make all raceways conveniently accessible.

10. Install communication conduits for intercom units and coaxial cables for TV between all teaching-learning areas and central control facilities in the educational media center and the administrative office areas.

11. Consider installation of front-to-back communication control conduits in all teaching-learning areas in which audio or projection equipment is likely to be used.[19]

ADAPTING OLDER BUILDINGS FOR MODERN EDUCATIONAL PROGRAMS

"Made over" buildings and "made over" clothes never seem to fit as well as new ones, and the fewer alterations that are made the poorer the fit. With the rapid changes that are taking place in teaching-learning technology, many administrators throughout the country are forced to work with "hand-me-down" buildings that do not fit the educational program. This means that many thousands of boys and girls will receive an inadequate education.

There are really no short cuts to providing school facilities that foster the optimum use of learning resources. It is usually easier, however, to achieve a good teaching-learning environment in a new facility than in an old one. Regardless of time and efforts spent in remodeling—to use the clothes simile again—the fabric is old, and there is always the danger that it may give way at some weak point.

DECIDING WHETHER TO MODERNIZE

Throughout this section the term "modernize" is to be interpreted as meaning bringing a building up to present-day educational standards. Specifically, in relation to the topic under discussion, it means to rehabilitate a school facility so that optimum use may be made of all the new, as well as the old, educational media.

Perhaps school administrators and school boards are too timid. Instead of inquiring whether or not a building can be modernized, they should

---

[19]Adapted from Amo DeBernardis, *et al., Planning Schools for New Media* (Portland: Division of Education, Portland State College, 1961), p. 29.

decide to replace it. Unfortunately, the taxpayer does not always see things that way. Just as "hand-me-down" clothes are an accepted "fact of life" in many families, "hand-me-down" school buildings are expected to serve many generations. Consequently, for years to come school administrators and boards of education will be deciding whether to modernize school facilities or to abandon them. In making this important decision serious thought should be given to the following points:

1. The possibility of population shift, so that a school will no longer be needed in that location.
2. The feasibility of transferring to other buildings the pupils who live in the attendance area of the school under consideration.
3. The adequacy of the site in terms of location, size, and its potential for expansion at a reasonable cost.
4. The condition of the structure and its mechanical service systems as determined by competent consultants.
5. The obstacles likely to be encountered in the modernization of the structure as determined by competent consultants.
6. Deficiencies in the building with respect to state or local health and safety codes and space standards.
7. The approximate cost to modernize the facility and the cost to replace it as determined by competent consultants.
8. The adequacy of the modernized structure for a modern educational program as compared to the adequacy of a new structure.

In keeping with the theme of this book, the last item is of greatest concern. Unless the building has been rehabilitated so that conditions in all respects approximate those described throughout this text, it cannot be considered as modernized.

PLANNING FOR MODERNIZATION

In planning for the modernization of an older building, the same steps must be followed as those recommended for new facilities. The same individuals should be involved in developing the educational specifications and in planning the facilities.

The selection of an architect, environmental consultants, and consultants in electronic teaching-learning media is crucial. These individuals must have the kind of creative imagination that enables them to see great potential in existing facilities, and to transform them at a reasonable cost into workable new schemes and patterns that meet the requirements of this modern age of education.

No attempt will be made here to recommend short cuts to modernization of school facilities. The make-shift days are past. Unless a building can be modernized in the truest sense of the word it should be scrapped.[20]

20For excellent ideas on modernization, see Green, *et al., Educational Facilities with New Media*, Sec. B, pp. 58–67.

ENCOURAGING PROPER USE OF FACILITIES

The plain facts of life are that the man who insists on rowing his boat rather than using its motor, and anyone who hitches a mule to his Cadillac instead of filling it with gas would be considered a fool. In spite of this, analogous situations are taking place in thousands of schools throughout the land. Teachers are lecturing without even using the chalkboard, while a dust-covered overhead projector sits in the corner; and TV screens remain dark, while children fill in blanks in workbooks.

The point the authors wish to make is that unless the materials in the educational media center are used in the manner intended and the carefully planned sonic, visual, and thermal environments correctly maintained, a lot of money has been wasted, and the community is being shortchanged.

The responsibility for seeing that all facilities are properly used and maintained rests with the administrative and supervisory staff.

SPECIFIC LEADERSHIP TASKS

The administrator who takes the following tasks seriously is less likely to have unused facilities for teaching and learning:

1. Involve as many individuals as possible in the planning of school facilities and in the selection of equipment.
2. Keep all members of the staff informed during the planning period.
3. Make copies of the educational specifications available to all staff members.
4. Encourage all staff members to follow the progress of the construction or modernization of the school facilities.
5. Plan and hold orientation sessions for professional staff members and for non-professional personnel to acquaint them with the new facilities after they have been completed.
6. Repeat the orientation process each year for new staff members and others who desire to attend.
7. Hold in-service workshops on the use of the new instructional media in the new facilities. Repeat the workshops periodically.
8. Compliment and encourage teachers who are making good use of the new facilities.
9. See that the building and equipment are properly maintained.
10. Don't forget the community—they also should be kept up-to-date on the new facilities.

SUMMARY

The planning of school facilities that make optimum use of learning resources possible is a cooperative enterprise. Representatives of all groups that will use the school plant should be involved at some stage in the planning. In addition, technical assistance will be needed in certain aspects of the planning.

Good educational specifications are essential in all school plant planning. Without them there is little likelihood that the new facility will be adequate.

To facilitate the maximum use of learning resources, environmental conditions as near ideal as possible should be provided. The visual, sonic, thermal, and aesthetic environments are critical in all the various learning areas in which specific environmental conditions are necessary for the most advantageous use of learning resources.

Space requirements for the various facilities must be carefully planned, and the locations and affinities of the areas given serious consideration. Particular attention must be given to the planning of the reading area in the IMC. The trend appears to be the provision of more reading space than formerly. The number, type, and location of student carrels also is of great importance.

Areas for large-group instruction must be planned wisely so that teachers will be able to use educational media effectively. Provisions for computer-assisted instruction also must receive consideration in the planning of a modern school facility.

Adequate display space is a great asset to the learning resources program. Innovative ways should be thought of to provide it.

In modernizing old facilities, the same thoughtful planning should take place. Unless the modernized building can serve essentially the same educational requirements as a new structure, continued use of the old facility is questionable.

Unless teachers and other personnel receive orientation to the new facility, it is unlikely that it will be used as originally planned. Each year new faculty members require a similar introduction to the special features of the building. The community also is entitled to an examination of their new school.

SUGGESTED ACTIVITIES AND PROBLEMS

1. Examine the educational specifications for an instructional materials center, including the library. Visit the facilities to determine how satisfactorily the architect has translated them into spaces and learning environments. Write a report on what you found.
2. Examine your building to discover the characteristics that facilitate the use of educational media and those that make their use difficult. Make recommendations for correcting the deficiencies.
3. Evaluate the visual and sonic environments of a school plant constructed in the past two years in terms of the use of learning resources. Report your findings.
4. Study the educational specifications and the floor plans of a school in the

initial stages to determine the provisions that are being made for the use of electronic equipment. Pay particular attention to the electrical wiring and the provisions being made for future equipment. Write a report including recommendations for any changes you think should be made in the plans with respect to the above.

5. Discuss the problems encountered in attempting to provide adequate visual and sonic environments and climate control to facilitate the use of educational media in an old building.

SELECTED READINGS

Acoustical Environment of School Buildings. New York: Educational Facilities Laboratory, 1963.

Beynon, John, *Study Carrels—Designs For Independent Study Space.* Stanford, Calif.: Western Regional Center of Educational Facilities Laboratories, Inc., 1964.

Boles, Harold W., *Step by Step to Better School Facilities.* New York: Holt, Rinehart & Winston, Inc., 1965.

Brubaker, Charles W., and Stanton Leggett, "How to Create Territory for Learning in the Secondary School: The Turf Concept for the Multischool," *Nation's Schools,* LXXXI, No. 3 (1968), 67.

Chapman, Dave, *Design for ETV: Planning for Schools with Television.* New York: Educational Facilities Laboratories, 1960.

DeBernardis, *et al., Planning Schools For New Media.* Portland: Division of Education, Portland State College, 1961.

Design for Paperbacks: A How-To Report On Furniture for Fingertip Access. New York: Educational Facilities Laboratories, n.d.

Green, A., *et al., Educational Facilities with New Media.* Washington, D.C.: Department of Audiovisual Instruction, National Education Association, 1966.

Guernsey, John E., "How Oregon School Keeps Out Airport Noise," *Nation's Schools,* LXXX, No. 5. (1967), 65.

Hartley, James M., "Designing a School for Audio-Visual System," *The American School Board Journal,* CLI, No. 4 (1965), 40.

NCSC Guide for Planning School Plants, Chaps. 7–10. Columbus: Council of Educational Facility Planners, 1964.

Neagley, Ross L., and N. Dean Evans, *Handbook for Effective Curriculum Development,* Chap. 10. Englewood Cliffs, N.J.: Prentice-Hall, Inc., 1967.

Nelms, Walter L., "Standardization of Educational Specifications," *The American School Board Journal,* CLI, No. 1 (1965), 44.

Oglesby, W. B., "Basic Elements of an Instructional Resources Center," *American School & University,* XXXX, No. 9 (1968), 59.

Wiman, Raymond V., and Wesley C. Meierhenry, eds., *Educational Media: Theory into Practice,* Chap. 10. Columbus: Charles E. Merrill Publishing Company, 1969.

7

Organizing Cooperative
Instructional Services

The chief school administrator with a student population of less than 6,000 pupils who is determined to bring about the changes necessary for curriculum development, effective administrative organization, and new teaching methods and resources to meet the needs of the learner, may soon find himself at his wit's end. "How," he may well ask himself, "can I provide all of the resources necessary to begin such a program?" How, indeed!

How can you be sure which of the national programs in biology, mathematics, or reading, for example, will best meet local curriculum objectives? Can you afford the computer system necessary to provide the data for effective evaluation of the educational program? Where do you find the consultants and specialists needed for the required in-service activities? Is it economically feasible to produce all instructional materials locally?

The problems posed by these and other pertinent questions brought about a rather unique conference of some 160 school administrators in southeastern Pennsylvania under the auspices of a group known as *Curriculum Area 9*.[1]

Formed in the sixties under a program of the Pennsylvania Department of Public Instruction which assigned geographic curriculum areas in Pennsylvania, *Curriculum Area 9* was very active in sponsoring a variety of educational conferences, local research projects, and in-service programs. Always alert to the changing needs of its members, the Steering Committee of *Curriculum Area 9* recognized that, with the technological revolution and the explosion of knowledge this revolution created, local school districts would very likely be unable to provide all of the services

[1] Located at West Chester State College, West Chester, Pa., *Curriculum Area 9* represented the Counties of Delaware, Chester, and Montgomery in southeastern Pennsylvania.

they would need in the near future. A conference for school administrators was held in late 1965, at which time it was agreed that a cooperative approach in such areas as Instructional Materials, In-Service Education, Curriculum Evaluation and Development, Consultant Services, and Educational Information Services might be practical. The Steering Committee was asked to conduct a more detailed analysis of the need for the services described above and to present its report as soon as possible.

A second conference involving 160 school administrators was then held in May, 1966, at which time the report was presented. Each of the 160 superintendents, assistant superintendents, supervisors, and principals in attendance was assigned to one of the five areas under consideration. That the conferees did some serious soul-searching is evident in the report resulting from the Conference, which is presented here:

A. *Instruction Materials*
1. *Application of materials.* We have a great deal of materials and other resources. One problem that must be solved is, How Can It Best be Applied?
2. *Individual use.* Attention must be given to the use of materials by individuals since some instructional materials might be more useful to one child than to another (in the same class during the same lesson).
3. *Analyses of automated instructional equipment.* A center could make available information that describes and explains purposes and uses of and evaluates equipment. Information could be catalogued and circulated.
4. *Maintain library of tapes of demonstration lessons by "experts."*
5. *Provide tape-duplication service.*
6. *Motivational games.* This could be developed and/or evaluated, catalogued and made available.
7. *Develop or locate materials emphasizing senses of sight and smell.*
8. *Mobile Demonstrations* (poetry, home economics, art, industrial arts). For example, provide an art mobile containing examples of prints and originals which would be too expensive for any one district to purchase.
9. *Employ commercial artists and other experts outside education.* They would help districts in the technical phase of producing visuals, etc.
10. *Develop plan for releasing school resource personnel.* The center could suggest a system that districts might use for releasing staff members to serve as resource people within their own system.
11. *Organize a closed circuit television network* (in cooperation with the Tri-State Instructional Broadcasting Council).
12. *Organize trips* to outstanding Instructional Materials Centers.
13. *Develop "packaged unit materials"* in a kit form in various subject areas (filmstrips, slides, tapes, other aids).
14. *Develop a regional instructional materials catalog* of materials available at center.

15. *Develop instructional materials that students may take home* (filmstrips, cartridges, tapes, etc.).
16. *Assist districts* in the establishment of learning centers in each school.
17. *There is a need for each district to have an A.V. supervisor* who will coordinate use of A.V. equipment.
18. *A center could help develop a program to motivate teachers* to understand and use instructional materials.
19. *A center could give greater direction to school architects* in the planning of light control and other matters pertaining to the use of instructional materials.
20. *Regional Service Centers* could gather exceptional visuals from local school districts, duplicate them, and disseminate them to many schools in the area.

B. *In-service education*

Definition: Planned experiences designed to improve the professional employees' effectiveness as a result of professional growth for individual and school.

1. *Leadership*
    A. There is a great need for guidelines for good in-service programs.
    B. In many cases district personnel [are] sole organizers and participants.
    C. It is suggested that trained "outside" personnel are available but their use depends on willingness of districts to provide time and money to get them.
    D. Leaders should be cognizant of tenets of group dynamics and should be "accepted" by teachers.
2. *Major purposes of in-service programs*
    A. Understanding the curriculum.
    B. Developing the curriculum.
3. *Types of programs for teachers presently in operation*
    A. Days provided for intra-district participation.
    B. Inter-district visitation.
    C. Consultants make presentations and conduct workshops.
    D. Suburban study council members share experiences.
    E. Continuous program with time provided during school day as a result of early dismissal.
    F. Departmental and team meetings.
    G. In-service days differ from school-to-school within a district (time and content).
4. *Suggestions for expansion of in-service programs*
    A. Utilize time during summer.
    B. In-service training should be an ongoing program throughout the year. Too often, in-service days are isolated fragments and not part of a total program for the year.

5. *Present programs for administrators and supervisors*
   A. County level meetings and workshops.
   B. Attendance at university programs, seminars, conventions.
6. *Suggestions for improvement of in-service for administrators*
   A. Area research center to provide more programs.
   B. Funds for administrators to attend sessions.
7. *Current training of instructional specialists*
   A. College and university courses and workshops.
   B. Programs provided within the district.
   C. Area film library program for A.V. personnel.
8. *Suggestions for improvement of specialist training*
   A. More programs at area level.
   B. Funds to provide programs within the district.
9. *Suggested time allotment for in-service work*
   A. Time during the school day when students are dismissed early.
   B. Several days to 6-8 weeks.
   C. Provide summer programs where teachers are paid to help develop curriculum and evaluate years of work.
10. *How could an area research and service center help?*
    A. There is a wide range of needs on the part of various "outside" schools in a district. County offices are not equipped to handle such large numbers.
    B. "Experts" could be provided as leaders and participants.
11. *Other suggestions*
    A. An entire year of in-service training could be devoted to a certain area of the curriculum when this is needed (new math, concept approach to teaching of social studies, etc.).
    B. Use in-service money to pay for graduate courses relating to topic of in-service programs.
    C. Study ways of putting decisions into operation once they are made through in-service programs.
    D. Building principals have the capabilities of conducting their own in-service programs. ·

C. *Curriculum, evaluation and development*
   1. *An area center is needed—it could:*
      A. Develop curriculum.
      B. Compile, evaluate, and share with others what is being done nationally in specific curricular areas (such as has been done by Greater Cleveland Council).
      C. Make information available through various channels of communication such as bulletins, publications, workshops, and face-to-face relations.
      D. Provide consultants to districts that have a special problem.
      E. Identify local districts and personnel that are employing innovations.
      F. Provide use of curriculum library.

     G. Help districts develop their own curriculum library.

     H. Train personnel in research skills necessary for curriculum development.

     I. Stimulate district leadership.

     J. Test curriculum innovations through pilot projects.

     K. Study what is needed in the transition from the "old" to the "new."

     L. Standardization of courses of study (will benefit students who transfer from one district to another).

  2. *Those stating that an area center is not needed indicated*:

     A. Give money directly to teachers since the "classroom" teacher's hunch is as good as research.

     B. Teachers know what is wrong in education. All they need is more time and money.

D. *Consultant Services*

  1. *What consultant services are available*

     A. Department heads and curriculum committees in each district.

     B. County office specialists.

  2. *Suggestions for improvement*

     A. Curriculum content should be kept within the local school's domain; consultants within the district are needed.

     B. Districts should have a "generalist" to coordinate curriculum.

     C. Consultants in specific subject areas provided by an area center could be used to assist.

     D. An area consultant could provide such activities as pilot programs, demonstration lessons and audio-visual services.

     E. Need for more pupil personnel, psychiatric, home-and-school visitor consultant services.

     F. Provide area services rendering advice in plant construction.

     G. Area data processing consultants.

     H. K-12 emphasis in curriculum construction.

     I. There may be a danger in too much consultant interference.

     J. More consultant service needed in the areas of mathematics, reading, public relations, psychiatry, psychology, and sociology.

     K. Consultants should offer theory and practice.

E. *Educational information service*

  1. Develop a regional computer center[2]

The conference report indicated quite clearly the need for cooperative services in the five areas, and also the willingness of many administrators to support a cooperative agency. Therefore, the Steering Committee immediately proceeded to develop (and to submit under Title III of the Elementary and Secondary Education Act of 1965) a proposal to:

[2]Anthony F. Pinnie, principal investigator, *A Study to Determine the Need for an Area Research and Service Center to Serve Delaware and Chester County Schools* (West Chester, Pa.: County Superintendent of Schools Office, 1966), pp. 21–26.

1. [Organize] existing instructional services outside the local school district in Chester, Delaware, and Montgomery Counties;

2. [Assess] current national and state activities affecting the instructional program, and the need for coordination of research findings for use at the local level; and

3. [Develop] a proposal for an Area Educational Research and Service Center . . . (to provide those instructional services which cannot be best supplied by a local school district . . .) .[3]

In analyzing existing instructional services in the three-county area, it was found that:

A. Cooperating curriculum research projects have been sponsored by:
   1. Area Nine Curriculum Center
   2. Suburban School Study Councils
B. Instructional materials services are now offered by:
   1. Delaware-Chester Regional Instructional Materials Center (West Chester State College)
   2. Southeast Suburban Regional Instructional Materials Center (Radnor Township School District, Wayne)
   3. Montgomery County Regional Instructional Materials Center (County Superintendent of Schools, Norristown)
   4. Curriculum laboratories at West Chester and Cheyney State Colleges
C. In-service education services
   1. NDEA in-service programs (County offices and DPI)
   2. Curriculum conferences sponsored by:
      a. Area Nine Steering Committee
      b. Department of Supervision and Curriculum Development, Southeastern Region, PSEA
D. Special services utilizing resource personnel (County offices)
   1. Curriculum consultants for subject areas, mainly reading
   2. Psychological services
   3. Speech improvement
E. District Library (West Chester State College Library available for regional community use)[4]

The assessment of National and State educational programs revealed the need for a cooperative agency to organize available information from the various national studies and centers on the subject of curriculum projects and research findings, and to disseminate this information to concerned educators in the local school districts.

The proposal for an Area Research and Service Center, which was approved for funding under Title III of the Elementary and Secondary Education Act of 1965, became the foundation of a survey to determine

3*Ibid.*, p. 6.
4*Ibid.*, p. 7.

the educational needs of some 'fifty school districts, consisting of over 9,000 educators and serving over 200,000 private, parochial, and public school pupils in Delaware and Chester Counties in southeastern Pennsylvania.[5]

Thus we see that what began as a genuine concern by a few educators over the increasing need for instructional services grew into a definite plan of action, supported by many educators, to provide these services.

In "A Study to Determine the Need for an Area Research and Service Center to Serve Delaware and Chester County Schools," a questionnaire (see Appendix 3) was distributed to over 9,000 educators within the two-county area. While the results of the questionnaire were being analyzed, visits were made by members of the project staff to several cooperative agencies in other states to determine specific services offered by these agencies. Following these visits a series of workshops was held involving School Principals, Curriculum Supervisors, Assistant Superintendents, and Chief School Administrators. At these workshops the results of the questionnaires and a review of the visits to other agencies were presented. The workshop participants were then asked to complete a "Consultant's Evaluation Form" (See Appendix 3) to determine what educational agency could best provide the needed services as expressed in the results of the questionnaire.

The conclusion of the study clearly indicated the need for an Area Service Center, and that this Center should provide the following services:

A. *Instructional materials*
   1. Facilities for the production of Audio-Visual Aids
   2. Materials for the production of Audio-Visual Aids
   3. Personnel for the production of Audio-Visual Aids
   4. Educational TV programs
   5. Instructional recordings and tapes
B. *In-Service education*
   1. Opportunities to participate actively in classroom research projects that test new ideas.
   2. Programs to keep the staff up-to-date on the psychological aspects of education.
   3. Opportunities to study and visit schools using newer techniques and organizational patterns.
C. *Curriculum evaluation and development*
   1. Specialists to assist in developing the curriculum.
   2. Specialists to help the classroom teacher to improve instruction.
   3. Methods used by the system in evaluating the effectiveness of the curriculum.
   4. Educational contributions of the state department of education.

[5]Because of the geographic boundaries established in Pennsylvania for the submission of Title III ESEA Projects, Montgomery County could not be included in the study.

    5. Educational contributions from national sources.
D. *Consultant services*
    1. Consultant service in techniques of teaching.
    2. Consultant services in the areas of child growth and development.
    3. Consultants to assist pupils who have psychological or related problems.
    4. Consultants in special education services (speech correction, partially sighted, brain damaged, etc.).
E. *Educational information services*
    1. The dissemination to teachers of sufficient data regarding current changes in education.
    2. Making available for curriculum development curriculum guides showing what other schools are doing.
    3. Making provisions for a curriculum library for teachers.
    4. Data processing services.[6]

The study also revealed many inadequacies in services which were determined as being solely within the province of the local school district. The conclusions of the study recommended that local school districts strengthen such items as supplementary textbooks, certain audiovisual services, and increased time for teachers to study and participate in curriculum evaluation and development.

DETERMINING NECESSARY COOPERATIVE SERVICES

Once you have asked the question raised earlier in this chapter—"How can I provide all of the resources necessary to begin such a program?"— you are on the way to providing these resources. At this point, however, too many educators decide that they cannot possibly provide the necessary resources and therefore quickly dismiss the subject. If instead they think beyond the boundaries of their respective school districts, the solutions to these and many other educational problems are readily apparent. All that is needed in many cases is the willingness of all educators in the area to discuss their needs openly, and then to determine which of these needs can be met by the local district and which might be more effectively met by a cooperative agency.

When the need for a cooperative agency is thus established, and the services to be provided by the agency are determined, then the process of developing and organizing it can begin.

DEVELOPING A COOPERATIVE LEARNING RESOURCES CENTER

Since this handbook is concerned primarily with learning resources, the process necessary for developing a cooperative learning resources center

[6]Pinnie, *A Study to Determine the Need for an Area Research and Service Center,* pp. 45–47.

will be discussed. However, many of the recommendations presented are applicable to the establishment of other cooperative services as well.

The decision to establish a cooperative learning resources center should not be taken lightly. To avoid serious pitfalls, a detailed plan of action for the implementation of the center should be made almost immediately. It is suggested that a committee representing the interested districts be established to determine:

1. The legal authority of the center.
2. The services to be offered by the center.
3. The personnel necessary to coordinate the program.
4. The necessary facilities and equipment.
5. The financial requirements of the program.
6. A program for evaluating the center.

(For more detailed guidelines see Appendix 4.)

The legal authority of the center must be established within the framework of any existing state laws. The variety and complexity of these laws preclude any definitive guidelines; however, the authors recommend as being very suitable those offered by McCarty and Hartsell:

A cooperative audio-visual program is one which extends services to two or more school districts in one or more counties. The audio-visual center may be organized under legal authority of the state legislature, state education agency, county board of education, and/or by mutual consent of the participating local school districts. The policy making body of the program may be a county board of education, and/or a board of school superintendents, or representatives of the schools participating in the financial support and services of the Cooperative audio-visual center.

The cooperative program may be financed by state funds, county funds, local funds, or any combination of these financial sources. In some cases higher education institutions contribute financial support, physical facilities, and administrative support to encourage the establishment and operation of the programs. The audio-visual services provided are generally limited to the schools participating in the program. The center does not necessarily serve all the public schools in the county or service area.[7]

The services to be offered by the center should be based upon the needs expressed by the supporting districts. Will the center provide only the acquisition and distribution of 16mm films, or will it offer a broader range of services extending from in-service programs through the acquisition, production, and distribution of materials and equipment, with provisions for television, a dial access system, or perhaps computer-assisted instruction? All of these are logical services of a cooperative center; but are they of immediate need in your area? Therefore, provisions must be

[7]Henry R. McCarty and Horace C. Hartsell, *The Cooperative Approach to Audio-Visual Programs* (Washington, D.C.: Department of Audio-Visual Instruction and Department of Rural Education, National Education Association, 1959), pp. 20–21.

made to survey *all* educators in the proposed service area to determine what services are needed immediately, and what will be needed in the future. Short- and long-range goals should be established, with priorities given for the implementation of these services.

An excellent example of a cooperative learning resources center is the Audio-Visual Service Center of the Department of Education, San Diego County, San Diego, California.

Audio-visual materials distributed (by the Center) include motion picture films, filmstrips, tape and disc recordings, art prints, exhibits, three-dimensional materials such as anatomical models, study prints, certain types of kits, and modular units. During 1964–65 the Audio-Visual Service distributed over 100,000 motion picture films and 60,000 filmstrips and other types of materials.[8]

The personnel necessary to coordinate the program cannot be overlooked. The number of professional, technical and clerical personnel should be determined for each service. Job descriptions for all personnel should be developed, based upon the services and activities they are expected to provide.

The professional staff, for example, while responsible for the administration of the center, should also be expected to provide a number of services for the cooperating school districts. These additional services should include:

*Stimulating teachers to use the materials available; helping them get maximum benefit from the materials they use.

*Serving with teachers and other consultants in curriculum planning and improvement.

*Conducting demonstrations, workshops, and other activities designed for the in-service development of teachers and administrators, especially their ability to plan, select, and use materials in the improvement of instruction.

*Organizing preview services and assisting teachers and school systems in the selection of audio-visual materials and equipment.

*Working with teachers in the planning and production of teacher-made or school-made audio-visual materials.

*Planning and carrying on research regarding the communicative value of various types of materials, their instructional value in concept development, in the retention of learning, and for similar aspects of the teaching-learning process—always seeking ways in which the process can be improved through the use of specialized materials.[9]

The technical and clerical personnel should engage in such activities as:

*Cataloging and organizing audio-visual materials for use.

*Scheduling materials for use.

[8]*Department of Education, San Diego County* (San Diego, Calif.: Department of Education, San Diego County), mimeograph.
[9]McCarty and Hartsell, *The Cooperative Approach to Audio-Visual Programs*, p. 39.

*Designing and preparing certain types of audio-visual materials.
*Maintaining and repairing mechanical equipment.
*Shipping, maintaining, and receiving and delivering materials.[10]

The staff organization chart for the Audio-Visual Service Center of San Diego County (see Figure 14) shows staff positions and related services.

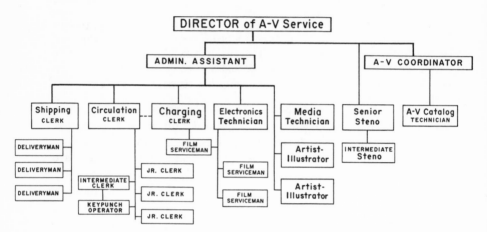

FIGURE 14.   Audio-visual service staff organization, Department of Education, San Diego County.

[During 1964–1965] The Audio-Visual staff [had] 3 professional and 21 clerical and technical personnel. The Section [had] seven operations: circulation, charging, maintenance, shipping, production, cataloging, and administrative services.[11]

The necessary facilities and equipment are now planned, based upon the center's objectives, services, and personnel.

A survey of the geographic region to be serviced should be made, locating any existing buildings which might be utilized and noting also the availability of any land which could be purchased in order to build new facilities, should this prove necessary.

The decision of whether to remodel an existing building or to begin construction on a new one should be made using the criteria presented in Chapter 6. In any event, a geographically central location is desirable for an efficient and economical operation. No attempt will be made here to prescribe any space allocations for the various operations of the center, since these can only be determined after all of the services are established

10*Ibid.*, p. 41.
11*Department of Education, San Diego County.*

and the activities which occur in each space determined. It is essential that professional consultants be retained before any remodeling or construction is attempted.

The reader is referred to Figure 15 which shows the audio-visual facilities of the Department of Education, San Diego County, California.

The financial requirements of the program can now be determined. The costs for each service should be delineated for both the short- and long-range goals (see also Chapter 8). While all potential sources of funds should be sought, i.e., national, state, county, foundation, and other institutions, it is essential that the local districts make a sound financial commitment to guarantee the continuation and success of the center.

A program for the evaluation of the center should be developed, carefully examining existing objectives and services relative to the changing needs of the local school districts.

The center's personnel should be evaluated in terms of their job descriptions and performance. Facilities and equipment should be evaluated relative to their suitability to perform required tasks and to their past maintenance records.

The cooperating school districts must also be prepared to evaluate the effects of the center's services on their program. For example, are teachers provided with released time to evaluate and help select materials to be distributed by the center? Has the school provided the necessary support personnel to coordinate the program within the district?

SPECIFIC LEADERSHIP TASKS

To effectively and economically provide all necessary instructional services, the school administrator must:

1. Discuss present instructional services provided by the district, with his district-wide curriculum committees, teachers, principals, and other personnel to determine the service's effectiveness.
2. Discuss with the above what additional services are needed now or in the near future.
3. Analyze present and additional services in terms of:
   a. Their affect on the school's educational program.
   b. The need for additional personnel and facilities.
   c. Financial implications.
4. Be willing to admit it if he finds the district cannot provide for all needed services.
5. Discuss needed services with other educators in the area with the specific intent of developing a cooperative service agency in the area.
6. Actively place the resources of his district behind the cooperative service agency which might ensue from these discussions.

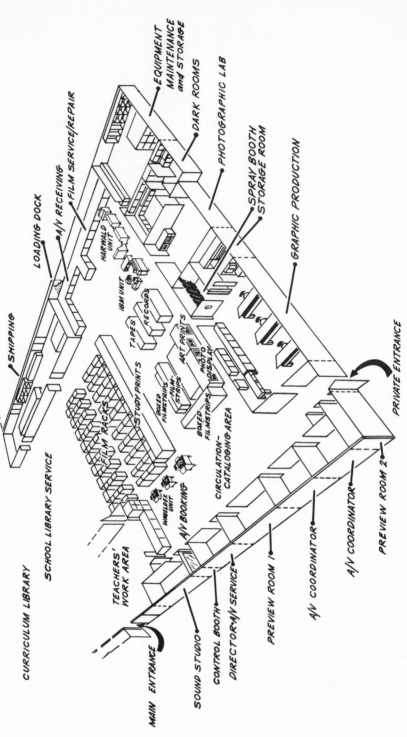

CURRICULUM LIBRARY

SCHOOL LIBRARY SERVICE

SHIPPING

LOADING DOCK

A/V RECEIVING

FILM SERVICE/REPAIR

EQUIPMENT MAINTENANCE and STORAGE

DARK ROOMS

PHOTOGRAPHIC LAB

SPRAY BOOTH STORAGE ROOM

GRAPHIC PRODUCTION

HARWALD UNIT

IBM UNIT

TAPES

RECORDS

ART PRINTS

PHOTO DISPLAY

STUDY PRINTS

BOXED FILMSTRIPS

FILM-STRIPS

BOXED FILMSTRIPS

CIRCULATION-CATALOGING AREA

FILM RACKS

A/V BOOKING

WINKLER UNIT

TEACHERS' WORK AREA

SOUND STUDIO

CONTROL BOOTH

DIRECTOR-A/V SERVICE

MAIN ENTRANCE

PREVIEW ROOM 1

A/V COORDINATOR

A/V COORDINATOR

A/V COORDINATOR

PREVIEW ROOM 2

PRIVATE ENTRANCE

FIGURE 15. Audiovisual facilities, Department of Education, San Diego County, Calif.

SUMMARY

The chief school administrator who is determined to bring about the changes necessary for curriculum development, effective administrative organization, and new teaching methods and resources, will soon find a need for a variety of instructional services. These instructional services will range from learning resources, in-service programs, and professional consultants to sophisticated computer information services, and may prove to be beyond the means of many districts—particularly those with less than 6,000 students.

If needed services cannot be provided by the local district, the school administrator must then be willing to go beyond the boundaries of his district and discuss these needs with other educators in the area, with the intent to establish a cooperative agency.

When the decision to establish a cooperative agency has been made, a thorough survey of all educators should be made to determine specific instructional services needed in the region. Instructional services which may already be in existence locally, state-wide, or nationally should then be determined and analyzed. Visits should be made to cooperative agencies in other parts of the country to examine their organization and services provided.

After needed instructional services have been determined and priorities have been assigned for their implementation, the process of developing and organizing the cooperative agency can begin.

A cooperative learning resources center is one of several instructional services which can be provided by several districts. The decision to establish such a center should not be taken lightly.

To avoid serious pitfalls, a committee representing participating school districts must determine the following: the legal authority of the center, the services to be offered by the center, the personnel necessary to coordinate the program, the necessary facilities and equipment, the financial requirements of the program, and a system for evaluating the center.

The establishment of a cooperative learning resources center will bring to the region a variety of programs and services ranging far beyond the capabilities of the individual district.

SUGGESTED ACTIVITIES AND PROBLEMS

1. Using as criteria the services outlined on pages 126–27, interview the chief school administrator of a district with less than 2,000 pupils. In your written report indicate (a) the degree to which the services are offered, (b) which of

these services he feels are necessary but are not provided, and (c) his reactions
to establishing a cooperative agency to provide the needed services.

2. Prepare a proposal for establishing a cooperative learning resources center
   which will provide 16mm films for several school districts having a combined
   pupil population of 25,000 (K–12) and 850 teachers and administrators. The
   center is to begin its service with 400 film prints.

3. Visit a cooperative service center in your area, interviewing the chief administrator of the agency and at least two school administrators from supporting
   districts. To what extent is the center meeting the needs of the districts? To
   what degree have additional services been added in recent years? What additional services do they feel are needed? In your written report analyze the
   degree of cooperation and communication between the center and the local
   school districts.

4. Write to three cooperative centers in different areas of the country, requesting
   the information necessary to determine the number of faculty and students
   served, the services offered, the number of personnel employed, and the financial requirements of their program. In your written report compare the results
   of your survey.

SELECTED READINGS

Brown, James W., and Kenneth D. Norberg, *Administering Educational Media,*
Chap. 13. New York: McGraw-Hill Book Company, 1965.

Isenberg, Robert M., ed. *The Community School and the Intermediate Unit,*
Yearbook, 1954. Washington, D.C.: Department of Rural Education, National Education Association, 1954.

McCarty, Henry R., and Horace C. Hartsell, *The Cooperative Approach to
Audio-Visual Programs.* Washington, D.C.: Department of Rural Education, National Education Association, 1959.

Neagley, Ross L., and N. Dean Evans, *Handbook for Effective Curriculum Development,* Chaps. 2 and 3. Englewood Cliffs, N.J.: Prentice-Hall, Inc.,
1967.

8

Guidelines
for Financing
Educational Media Programs

The title and theme of this entire handbook is the effective administration of learning resources. The ultimate test of effective administration is the extent to which the quality of education has been improved as a result of it. Effective administration suggests sufficient well-qualified personnel, ample high-quality instructional supplies, the latest educational media, and modern physical plant facilities to house the educational program. This all costs money—lots of money. It therefore will be the purpose of this chapter to discuss some general principles of budgeting for a quality educational program, to give a brief review of sources for financial support of education, and finally to suggest some guidelines for financing the educational media program.

The Budget As The Key To A Quality Educational Program

The term "budget" over the years has developed a connotation of restriction. From the time they are quite small, children hear their parents discuss the family budget. They also are placed on an allowance and cautioned to stay within the budget. In this restricted sense, a budget is merely a formal statement of proposed expenditures for a given period and the anticipated revenues for financing them. In the case of the household budget, the anticipated revenue is usually taken as the starting point because it is fixed. In government, business, and industry, if the leadership is of high quality, the needs of the enterprise are determined and the necessary revenue found to finance them. Too frequently, boards of education have started with the wrong dimension by determining how much money they dare raise and then planning the budget based on this limited amount. This, of course, is what happens in the case of the family budget, although it must be acknowledged that many families live beyond their means.

The discussion in this chapter is concerned with a much broader concept of the budget than the one just described. According to Ovsiew, *et al.*,

A budget may be defined as a specific plan for implementing organizational objectives, policies and programs for a given period of time. It embodies (1) descriptions of organizational activities and services requisite to attainment of organizational goals; (2) estimates of expenditures and their allocations; and (3) forecasts of fiscal resources available to support the plan.[1]

Budget preparation for schools has improved in recent years. As school administrators have become better prepared, they have learned more about the budgeting process. They have become aware of the fact that the budget is the key to quality educational programs.

In discussing the foundations of effective budget development, Ovsiew and Castetter suggest the following principles of budget development:

1. Budget considerations begin with educational objectives.

2. Budget development requires continuing appraisal of the present status of the educational program.

3. A well-organized budget contains (a) a description of the *educational plan*, and the objectives upon which it is based, including the manner in which the budget requests are designed to accomplish the objectives—new or revised offerings, additional services, supplies, equipment, and the quality of personnel involved in the progam; (b) a precise *expenditure plan* showing the budget categories to which the various expenditures will be distributed, and explanations of increases or decreases in the various budget items with supporting data to indicate the appropriations necessary to carry out educational plans; and (c) a *revenue plan* which describes the amounts and sources of funds proposed for financing the estimated expenditures.

4. Effective budget development involves extensive utilization of the special capacities to be found among staff personnel and citizens generally.

5. Sound budget development is based on unit control, which means that the board of education should delegate to a single educational authority, the superintendent of schools, the responsibility for initiating and coordinating budget planning.

6. An imaginative approach to budget development encourages public understanding and support of the policies and practices reflected in the budget proposal.

7. Efficient budget development involves planning beyond a single fiscal year.

8. If a budget is to be really useful, it must be properly administered, however well-conceived and adequate it may also be.[2]

[1]Leon Ovsiew, William B. Castetter, and Adolph J. Koenig, "Budgeting," in *The Theory and Practice of School Finance*, eds. Warren E. Gauerke and Jack R. Childress (Chicago: Rand McNally & Company, 1967), p. 209.

[2]Leon Ovsiew and William B. Castetter, *Budgeting for Better Schools* (Englewood Cliffs, N.J.: Prentice-Hall, Inc., 1960), pp. 16–18.

Various procedures have been followed by school-district and other officials in the preparation of budgets. One well known but questionable practice is that of padding the budget. In the public schools this has been done because of lack of confidence in one or more of the individuals or groups having control over budget requests or appropriations. In this category may be found state agencies, the electorate, boards of education, and administrators. If an individual who is preparing his budget requests believes that anywhere along the line these requests may be cut, there is a great temptation to ask for more than is actually needed. This practice is both indefensible and reprehensible and should not be tolerated. If good budgetary procedures are followed and real educational leadership exercised by those in authority, this practice will have no place in the scheme of things.

A good procedure to insure that budgets will not be padded is to prepare a "justified budget," requiring all individuals submitting requests to justify in writing the items they desire. In discussing this procedure Ovsiew and Castetter state:

A written justification for each budget item has two values, each of which forces the superintendent to test his judgment: first, by specifying the purpose of the expenditure, the justification defines the educational use of the item and, second, by specifying the elements of the computation used in assigning the dollars, the justification offers a prudential check on assumptions and computations.[3]

The same authorities suggest that establishing priority is closely associated with the writing of justifications. This may be considered as an effort to rate each item in its order of importance to the educational plan. A system of priority ratings is a refinement of the selection function. Refined in this manner, selection is subjected to its complementary act, evaluation. When used together, priority rating and justification contribute to making the budget trenchant and persuasive.[4]

EDUCATIONAL MEDIA PROGRAMS AND THE BUDGET

In Chapter 4 the authors took the position that financial requirements for media are a direct result of the professional decisions made in the curriculum council and in the offices of the assistant superintendent in charge of instruction. This implies that, regardless of whether the administrative structure suggested in this handbook is followed, the assistant superintendent in charge of instruction is responsible for preparing the budget for financing the educational media program. All departmental,

[3]Ovsiew and Castetter, *Budgeting for Better Schools*, p. 35.
[4]*Ibid.*, pp. 35–36.

building, and special services budgets feed into his office. In school systems that have not as yet unified their educational media programs, there will be considerable overlapping of requests, and the resolution of these conflicts will require a considerable amount of tact and diplomacy on the part of the superintendent in charge of instruction.

The authors are not suggesting that the superintendent in charge of instruction personally make up the budget for the educational media program—many persons will contribute to the budget-making process. The coordinator of learning resources will be quite influential in determining what items are finally included in the budget; principals and subject area curriculum coordinators also will make their influences felt. A good budget usually results from a cooperative venture. It is the team approach discussed in Chapter 2 that really produces a worthwhile realistic document.

Budgeting and financing the educational media program. Although later on in this chapter some specific recommendations will be made with respect to expenditures, the authors are more concerned with procedures than with actual allotment amounts. Budget allocations, like space assignments, depend upon the educational program. Therefore, with the focus on procedures, rather than budgetary details, the following principles of budgeting and financing the educational media programs are enumerated:

1. An educational media program should operate from a central budget which is prepared and defended by representatives of the educational media services.
2. An educational media program should be financed entirely from regularly appropriated school funds.
3. A school system should have clear-cut policies concerning allocation, income, and charges against the educational media budget.
4. The budget of an educational media program should be based on both the schools' long-range goals and immediate educational media needs.
5. Long-range budget planning should provide for improvements to be made gradually until the full media program goals are realized.
6. Long-range financial plans should include provisions for the expansion of media services as required by the improvement of quality and scope of the instructional program.
7. The budget of an educational media program should provide for increased scope of services, expansion of services to meet increased enrollments, and the needs created by the addition of new structures.
8. There should be a definite plan for gaining administrative and community support for the media program. The plan should include evaluation of the program, determination of media needs, long and short range planning, and presenting facts about media needs to administrators and governing boards.
9. All costs relating to procurement or production of materials, purchase of

equipment, and employment of staff for use in the schools' educational program should be completely subsidized through a centralized budget.

10. Teachers should be able to use educational media from the media center with no more restrictions than those imposed on the use of the book library or similar school services.

11. The selection of all materials and equipment for purchase by the educational media center should be based on predetermined specifications formulated by the media staff.

12. Provisions should be made in the educational media budget for systematic replacement of obsolete or worn-out media.[5]

The above 12 principles make a lot of sense and should receive serious consideration by all individuals responsible for budgeting and financing an educational media program in the schools. The principles are self-explanatory and consequently require no extensive elaboration. Brief comments will be made, however, on several of the principles.

The first principle states that the educational media budget should be prepared and defended by representatives of the educational media service. The authors concur, but wish to suggest to the reader that if the budget items are accompanied by adequate justification, the assistant superintendent in charge of instruction, the superintendent of schools, and the board of education are all much more likely to approve them.

Principles 4 and 5 suggest the desirability of both long-range and immediate goals and needs. Here again, if those who must endorse the budget requests see immediate needs in relation to long-range goals and understand that improvements are to be made gradually, there is greater probability of budget approval.

Principle 6 relates the expansion of media services to the improvement of the quality and scope of the instructional program. It would seem that this is the key to the entire budgetary process. Unless the expenditure of public funds gives evidence of some tangible results, difficult as they are to measure, continued support for the educational media budget may be difficult to obtain.

Justification of educational media budget items. Earlier in this chapter the advantage of a written justification for each item of the budget was explained. One AV authority concurs by stating:

The best way to build, maintain, and expand an AV program is by what I call a "justified budget." It is the hardest type to prepare because it requires time, research, and decision making on the part of the AV director. . . . A justi-

[5]W. R. Fulton, *Criteria Relating to Educational Media Programs in School Systems* (Norman, Oklahoma: University of Oklahoma. Developed as part of a study performed pursuant to a contract with the USOE, Department of Health, Education and Welfare, under the provisions of Title VII, Public Law 85–664, mimeographed, n.d.), pp. 8–9.

fied budget is exactly what the name implies; every item must be justified on its need for the coming year. Asking for what isn't essential is the surest way I know to hand the board of education an axe with which to chop down the AV budget.[6]

Although the following material illustrating justification of items in an educational media budget is hypothetical, it does exemplify this important procedure in budget making.

PAGE FROM HYPOTHETICAL BUDGET ILLUSTRATING THE JUSTIFICATION OF BUDGET ITEMS

EDUCATIONAL MEDIA

Educational TV: Funds are being requested again this year for membership in the Tri-State Educational TV Council. It should be noted that the amount requested represents approximately a 30 per cent increase over the amount budgeted last year. Part of this increase is due to a rise in operational costs—the additional increment is the result of increased services.

During the past year, 2,200 individual programs were viewed by students in the secondary schools, or an average of two programs per student each week.

In the elementary schools the corresponding figures were 3,500 and three. A majority of the teachers used the programs as intended. They made good use of the "Teachers' Guide" for the TV series. All teachers participated in one or more educational TV workshops.

The additional services planned for next year include a series of educational TV programs on African History. This, you will agree, has been a real need that we have been unable to meet because of lack of instructional materials.

Filmstrips: The budget item for filmstrips also represents an increase over last year. Filmstrips, unlike films, are purchasable only. Consequently, like textbooks they wear out, become outdated, and must, therefore, be replaced. Justification for selection of particular filmstrips is based upon the following characteristics:

1. Filmstrips that correlate with particular texts in use in the school system.
2. Filmstrips that illustrate certain concepts being taught in a given area of study.
3. Filmstrips especially prepared for small-group and individualized learning.
4. Filmstrips illustrating concepts that require a pictorial presentation in order that they may be understood.

Justification for extensive purchase of filmstrips is based on the following:
1. They will be available when needed.
2. They can be used over and over again.
3. Multiple prints of frequently used filmstrips are justified on the basis of making them more readily available at the time and place needed.

[6]Thomas H. Boardman, "Budget Preparation and Presentation," *Audiovisual Instruction*, XII, No. 3 (1967), 238.

In an actual budget, many additional items would be included, but the justifications for the above items would be sufficient to illustrate the procedure.

Use of the performance budget. Another type of budget that has possibilities for educational media is known as the performance budget. According to Thomas a performance budget would include statements about anticipated revenue, expenditures, and pupil performance. He admits that there are many difficulties in applying the concept of the performance budget to schools, because of the complexity of educational enterprises and the fact that they seek a multiplicity of objectives. He further admits that it is difficult to identify rank and to measure the outcomes of education. In spite of these difficulties, however, Thomas believes that performance budgeting can be used in the schools in the following specific cases: (1) in budgeting for a special educational project, (2) in approaching cases where marginal increments in expenditure are planned—as, for example, a proposal to increase the instructional budget might have as a primary goal the improvement of written English by employing theme readers, and (3) in making an analysis of specific aspects of the school's program. In the third case, he suggests that in a given year the senior mathematics program might be budgeted on a performance basis.[7]

The practicing school administrator and the student in educational administration should have little difficulty in seeing the relationship of the three cases cited above to the use of performance budgeting in the educational media budget. For example, the special project budgeted for under case (1) might be the use of computer assisted instruction in the teaching of mathematics. In case (2), the primary goal for increasing the operating rate of taxation could just as easily have been the improvement of foreign language teaching by the installation of a language laboratory. In the final case given above, each year a different item might be budgeted on the performance basis, and research conducted to determine its relationship to improved learning in a given area of the curriculum.

Presentation of the educational media budget. The most carefully made budget is of little use unless it is finally approved by the board of education, and in some states the electorate. Although the assistant superintendent in charge of instruction is the key person to work with in the preparation of the educational media budget, the superintendent of schools is the individual who must secure final approval for the entire

---

[7]Adapted from J. Alan Thomas, "Educational Decision-Making and the Budget," in *School Administration: Selected Readings,* eds. Sherman H. Frey and Keith R. Getschman (New York: Thomas Y. Crowell Company, 1968), p. 415.

school budget by the board of education. In discussing the presentation of the budget, Boardman suggests that individuals responsible for the AV budget can assist the superintendent in his preparation for budget presentation by:

1. Explaining the meaning of "justified budget."
2. Proving their budget figures are highly reliable.
3. Emphasizing that there is no padding.
4. Helping him to understand why a justified budget may vary considerably from year to year.
5. Assisting him to comprehend why a per-pupil allocation will not provide the AV program that really achieves the desired educational goals.
6. Making it clear that "priority" does not always apply.
7. Encouraging him to make use of the AV departmental services in his total budget presentation.[8]

The above suggestions assign an important role to the audio-visual services personnel, but they are applicable to all personnel concerned with the entire educational media program. In fact, the suggestions could be followed advantageously in preparing for the presentation of all areas of the budget.

FINANCING THE EDUCATIONAL MEDIA PROGRAM

In the USA education is a state function, the responsibility for which has been delegated to the local school district. Although the federal government has demonstrated its concern from time to time by providing funds for special purposes, it has only been in the past decade or so that a major concern has been shown by the appropriation of considerable sums of money for the support of education.

At various times and in different locales industry and business have shown their interest in education as a means of improving the national economy. Foundations established by business, industry, and wealthy families have contributed large sums to special educational projects, which in many instances were focused on the improvement of the teaching-learning processes.

A good instructional media program is expensive, but in most school districts alert, enthusiastic school administrators can find the necessary funds to finance one if they are willing to expend the necessary time and energy. When they assume the important role of administrative leadership, superintendents, principals, and other school administrators should keep in mind the findings of Brickell, which clearly reveal that instruc-

[8]Adapted from Boardman, "Budget Preparation," p. 241.

tional changes of any significance depend almost entirely upon administrative initiative.[9]

This truth is attested to below in this chapter when figures are quoted indicating the wide range of expenditures for educational media in different school systems.

STATE AND FEDERAL SOURCES

The constitution of all 50 states charge their legislatures with the responsibility of providing for the education of their children and youth. Although, with the present exception of Hawaii, the states have delegated this responsibility to the local school districts, it has become necessary over the years for the states to assume an increasingly larger share of the local school budget.

According to a recent study by Collins, the percentage of revenue for public elementary and secondary schools received from state governments varies dramatically. For the school year 1967–1968 the state of Delaware led the list with an average contribution of approximately 80 per cent, while Nebraska was at the bottom with about 5 per cent. On the national scene, the average state support of education was 40 per cent, excluding federal aid distributed through the states.[10]

A recent publication of the NEA mentions that state funds for education are of the following types: (1) flat general-purpose grants, (2) flat special-purpose grants, (3) equalizing general-purpose grants, and (4) equalizing special-purpose grants. The same report further reveals that in a majority of the states some state funds are distributed by the equalization method and some made available by the flat-grant method. In some of the state foundation programs an incentive feature has been added to the basic state grant. Under this plan, the state contributes additional funds to match any additional local funds raised above the minimum amount required.[11]

As the demand for better education grows, the states will have to assume a much larger share of the costs, particularly in those states that are below the national average and, hopefully, in most of the others as well. Many of our big city school systems are in dire financial straits. The states in which they are located must find new methods for providing revenue to meet the big city schools' increasing needs.

In discussing basic state action in financing schools, the NEA report

[9]See Henry M. Brickell, *Organizing New York State for Educational Change* (Albany, N.Y.: State Education Department, 1961), p. 23.

[10]George J. Collins, "How Schools Budget 1967–68," *Nation's Schools*, LXXX, No. 6, 38.

[11]*What Everyone Should Know About Financing Our Schools* (Washington, D.C.: Committee on Educational Finance, National Education Association, 1966), p. 46.

cited above recommends that, in connection with the distribution of state school funds to the local districts, the following objectives should be achieved:

1. Educational opportunity should be provided for all children and youth by establishing an adequate minimum or foundation of financial support per pupil in all school districts.

2. Local interest and initiative in education should be preserved by requiring all local districts to make an equitable contribution toward the financing of schools in terms of local financial ability.

3. The required local contributions should be such as to leave tax leeway in the community available for local innovation and experimentation in the schools.

4. The cost of the schools should be equitably distributed over all forms of taxable capacity.

5. The total amount available for the schools should be sufficient to permit the financing of a quality program of education.[12]

The time is ripe for a rearrangement of the role played by each of the triple partners in the financing of education in the United States. Adequate financial support of public education cannot be expected when the local district, which is the least able partner in taxing power, is carrying the "lion's share" of the costs in most states. The state, although only second in taxing ability, picks up most of the remainder of the cost of education, while the federal government, with the greatest taxing power, has contributed the least financial support.

Federal financial support for education. Participation by the federal government in the financing of education is not new. The land grant acts, vocational education acts, impacted areas acts, and GI legislation are all familiar to the student of school finance. Beneficial as they were, their impact on the total educational scene was slight. Now it appears as though the role of the federal government in supporting education in our nation may be changing.

Importantly, much of the new legislation that portends this change has made funds available for the improvement of the educational media program. The beginning of a movement for increased federal support by means of categorical aids dates back to the year 1958. Under the threat of Russian technological advances, as demonstrated by Sputnik, the National Defense Education Act gave generous federal support for projects in science and mathematics. Foreign language instruction also received a considerable boost under Title III of the NDEA. This section enabled local school districts to purchase instructional resources in science, mathematics, and foreign languages by matching the federal funds

[12]*Ibid.*, p. 47.

made available to them through state coordinators. In 1964 the expansion of the basic Act to include financial support for instructional materials in the social studies and English fields restored once again a balance in the curriculum. Of even more direct concern to the subject of this handbook was a separate title of the NDEA which made possible the development and expansion of new educational media. Under this section of the Act funds were provided to pay for educational media such as educational television, transparencies for overhead projectors, and 8mm sound films for classroom use. Three other recent federal acts contributing to the improvement of education are the Cooperative Research Act of 1954, the Vocational Education Act of 1963, and the Economic Opportunity Act of 1964.

Another landmark in federal aid to education that had great implications for the media program was the 1962 Educational Television Facilities Act. This Act authorized the expenditure of $32 million during a five-year period. Funds were distributed on a matching basis for the construction of or additions to educational TV broadcasting facilities. A limit of $1 million was placed on the amount that might be allocated in any one state.

However, the real milestone in federal aid to education was the passage of the Elementary and Secondary Education Act in 1965.

Title I provides for the largest amount of funds under the ESEA and allows local school districts the greatest amount of freedom in deciding how to use the money. The main purpose of Title I is to provide financial aid to local educational agencies that are serving areas in which there are concentrations of children from families with low incomes. The objective is to meet the special needs of educationally deprived children. Although the emphasis is on the needs of children from families with low incomes, all children with similar needs from both public and non-public schools are enjoying the benefits of the new programs that have evolved. Illustrative of acceptable programs under Title I are pre-school programs; community study centers; remedial programs; cultural enrichment activities; after-school tutoring; summer school and Saturday classes; classes for talented pupils; educational radio and television; use of films, tape recorders, and other equipment; mobile facilities such as libraries and laboratories; and in-service education experiences for teachers. Although it is not safe to generalize concerning the effects of Title I on educational media programs, it is probably fair to assume that some improvement resulted. Certainly, no one would question the potential inherent in the last four categories listed above.

Title II of the ESEA potentially could have considerable influence on the use of educational media in the schools. This section of the Act provides money through the states for the purchase of textbooks and library books, periodicals, documents, charts, maps, globes, magnetic tapes, transparencies, films, phonograph records, and other printed and published instructional material. Equipment, however, may not be purchased under Title II.

Title III seems to hold the greatest promise for improving teaching and learning, because it was designed primarily to stimulate local imagination and creativity. The intention of this Title is to assist local districts to relate research to practice by supporting creative, innovative, supplementary centers and services.

Considerable latitude is permitted, although each project must be approved individually by the U.S. Office of Education. Among the types of projects funded under this Title that relate to educational media are learning laboratories, instructional materials centers, mobile libraries, mobile science laboratories, home study courses incorporating new techniques of learning, and innovative educational radio and television programs. Some of the above activities are being conducted on a cooperative basis—e.g. the establishment of a regional instructional materials center serving several counties or a combination of school districts. A good example of this is the Southwest Iowa Learning Resources Center, the plan of which is found in Figure 9 of Chapter 6 of this text.

Title IV of the Elementary and Secondary Education Act amended the Cooperative Research Act of 1954 by enlarging it, and by calling for the establishment of a national network of educational laboratories to engage in and implement educational research. Title IV is making its contribution to the improvement of learning resources by carrying on research in the areas of curriculum and instruction. Studies on the content of the curriculum and methods of instruction are receiving high priority in the regional laboratories. The sharing of research findings through cooperative data processing systems is another objective of these national and regional research facilities.

Title V of the ESEA is aimed at strengthening state departments of education. Although it does not involve local districts directly, any improvements in the state departments' ability to provide professional counsel and leadership ultimately will benefit at least some local school districts within each state participating in the program. Grants may also be used for educational research and demonstration projects and the publication and distribution of curriculum materials, and projects of this nature would have some potential for affecting the ways in which educational media are used in the schools.

Charged with the responsibility for administration of the new federal programs in education, the U.S. Office of Education is taking on a very significant role in shaping our nation's schools. .

Some educators are concerned that this eventually may result in a national system of education; others feel that is a long overdue move in the right direction. In order to preserve the state and local control of education, the NEA Committee on Educational Finance suggests the following criteria:

1. The major contribution of the federal government to the partnership should be made through a basic financial program of support to the states.

2. The federal share of fiscal support of elementary and secondary schools when combined with state and local tax resources should be sufficient to provide adequate educational services and facilities in all state-local school systems.

3. The amount of aid should be generally predictable for long-range planning and specifically predictable for year-to-year planning.

4. The amounts of federal funds to which individual states or local school districts are entitled should be determined by objective formulas, reducing to a minimum the discretionary power of federal officials. The formula for distributing federal funds should recognize the wide variation in the states' ability to finance education.

5. Federal funds for education should be allocated to state governments to be distributed by them to local schools in accordance with state plans.

6. The accounting and auditing safeguards for federal grant funds should be applied at the state level by utilizing the procedures required by the states to safeguard state grants to local school systems.

7. Special purpose grants appropriately supplement general purpose grants to stimulate the development of educational programs of critical national concern; to finance the research development, and demonstration phases of special educational problems; or to meet the federal government's obligations as a landowner and employer for payments in lieu of local property taxes. Special grants should be limited in number, comprise a small portion of the total federal aid, and be reviewed by Congress periodically.

8. All federal educational programs should be administered by the U.S. Office of Education at the federal level, by the state educational agency at the state level, and by the local educational agency at the local level.[13]

Under present world conditions, it is difficult to predict accurately how large a role the federal government will play in the financing of education during the next decade, and how soon the above criteria can be met. So much depends upon how quickly our nation can get back on a peace economy, and how long it can avoid other military entanglements. Once peace is restored, education will become a top national priority, in fact as well as in name. Then the flood-gates on the dam of federal dollars, which allowed only a trickle to ooze out in the mid-sixties, will open wide and inundate the field of education. Perhaps this is "wishful thinking," but it certainly is within the realm of possibility.

[13]Erick L. Lindman, "Criteria for Evaluating Federal Education Programs," in *The Challenge of Change in School Finance* (Washington, D.C.: Committee on Educational Finance, National Education Association, 1967), p. 30.

However, school districts should be prepared for this eventuality with plans for research, innovation, expansion of programs, and other improvements in education—so that there would not be a delay in putting federal funds to work in worthwhile, well-planned projects.

INDUSTRY AND FOUNDATION SOURCES

Industry and business have long recognized the importance of education to the national economy. They know that there is a direct positive relationship between education and full employment, high national income, and general well-being. They also acknowledge that democracy as a form of government cannot achieve its full stature unless the populace is literate. Therefore, in addition to carrying part of the taxation load for education, industry and business have contributed directly to the improvement of the teaching-learning process. They have accomplished this by sponsoring research, encouraging experimentation in the use of their products, developing new materials and equipment, and providing free instructional materials that include an advertising message. Many of these free materials are useful educational media consisting of such items as transparencies, films, filmstrips, recordings, posters, charts, pictures, models, and demonstration kits.

It is difficult to estimate the effect of industry and business on curriculum and instruction. For years in many classrooms the basic textbook largely determined what was taught in a given area of the curriculum. Now that the purveyors of "software" have also become peddlers of "hardware" the influence of textbook companies on education could be tremendous.

Companies specializing in school equipment, both instructional and other types, continue to make their influence felt. In the purchase of audio-visual equipment, for example, the personality and skill of the sales personnel have frequently been influential in the selection made— at least on items not requiring bids. Then too, the excellent exhibits and displays of manufacturers held at national, state, and regional educational meetings offer a wonderful opportunity for school administrators and other school personnel to inspect the nation's wares and consequently to select the educational media and equipment that will give the greatest value.

Local industries have been willing, on occasion, to contribute funds directly to local schools and regional groups. One of the best examples of this is The Greater Cleveland Area Research Council, which got its start with the assistance of industries in that area. If a recent U.S. district court decision[14] becomes common knowledge and is not overruled by a higher

---

[14]Case cited in article is Jefferson Mills, Inc., *v.* United States, 259 F. Supp. 305.

court, many schools may be receiving tax-free dollars from local firms. In the case cited below, the court accepted the plaintiff's argument that its concern with education grew out of a desire to further its own interests and therefore, held that the funds were a "business expense."[15]

Private foundations have poured and continue to pour millions into the support of educational projects—most noteworthy of those related to educational media are projects underwritten by the Ford Foundation in educational television. Their contributions to this educational media are far too numerous to mention in a work of this limited scope; it is sufficient to say that over $50 million has been spent.

A recent study conducted as a preliminary survey to a doctoral dissertation revealed that there are approximately 114 foundations making annual grants of $10,000 or more that contribute to the improvement of curriculum and instruction. Many of these grants can and do influence the educational media program.[16]

THE COST OF EDUCATIONAL MEDIA PROGRAMS

In Chapter 6 on the school plant the authors took the position that to quote figures, even as minimum standards, can be dangerous if school districts take them as gospel rather than as guides. The same is true with respect to cost figures for educational media; the important facts are not what other districts are spending, but rather how much does each district need to spend in order to provide the best available educational media for its students and teachers. It does, however, help districts to plan their purchasing of educational media if they know how much other districts are spending. It also is advantageous for them to know what authoritative sources consider to be necessary expenditure levels to provide adequate instructional materials and equipment.

This section of the chapter will be concerned with the above topics. All figures must be considered as guidelines and nothing more.

What is being spent for educational media? One of the best sources of information concerning total school expenditures over a period of several years is a recent survey made of more than 1,200 school districts throughout the country and reported in *School Management*. In computing school district expenditures, the study uses "Expenditure Pupil Units" (EPUs) rather than the actual number of pupils. These units take into account the fact that it costs more to educate a secondary school student than it does to educate an elementary school pupil. A district's EPUs were computed by multiplying the Average Daily Attendance of its sec-

[15]Lee O. Garber, "Schools Can Get Tax-free Dollars from Local Firms," *Nation's Schools*, LXXX, No. 6 (1967), 50.
[16]Preliminary data collected by Richard Reiff and used by permission.

ondary school students by 1.3 and adding this figure to its elementary ADA.

Analysis of the data collected reveals that national median districts spend $5.10 per EPU for textbooks and $14.75 for other teaching materials; a fourth of the districts $7.04 and $18.94; and ten per cent expend $9.19 and $24.98 per EPU, respectively. An extremely interesting finding of the study was that although wealthier districts do spend more than poor districts for instructional materials, the difference is very slight. One additional item from the study that should be of interest is that for all districts studied the cost of textbooks represented 1.1 per cent of the net current expenditures and other teaching materials 3.2 per cent. The comparable figure for all costs of instruction including salaries was 78.4 per cent.[17]

In a study on budgeting for the 1967–1968 school year Collins reports the relationships of expenditures for instructional materials to the total instructional budget by different levels of per pupil expenditure to be as follows:

1. In districts with a per pupil expenditure of less than $500 the range is from 2.30 per cent to 24.73 per cent.

2. In districts spending $501 to $700 per pupil the range is from 2.64 per cent to 18.25 per cent.

3. In districts spending more than $700 per pupil the comparable figures are 3.09 per cent and 15.69 per cent.[18]

It should be noted that in calculating the per pupil costs in the above study the secondary school pupils were not weighted as in the previous study.

Although it is not as recent as the other two studies reported, a very comprehensive survey of the cost of audio-visual instruction covering the period 1962–1963 to 1965–1966 inclusive can be found in another issue of *School Management*. This study again uses the weighted secondary school pupil. As is also true of the other articles mentioned, the entire article must be studied to appreciate its implications. It should, however, be of value to report here the amounts spent per EPU in 1965–1966 for each of the following categories of audio-visual materials:

1. For 16mm projectors 65.5 per cent of the districts spent 37 cents.
2. For 16mm film 31.0 per cent of the districts spent 41 cents.
3. For film rental 83.1 per cent of the districts spent 25 cents.
4. For filmstrips 82.4 per cent of the districts spent 18 cents.
5. For record players 80.2 per cent of the districts spent 15 cents.

[17]Adapted from "The Cost of Education Index 1967–1968: How the School Dollar is Being Spent," *School Management*, XII, No. 1 (1968), 90.

[18]Collins, "How Schools Budget," pp. 44–45.

6. For phonograph records 78.0 per cent of the districts spent 8 cents.

7. For overhead projectors 80.2 per cent of the districts spent 35 cents.

8. For language laboratories 25.6 per cent of the districts spent 31 cents.

9. For television receivers 25.2 per cent of the districts spent 16 cents per Expenditure Pupil Unit.[19]

In interpreting the above figures it is important to remember that in 1965–1966 most of the districts probably were heavy recipients of funds under the ESEA.

How much does a good educational media program cost? Many individuals and groups stand ready to inform districts how much they should spend for instructional media and what materials and equipment should be purchased. As guidelines, these pronouncements serve their purposes. However, school districts do vary in many respects, and consequently each district must determine its educational program in the light of its educational philosophy and objectives, pupils' needs, staff's qualifications, community's aspirations, and, realistically, its financial resources.

One difficulty in reporting authoritative opinion on the costs of a good educational media program is due to the fact that categories of materials are not always the same. This is highlighted in a recent report when the following definition of "printed instructional materials" is stated as follows:

By definition, the items . . . include hard-cover textbooks, workbooks, programed books, paperbound supplementary books, and dictionaries. Where films, filmstrips, and audiovisual materials are an integral part of texts, they are included in this definition. Certain other items normally included in the 220 Account (Textbooks) such as atlases, maps, globes, encyclopedias, classroom periodicals, tests, and manipulative materials are not covered by the above definition.[20]

On the basis of the definition just cited, the same source believes that the following cost figures are financially realistic now and will probably remain so until 1970:

1. For each new elementary pupil, grades 1–6, the initial outlay to equip him with a supply of printed instructional materials should be $42. The corresponding figure for each new secondary school student in grades 7–12 should be $63.

2. For each elementary pupil, grades 1–6, now enrolled in school, the annual current expenditure to provide for the yearly replacement cycle of printed instructional materials should be $14. The matching figure for each secondary school student now enrolled in grades 7–12 should be $21.[21]

[19]Adapted from "The Cost of Audio-Visual Instruction," *School Management,* X, No. 6 (1966), 111.

[20]*Guidelines for an Adequate Investment in Instructional Materials* (Washington, D.C.: National Education Association, 1967), p. 5.

[21]*Ibid.,* p. 4.

The above figures must be increased to incorporate the other items usually included in the 220 Account if districts desire to budget adequately for these vitally important educational media. School districts also must budget for library books and other items considered part of the educational media center.

The most recent standards for school libraries suggest that after a base collection has been established, districts should spend annually approximately $18 per student.

Minimum standards for the size of library book collections in schools with 250 or more pupils are 6,000 to 10,000 books.[22] In schools with enrollments of 1,000 or more, ten books per student are considered as the minimum collection.

Some authorities believe the above figures are entirely too low, particularly for secondary school libraries. They believe that a high school student should have access to a collection of 40,000 to 50,000 carefully selected titles.

Audio-visual materials also must have an allocation in the budget each year. One authoritative reference states:

To provide for a well-rounded [*audiovisual*] materials program it is recommended that the basic complement of films, filmstrips and recordings be considered capital equipment and be purchased with such funds. To provide for the on-going materials program, including maintenance and replacement but not expansion, no less than 1 per cent of the average per pupil cost in the school unit should be spent per year per student. The 1 per cent amount would include film rentals if no basic collection is started and subscription television. . . , but would not include salaries, building construction or remodeling, CCTV installations, or electronic learning centers. To provide an advanced materials program the 1 per cent figure should be increased to 1.5 per cent.[23]

According to the pupil expenditure units quoted earlier in this chapter, the 1 per cent figure would be equivalent to the expenditure of approximately $3 to $8 per pupil annually.

The authors believe that a more realistic figure would be 2 to 3 per cent of the average per pupil cost, if a good audio-visual program is to be maintained.

The source which is considered to be the single most authoritative in the field of educational media suggests the following guidelines for expenditures:

To maintain an up-to-date collection of materials in the Media Center not less than 6 per cent of the national average for per pupil operational cost

[22]*Standards for School Media Programs* (Washington, D.C.: American Library Association and the National Education Association, 1969), p. 30.

[23]*Quantitative Standards for Audiovisual Personnel, Equipment and Materials* (Washington, D.C.: Department of Audiovisual Instruction, National Education Association, 1966), p. 4.

[ADA] should be spent per year per student. . . . This figure does not include funds for school-adopted textbooks, reference materials housed permanently in classrooms, closed circuit television installations, subscription television, electronic learning centers, distribution systems, supplies, equipment, and the processing of materials. . . . [In addition] special programs and curricular experimentation may require an upward revision of the amount suggested. . . . There should be flexibility [in] purchasing procedures so that materials can be ordered throughout the year.[24] (See Appendix 6.)

SPECIFIC LEADERSHIP TASKS

There are numerous leadership tasks that are implied throughout this chapter, only a few of which will be enumerated here.

1. Budget on the basis of the requirements of the educational program, both present and long-range.
2. Budget for sufficient funds in all categories directly affecting the educational media program.
3. Do include in the budget funds for research and development of the educational media program.
4. Do involve teachers in making decisions about the educational media budget.
5. Be certain to provide a justification for each item requested and don't pad the budget.
6. Become familiar with the latest guidelines recommended for expenditures in the various categories of educational media, but don't consider them as maximum.
7. Become thoroughly knowledgeable about all sources of revenue available for purchasing educational media. Investigate local, state, national, federal, foundations, business, and industry resources.
8. Know about the quality of educational media equipment and materials distributed by different firms, and always select the quality goods that will best serve your educational requirements.

SUMMARY

The preparation of the budget begins with the educational objectives. The budget is the key to a good educational media program. It should be prepared under the supervision of the assistant superintendent in charge of instruction. Principals, educational media specialists, and teachers should be involved in its preparation. The budget is an educational plan and should take into account both short-term and long-range goals. Each item should include a justification. School administrators should consider the advantages of a performance budget.

In financing the educational media program, all sources of revenue—

[24]*Standards for School Media Programs* (Washington, D.C.: American Library Association and the National Education Association, 1969), pp. 35–37.

local, state, federal, industry and business, and foundations should receive consideration.

The alert administrator will keep abreast of the latest developments in federal aid and seek other financial resources.

School districts need to be aware of what other districts are spending for educational media and must know what authoritative sources recommend should be spent in the various categories. However, these figures should be considered only as guidelines, for in the final analysis the expenditures for educational media should be determined by the needs of the district.

SUGGESTED ACTIVITIES AND PROBLEMS

1. Examine an educational media budget of a school district. Interview a school official to determine the steps followed in its preparation. Write a short critique of the budget and of the procedures used in its development.
2. Assume that you are the assistant superintendent in charge of instruction in a school district with 2,800 pupils in grades 1–6 and 2,200 students in grades 7–12. Prepare the budget figures for educational media and indicate how you arrived at your figures.
3. Make up a budget for educational media in your school or school district and write a justification for each item.
4. Read widely in the literature about the provisions of Title III of the ESEA. Outline and describe an innovative project requiring the use of educational media.
5. Investigate the possibilities of securing aid from a foundation or local industry for a research project involving the use of educational media.

SELECTED READINGS

Boardman, Thomas H., "Budget Preparation and Presentation," *Audiovisual Instruction*, XII, No. 3 (1967), 238.

The Challenge of Change in School Finance. Washington, D.C.: Committee on Educational Finance, National Education Association, 1967.

"Cost of Audio-Visual Instruction," *School Management*, X, No. 6 (1966), 111.

Exton, Elaine, "Will Profit-Oriented Industries and Uncle Sam Determine What's Taught in American Schools?" *The American School Board Journal*, No. 3 (1966), 15.

Gauerke, Warren E., and Jack R. Childress, eds., *The Theory & Practice of School Finance*. Chicago: Rand McNally & Company, 1967.

Guidelines for an Adequate Investment in Instructional Materials. Washington, D.C.: National Education Association, 1967.

Guidelines for Textbook Selection, rev. ed. Washington, D.C.: National Education Association, 1967.

Standards for School Media Programs. Washington, D.C.: American Library Association and the National Education Association, 1969.

Lindman, Erick, *The Federal Government and Public Schools.* Washington, D.C.: American Association of School Administrators, National Education Association, 1965.

Local, State, Federal Partnership in School Finance. Washington, D.C.: Committee on Educational Finance, National Education Association, 1966.

Loughary, John W., *Man-Machine Systems in Education.* New York: Harper & Row, Publishers, 1967.

Ovsiew, Leon, and William B. Castetter, *Budgeting for Better Schools.* Englewood Cliffs, N.J.: Prentice-Hall, Inc., 1960.

Planning Your Purchases of Educational Materials 1966–1969. New York: The American Textbook Publishers Institute, 1966.

Quantitative Standards for Audiovisual Personnel, Equipment and Materials. Washington, D.C.: Department of Audiovisual Instruction, National Education Association, 1966.

"A Survey of Textbook Purchasing Practices," *School Management,* X, No. 3 (1966), 4.

"Title 12345: An Administrator's Guide to the Elementary and Secondary Education Act," *American School and University,* XXXVIII, No. 6 (1966), 39.

What Everyone Should Know About Financing Our Schools. Washington, D.C.: Committee on Educational Finance, National Education Association, 1966.

9

Evaluation and the
Learning Resources Program

One of the weakest links in our educational chain is the failure to stop periodically to see if we are going in the direction we started to go and how close we are to our destination. Too frequently, we behave like the motorist who asks his automobile association to map out a travel route and then, instead of following it, drives on the back roads and wonders why he never arrives at his destination. Some of us, unfortunately, never planned a route or a destination and, consequently, don't know where we are going, but only that we are on our way.

Whether travel or education is the topic, the results can be disastrous if no destination or goals and objectives are selected, if the route or procedures are not carefully planned, and if periodic checks are not made to determine our progress.

The topic of concern here is, of course, evaluation. How much longer will John Q. Public, the taxpayer, be willing to foot the bill for expensive educational media and services if he doesn't know whether or not they produce results that are superior to the more conventional educational methods of instruction, or even the slate and copybook, for that matter?

It is not only important to determine whether improvement in learning is taking place as a result of the use of educational media, but also to scrutinize continuously all aspects of the learning resources program. This overall examination of learning resources should encompass: (1) their organization and administration, (2) their relationship to curriculum development and instruction, (3) the extent to which they are being used, (4) the suitability of the physical facilities for educational media, and (5) the adequacy of the budgetary procedures and financial support for them.

The intent of this chapter, therefore, will be to discuss briefly the process of evaluation, and then to demonstrate its relationship and use in respect to the various aspects of learning resources discussed in this handbook. Specific guidelines and procedures for evaluating a media program will be presented.

EVALUATING THE LEARNING RESOURCES PROGRAM

Comprehensive, continuous evaluation is an important component of any educational, system. Sophisticated learning programs involving a variety of media, teaching methods, and facilities require careful measurement of student behavior to determine if the learning outcomes match the stated performance objectives. It is extremely difficult to isolate and assess the effect of media on a particular learning sequence. However, an attempt must be made to find some of these relationships of educational media to learning. Administrators must be able to give some assurance that the learning resources programs in their district are effective. This can be done only by the use of evaluative techniques.

A BROAD VIEW OF EVALUATION

Evaluation must be considered from a broad point of view. The effectiveness of the learning resources program should be judged in terms of the results obtained throughout all levels of the school system by all types of educational media. Ideally, we ought to know what kinds of changes are taking place in children and youth as a result of their exposure to ETV, CAI, films, good books, and other media. If this could be done accurately, we could easily prepare the performance budget discussed in Chapter 8.

EVALUATING THE TOTAL SCHOOL SYSTEM

Knowledge of what is happening in any one segment of the school system or school program as a result of any particular phase of the learning resources program is not sufficient. It is the entire picture that we need to see. It is true that the scene may be too large for us to view at one time; but, as with a moving picture, we can splice together a number of separate scenes, run them through the projector—or our mind—and thus get the broad view. To know the effects of learning resources on preschool and kindergarten-primary children is just as important as to be aware of what happens to children and youth in the middle and upper levels of the school system after exposure to educational media. How slow learners react to teaching-learning aids is of as great significance as the manner in which the gifted respond. And the imprint instructional materials leave on the culturally deprived learners actually may be of greater consequence to the welfare of our nation than any changes wrought in the so-called middle-class students.

Evaluating the whole child. A well-known educational cliché states, "Teach the whole child." Thousands of teachers have believed this statement and have sincerely tried to practice it. Others in the field of education and outside have ridiculed the idea. Although we have, throughout the past 50 years, alternately emphasized the subject-matter approach, the experience approach, and the discipline approach to learning, as well as others—the solutions to many of our social problems appear to depend upon changes in attitudes, rather than in acquisition of knowledge alone. The experience approach seems to emphasize this aspect more than do the other approaches to learning.

What, then, are the implications for the evaluation of learning resources in terms of the whole child? Plainly stated, the contributions of educational media must be examined in terms of the behavioral changes that take place in the learner. Does the statement, "A picture is worth a thousand words," mean only that, or is there more? Do the "thousand words" represent knowledge only, or do they cover attitudes, appreciations, and even skills? To what extent are pupils encouraged to be creative as a result of their experiences with learning resources? Are we using our audio-visual media so extensively that pupils become listeners and viewers (spectators) rather than doers? These are the kinds of questions we must ask as part of our evaluation of the effectiveness of our educational media programs.

The student as an evaluator. Never has there been a greater opportunity for students to participate in the evaluation process. The trend toward independent learning and study is gaining tremendous momentum. The individualized instruction talked and written about for so many years is at last possible. Programmed texts, teaching machines, tapes, records, films, and filmstrips of all types are as available for pupils to work with independently in their study carrels as are textbooks and library books. Looking to the future the AASA Committee on Electronic Data Processing suggests:

> When EDP comes of age in schools, computer terminals will be at least as common as TV sets are presently, and probably more so. At present, high programing and equipment rental costs have confined computer-assisted instruction to experiments. However, this is only a short-term effect; over the long term, computer-assisted instructional sequences for many subjects and for learners with different problems will be available in abundance.[1]

The implications seem to be clear. If the student participates in formulating his own goals and objectives, and works toward them independently at least part of the time—then he must also assume some of the

[1] *EDP and the School Administrator* (Washington, D.C.: American Association of School Administrators, 1967), p. 38.

responsibility for self-evaluation. In the future the student engaging in computer-assisted instruction will also be aided in the self-evaluation process by this electronic marvel.

Another task of the student in his new role as an evaluator will be to appraise the instruction he is receiving in groups or individually. Although many good teachers in the past have involved pupils in the evaluation of their learning experiences, the freedom to criticize and make suggestions really never existed in most classrooms. Now with the wide use of learning resources and much pupil time spent in individualized learning, the evaluation can be made of a film or TV program; and programmed materials can be evaluated, whether presented by text, teaching machine, or computer. Plainly stated, pupils should be encouraged to assist in the evaluation of the learning resources program.

Testing, measurement, and evaluation. There is considerable confusion in the minds of teachers, pupils, and lay persons concerning the distinctions between *testing, measurement,* and *evaluation.* Most frequently the confusion arises over the difference between measurement and evaluation.

Simply stated for the purpose of the discussion in this chapter, the distinctions are as follows:

Testing. A procedure used to measure certain qualities and/or characteristics of a person, place, or thing. In its application to education, it is most frequently thought of as a form of questioning used to ascertain the extent of knowledge retention. Testing in relation to use of audiovisual equipment would have a different connotation.

Measurement. The process of obtaining evidence about some characteristic of a person, place, or thing by the use of objective and scientific means. Normally the data are expressed in quantitative terms.

Evaluation. A procedure in which data collected by measurement and/or other means are used as a basis for making judgments about the person, place, or thing tested, measured, or examined. Usually, some value is placed on a particular level of achievement, accomplishment, or adequacy.

The distinctions should be easier to make after thinking through the following example involving learning resources. Assume that your school decides to evaluate the effectiveness of a series of ETV programs on African culture. The objectives of the series are concerned with helping children gain some background information and understandings regarding African culture, with the hope that their attitudes toward minority groups might be improved.

Prior to the series of programs, measurement of the knowledge pupils already possessed about African culture and their attitudes toward minority groups was conducted by testing and by the use of an attitude scale. The pupils were then exposed to the series of ETV programs. During this period, staff members in charge of the project discussed various ways of measuring the extent to which the objectives of the series were being realized. It was decided to accomplish this by testing, through the use of alternate forms of the same devices employed in the pre-testing.

The results indicated that although the median score for the knowledge test rose appreciably, there was only a slight improvement in attitudes. In fact, some students evidenced more negative attitudes after the series than before.

Now is the time for the evaluation phase. On the basis of scores obtained by testing as a measurement procedure, someone must examine the measurement data and use them as a basis for judging the value of the ETV series in terms of the original objectives. Certainly, the knowledge gain was considerable, but the attitude change appeared insignificant. On the basis of the evidence collected, the series would receive a high rating for knowledge gains, but a low score on attitude changes.

From a learning resources point of view, it would seem desirable to carry the study described above several steps further. Perhaps the same series of programs might be repeated with other groups of children. Certainly, attempts should be made to ascertain why attitudes did not improve. Here the pupils can be of great help. What incidents in the series produced negative feelings in some pupils? What episodes were most helpful in developing positive attitudes? Were the teaching plans carefully followed? Did the teachers rely too much on the TV programs and not enough on small group discussion?

It should be noted from the above example that testing is one form of measurement, and it in turn is a necessary ingredient in evaluation. Measurement supplies the data on which evaluation is based. It, therefore, encompasses more than measurement. Measurement provides the facts, and evaluation makes a qualitative assessment about these facts.

It should always be kept in mind that evaluation must be made in terms of goals, objectives, functions, and/or purposes. (Without stated objectives the ETV series could not have been evaluated.) The administration of learning resources must be evaluated in terms of functions and purposes. Curriculum development, instruction, and the supporting learning resources must be judged on the basis of aims and objectives. The school facilities and equipment should relate to their special purposes and be evaluated accordingly. The budget must be examined to determine whether sufficient funds are being provided to maintain a high level in the instructional resources program.

From this basic discussion on evaluation, let us now consider some specific guidelines for appraising the impact of media in a school system.

How To Evaluate Specific Aspects Of A Media Program

It is vital that the administrator have some guidelines and procedures for evaluating the growing media program in his school district. How does a superintendent know if the investment in a sophisticated dial access system can be justified? Can it be proven that learning has been enhanced by the use of a new student response system in the large-group lecture hall? Is biology a better course since the regional instructional materials center has acquired a set of color films keyed to the major textbook series?

Of one thing the authors are certain—and the reader is well aware of this point by now—learning resources programs cannot be effectively evaluated apart from the total instructional process of which they are (or should be) an integral part. The school administrator who would assess the effectiveness of educational media needs to look closely at three major integrative functions: (1) the role of personnel, (2) the thrust of curriculum development and instruction, and (3) the role of software and hardware. And these three are obviously affected by decisions involving facilities and finance.

EVALUATING ADMINISTRATIVE AND TEACHING PERSONNEL

All administrative and teaching staff members who have any responsibility for the production and application of learning resources should be continuously and comprehensively evaluated. In an age of automatic salary increments regardless of the quality of performance, evaluation is often a nasty word. However, the chief administrator, supervisor, or principal who is earning his salary will insist on a planned program of democratic, systematic evaluation of all personnel.

Ideally, self-evaluation is the best kind and should be universally encouraged—at least once a year on a formal basis. Each professional—principal, assistant superintendent, coordinator of learning resources, curriculum coordinator, and teacher—writes out an appraisal of his own performance in terms of the job description for his position. This evaluation is then discussed with the immediate supervisor in a frank conference where strengths and weaknesses are discussed. For example, the assistant superintendent in charge of instruction might conclude in his self-evaluation that he did not spend sufficient time in studying the latest research and technical developments in learning resources. He might further resolve to attend more meetings of the district curriculum council, since his leadership is really needed there. The superintendent, in a joint evaluation conference, may commend the assistant superintendent for his excellent rapport with the new district coordinator of learning resources, while agreeing that more attention might be directed to the district curriculum council.

A teacher might well be evaluated in part on his perception of the learning process and the relationship of the new media to it. His willingness to change or adapt teaching methods and materials in the face of new research may be a significant factor in his rating. In any event, a regular review of the teacher's use of pertinent media should be an integral part of the district program of faculty evaluation.

In Chapters 4 and 5 of this handbook, the reader may use the specific leadership tasks identified for each position as a basic criteria for evaluation of job performance. Some administrators will want to develop their own evaluation instruments and procedures for the regular appraisal of professional personnel. Regardless of variations in technique, it is imperative that the job be accomplished as an integral part of the evaluation of the total learning resources program.

The effectiveness of groups of persons working together needs to be assessed as well. For example, the district curriculum council and the subject area curriculum committees should be evaluated in terms of their contributions to the achievement of the total school program. The chairmen, on occasion, might conduct self-evaluation discussions, and try to lead the groups to reflect on their accomplishments and shortcomings. Such soul searching should include an honest appraisal of the leadership of the group, with suggestions for improvement.

EVALUATING MEDIA—CURRICULUM—INSTRUCTION

Any attempt at estimating the value of media apart from curriculum and instruction is meaningless. The most beautiful, professionally produced color motion picture is useful *only* if it contributes to the success of the instructional program. No learning resources can be fruitfully evaluated in isolation. Media always need to be considered in the light of their contribution to the achievement of the goals of instruction. More specifically, in modern learning sequences there must be a direct relationship between the instructional methods and materials and the behavioral objectives sought.

As indicated in Chapter 3, the initial concern in curriculum development is the identification of values, which are the basic determinants of the remainder of the process. Next comes a statement of school district philosophy followed by a declaration of institutional goals. Then, specific objectives are developed in behavioral or performance terms. In the continuing process of curriculum design, learning resources are identified to help the learner achieve certain behavioral outcomes. But how do we know which factors helped him to attain the desired behaviors? While the Chinese may have indeed believed that the picture is worth 1,000 words, we educators need more evidence to justify the expenditure of thousands of dollars on a dial access system. And this brings us to the "Achilles' heel" of media evaluation. It is often very difficult to prove that a single concept film, for example, contributed significantly to the achievement of certain objectives in physics. The student could have learned the content from his textbook, from a fellow student, or from his teacher in the laboratory.

Only by carefully and scientifically programming each instructional sequence in the future are we going to be able to develop any sophisticated and accurate measures of the effect of media on instruction. The field is wide open for research; each institution must be willing to conduct some of its own and contribute to cooperative action research.

Modern educational media centers can generate a plethora of media. But the ultimate justification of any resource can be found only in the crucible of goal identification and fulfillment. And we must constantly seek to prove more realistically the relationship of media to the achievement of learning objectives.

EVALUATING SOFTWARE AND HARDWARE—ADMINISTRATIVE, BUDGETARY, AND PLANT IMPLICATIONS

The exigencies of the continuing technological revolution force educators to weigh many factors before filling their schools with computers and other electronic marvels. We have to continually remind ourselves that no projector, student response system, or any other piece of hardware will itself enhance the learning experiences for students. The hardware is simply the carrier of the program (or software), which *may* contribute to the learning process if properly related to the behavioral objectives. A rational teaching-learning setting will usually employ a balance between software and the hardware necessary to program it.

SPECIFIC LEADERSHIP TASKS

The following procedures should help the administrator to evaluate and improve the process by which technological equipment and accompanying programs are selected.

1. Organize a systems approach to instruction for the school district. The role of educational hardware and software will gradually become more apparent.

2. Always investigate to determine if a simpler or less expensive piece of equipment can accomplish the objective. For example, a short motion picture projected into a rear screen carrel projector may be just as effective as the same movie fed into an expensive dial access system. Insist on justification for more expensive methods of media delivery.

3. Have available some objective criteria for evaluating instructional equipment. As discussed in Chapter 3, the Montgomery County, Maryland, Public Schools have produced a guide, *Review and Evaluation Procedures for Textbooks and Instructional Materials.*[2] This publication includes specific criteria for the review and evaluation of instructional equipment, including amplifiers, listening stations, record players, tape recorders, cameras, microscopes, projectors, television equipment, and teaching machines.

4. Move into the new technology gradually. For example, consider the purchase of one bank of dial access equipment initially, and then add the second generation as the hardware improves. In this way, your school will always have some of the latest equipment and will be in a position to phase out the most obsolete items without making a large hole in the annual budget. The technology is changing so rapidly that very large expenditures for certain fixed items of equipment are increasingly difficult to justify.

5. Use some of the newer devices as motivating factors with the faculty. While it is unwise to purchase or lease large quantities of hardware in the hope that someone will use it, judicious investments in newer equipment will often stimulate interest in programming and ultimate use in learning situations.

6. Take a positive attitude toward experimentation and research. Many faculty members will be inclined to try new instructional media if they know that the administrators assume a healthy leadership posture toward innovation.

7. Make sure that school district and individual building facilities are adequate to insure the delivery of software and equipment to the teacher when and where he needs it.

A helpful checklist for evaluating educational media programs has been developed by W. R. Fulton.[3] Reproduced in Appendix 5, this evaluative checklist includes items on: school system educational media services, curriculum and instruction, the educational media center, physical facilities, budget and finance, and the educational media staff.

The evaluation of a media program is a complex, continuing task. Much of it is subjective, requiring the careful attention of all administrators and teachers whose roles are described in this handbook. In the last analysis, the value of any learning resource lies in its contribution to the total learning process.

[2]*Review and Evaluation Procedures for Textbooks and Instructional Materials* (Rockville, Maryland: Montgomery County Public Schools, 1968).
[3]W. R. Fulton, *Evaluative Checklist—An Instrument for Self-Evaluating an Educational Media Program in School Systems* (Norman, Oklahoma: University of Oklahoma, n.d. Developed as part of a study performed pursuant to a contract with the USOE, Department of Health, Education and Welfare, under the provisions of Title VII, Public Law 85–664), mimeographed.

There is no doubt that students in the teaching-learning centers of the future will require highly sophisticated instructional resources to assist them in achieving their performance objectives. Those who administer educational media programs must insist that the learner's goals and values, and those of our democratic society, be given top priority. In the exciting process of dynamic curriculum design and instructional systems development, the future role of learning resources will be found. Under the sensitive guidance of the true professional, educational media will emerge as a vital component of the teaching-learning process.

SUMMARY

Evaluation of the learning resources program should encompass: organization and administration, the relationship to curriculum development and instruction, the suitability of physical facilities, and the adequacy of budgetary and financial support.

A broad view of evaluation requires knowledge of the total school system and an approach to evaluating the whole child. The contributions of educational media must be examined in terms of the behavioral changes that take place in the learner.

With the advent of significant independent learning and study in schools, the student is becoming an evaluator of his own learning experiences.

It is important to note the distinctions between testing, measurement, and evaluation. Testing is a procedure used to measure certain qualities and/or characteristics of a person, place, or thing. Measurement is the process of obtaining evidence about some characteristics of a person, place, or thing by the use of objective and scientific means. Evaluation is a procedure in which data collected by measurement and/or other means are used as a basis for making judgments about the person, place, or thing tested, measured, or examined.

Learning resources programs cannot be effectively evaluated apart from the total instructional process. The school administrator needs to look closely at three major functions: the role of personnel, the thrust of curriculum development and instruction, and the role of software and hardware.

SUGGESTED ACTIVITIES AND PROBLEMS

1. Using criteria discussed in this chapter, conduct an evaluation of a major phase of the learning resources program in a school district.
2. Develop a plan for student involvement in the evaluation of an educational media program.

3. Interview an assistant superintendent in charge of instruction and a teacher from the same school district. Ask them about the prevailing attitudes toward research and experimentation in the schools and learning centers of the district. Compare their responses in an analytical paper.
4. Interview the coordinator of learning resources in a school district. Ask him to justify his largest hardware purchase of the past year by relating use of curriculum objectives. Summarize your findings.

SELECTED READINGS

Bloom, Benjamin S., ed., *Taxonomy of Educational Objectives: Cognitive Domain.* New York: Longmans, Green and Co., 1956.

Brown, James W., and Kenneth Norberg, *Administering Educational Media,* Chaps. 3, 7, 11, and 16. New York: McGraw-Hill Book Company, 1965.

Erickson, Carlton W. H., *Fundamentals of Teaching with Audiovisual Technology,* Chaps. 3, 4, and 5. New York: The Macmillan Company, 1965.

Green, Adam C., ed., *Educational Facilities with New Media.* Troy, N.Y.: Rensselaer Polytechnic Institute, Center for Architectural Research, 1966.

Krathwohl, David R., Benjamin S. Bloom, and Bertram B. Masia, *Taxonomy of Educational Objectives: Affective Domain.* New York: David McKay Co., Inc., 1964.

Mager, Robert F., *Preparing Instructional Objectives.* Palo Alto, Calif.: Fearon Publishers, 1962.

——, and Kenneth M. Beach, Jr., *Developing Vocational Instruction.* Palo Alto, Calif.: Fearon Publishers, 1967.

Neagley, Ross L., and N. Dean Evans, *Handbook for Effective Curriculum Development,* Chap. 11. Englewood Cliffs, N.J.: Prentice-Hall, Inc., 1967.

Oliver, Albert I., *Curriculum Improvement: A Guide to Problems, Principles and Procedures,* Sections III and IV. New York: Dodd, Mead & Co., 1965.

Review and Evaluation Procedures for Textbooks and Instructional Materials. Rockville, Maryland: Montgomery County Public Schools, 1968.

Appendix 1

CRITERIA FOR THE REVIEW AND EVALUATION OF INSTRUCTIONAL MATERIALS, MONTGOMERY COUNTY PUBLIC SCHOOLS, ROCKVILLE, MARYLAND[1]

CRITERIA FOR THE REVIEW AND EVALUATION OF GLOBES

I. Is the material authentic?
    A. Is the material factually accurate?
    B. Is the material up-to-date?
    C. Are the author and/or producer well qualified?
II. Is the material appropriate?
    A. Does it promote the educational goals and objectives of the curriculum of Montgomery County?
    B. Might the material be considered objectionable?
    C. Is it appropriate to the level of instruction intended?
       1. Is the vocabulary appropriate?
       2. Are the concepts appropriate?
       3. Are the methods of development appropriate?
    D. Is controversial material presented impartially?
    E. Is this material suitable to the curriculum?
    F. Does this material present information that other approved sources do not?
    G. Does this material give a new dimension or direction to currently approved sources?
III. Will the material catch and hold the interest of the users?
    A. Will the material stimulate the curiosity of the user?
    B. Will the material appeal to many students?
IV. Is the content of this material well organized and well balanced?
    A. Is the material presented logically and clearly?
    B. Does the material achieve its stated purpose?

[1]From *Review and Evaluation Procedures for Textbooks and Instructional Materials,* produced by the Montgomery County Public Schools, Rockville, Maryland.

    C. Are latitude and longitude lines or indicators provided?

    D. Are color symbolizations pleasing but distinctive in quality?

    E. If raised-relief technique is used, is vertical exaggeration excessive?

V. Is the technical quality of this material acceptable?

    A. Will materials used in the construction of the globe resist denting and breakage?

    B. Are jointures on globe smooth and relatively unnoticeable?

        1. Are map segments well registered?

        2. Are places where parts of globe are jointed in construction prominent?

    C. Is the base firm and heavy enough to resist tipping in use?

    D. Will connections of movable parts deteriorate or become separated through use?

    E. Is there an axis provided for the globe?

    F. Is a place provided for the storage of an axis pin if it is removable?

    G. Is the surface soil-resistant and cleanable?

    H. Is the surface made to be marked upon?

VI. Is the cost of this material justified?

CRITERIA FOR THE REVIEW AND EVALUATION OF FILMS, FILMSTRIPS, SLIDES, AND TRANSPARENCIES

I. Is the material authentic?

    A. Is the material factually accurate?

    B. Is the material up-to-date?

    C. Are the author and/or producer well qualified?

    D. Are translations and retellings faithful to the original?

II. Is the material appropriate?

    A. Does it promote the educational goals and objectives of the curriculum of Montgomery County?

    B. Might the material be considered objectionable?

    C. Is it appropriate to the level of instruction intended?

        1. Is the vocabulary appropriate?

        2. Are the concepts appropriate?

        3. Are the methods of development appropriate?

    D. Is controversial material presented impartially?

    E. Is this material suitable to the curriculum?

    F. Does this material present information that other approved sources do not?

    G. Does this material give a new dimension or direction to currently approved sources?

III. Will the material catch and hold the interest of the users?

    A. Will the material stimulate the curiosity of the user?

    B. Will the material appeal to many students?

IV. Is the content of this material well organized and well balanced?

    A. Have the principles of learning been followed in developing the material, e.g., reinforcement—transfer?

B. Is the material presented logically and clearly?
C. Does the material achieve its stated purpose?
D. Is the content appropriate for this type of presentation?
E. Are the data sufficiently comprehensive to be useful?
F. Is there extraneous or unnecessary material?
G. Is the sequence developed adequately?
H. Is the material imaginative, when imagination is really needed?
I. Is the quality of the script or commentary satisfactory?
J. Is the music or background satisfactory?
K. Are the titles, labels, or captions appropriate?
V. Is the technical quality of this material acceptable?
  A. Is the visual image satisfactory?
    1. Is the photography clear and artistic?
    2. Does it have enough close-ups?
    3. Are printed items adequate in size?
  B. Is the quality of sound clear and intelligible?
  C. Is color used effectively?
  D. Are sound and visual image synchronized?
VI. Is the cost of this material justified?

CRITERIA FOR THE REVIEW AND EVALUATION OF PROGRAMMED MATERIALS

I. Is the material authentic?
  A. Is the material factually accurate?
  B. Is the material up-to-date?
  C. Are the author and/or producer well qualified?
II. Is the material appropriate?
  A. Does it promote the educational goals and objectives of the curriculum of Montgomery County?
  B. Might the material be considered objectionable?
  C. Is it appropriate to the level of instruction intended?
    1. Is the vocabulary appropriate?
    2. Are the concepts appropriate?
    3. Are the methods of development appropriate?
  D. Is controversial material presented impartially?
  E. Is this material suitable to the curriculum?
  F. Does this material present information that currently approved sources do not?
  G. Does this material give a new dimension or direction to currently approved sources?
III. Will the material catch and hold the interest of the users?
  A. Will the material stimulate the curiosity of the user?
  B. Can the material be used to satisfy curiosity?
IV. Is the content of this material well organized and well balanced?
  A. Have the principles of learning been followed in developing the material, e.g., reinforcement—transfer?
  B. Is the material presented logically and clearly?

C. Does the material achieve its stated purpose?

D. Is the program consistent with the behavior which is desired?

E. Does the program emphasize the major objectives of the course content?

F. Does the program offer the type of response, e.g., multiple choice, constructed response, that is desired?

G. Does the program orient the student to a problem and prepare him for new information?

H. Does the program use interesting and novel cues?

I. Are those cueing techniques being used most appropriate for the kind of behavioral outcomes desired?

J. Is the program overcued?

K. Does the program raise questions for discussion at different intervals in order to further learning?

L. Can the teacher develop problems from the programmed activities to be performed as follow-up activities in the program?

M. Is there an efficient way to refer to specific content?

V. Is the technical quality of this material acceptable?

A. Does the program provide a record of the performance of the participant which can aid in diagnosis of individual learning problems?

B. Does the program require a separate answer sheet?

C. Does the learner participate actively at each step in the program?

D. Does the program "reinforce" after each student's answer by telling him immediately whether he has responded correctly or not?

E. Does the program provide too many responses within a frame before correction or reinforcement?

F. Does each frame provide too much reading?

G. Is the program easy to handle physically?

H. Is the size of type appropriate for the grade level?

VI. Is the cost of this material justified?

Appendix 2

ELEMENTARY SCHOOL TEXTBOOK EVALUATION SCORECARD,
LANSDOWNE-ALDAN JOINT SCHOOL SYSTEM, LANSDOWNE, PENNSYLVANIA[1]

LANGUAGE TEXTBOOKS OR WORKBOOK TEXTS

Rating of Book

Title _____ Superior _____
Author _____ Good _____
Publisher _____ Average _____
Copyright date _____ Price _____ Poor _____

Scale for rating each item: 3-Superior; 2-Acceptable; 1-Not acceptable; 0-Not included

ITEM	RATING
	3 2 1 0

A. *Authorship and Point of View*
   1. Are the authors well qualified in training and experience?
   2. How acceptable is the underlying philosophy of the series?
   3. Is the philosophy clearly and consistently demonstrated in the presentation and use of the contents?
   4. Does the textbook follow and interpret the objectives of the course of study?
   5. Is the series based on important research?

B. *Content*
   1. Does the material arouse the interest of the children?
   2. Is it related to the children's experiences in speaking, writing, reading, and spelling?
   3. Is there adequate emphasis on *fundamental* English skills? Is enough functional grammar provided?
   4. Are stories, poems, and children's literature appropriate and of high quality?
   5. Is there correlation with the other subject areas of the curriculum?
   6. Is there proper balance between oral and written expression and listening experiences?
   7. Are the vocabulary and sentence structure well adapted to the grade level?

   8. Are ideas developed skillfully?

   9. Is the development of social competence emphasized?
Are the social amenities taught in due perspective to the communicative skills?

  10. Is there provision for creative work in language?

C.   *Presentation of Material and Organization*
1. Is readiness developed for each new topic?
2. Are skills developed in natural settings and with purposeful practice?
3. Is the presentation clear, understandable, and stimulating?
4. Is the organization flexible?
5. Is the development of content easy to follow by pupils and teacher?

D.   *Practice and Drill Material*
1. Is practice preceded by careful development?
2. Is the book adequately equipped with practice material?
3. Is sufficient practice provided for initial mastery of new processes or understandings?
4. Is the drill distributed to insure maintenance of skills?
5. Are there recurring reviews and tests?
6. Is there sufficient variety to insure interest?
7. Do the practice exercises embrace real-life experience?

E.   *Provisions for Individual Differences*
1. Is supplementary enrichment material provided for rapid learners?
2. Are diagnostic tests provided to discover specific weaknesses?
3. Is remedial instructional material provided?
4. Is there provision for pupils to evaluate their work?

F.   *Teaching Aids*
1. Is there a helpful manual provided for the teacher?
2. Does the book have a well-organized index and table of contents?
3. Is the material well illustrated?
4. Do the pictures, charts, and guides offer valuable aids?
5. Do the pictures make a direct contribution to learning?

G.   *Physical Features*
1. Is the book modern and attractive?
2. Does it have a durable binding?
3. Is the quality of the paper good?
4. Are size and spacing of type satisfactory?
5. Are the pictures, charts, and guides attractive, well placed, and functional?
6. Is the book of convenient size for use on the desk?
7. Does the book open well and stay open?

Appendix 3

QUESTIONNAIRE TO ASCERTAIN EDUCATIONAL NEEDS AND SERVICES. FROM *A Study To Determine The Need For An Area Research And Service Center.*

Educational Service Center, Chester and Delaware Counties. In each of the classifications given below, place an "X" before the category which most nearly describes your situation:

Position	*Grade Level*	*Yrs. of Service*
☐ Chief School Administrator	☐ Primary (K–3)	☐ First year
☐ Curriculum Coordinator	☐ Intermediate (4–6)	☐ 2–5 years
☐ Other Administrator/Supervisor	☐ Junior High (7–9)	☐ 6–15 years
☐ Building Principal	☐ Senior High (10–12)	☐ 16–25 years
☐ Classroom Teacher	☐ All Grades (K–12)	☐ over 25 years

If existent, rate on the basis of the DEGREE OF EFFECTIVENESS IN IMPROVING INSTRUCTION

In the row of blocks following each item, place an "X" in the position which most appropriately expresses your feeling. Mark only *one* of the six blocks for each item.

	Nearly Nonexistent *But Needed*	Nearly Nonexistent *Not Needed*	Excellent	Good	Fair	Poor
A. *Instructional Materials*						
1. Available basic textbooks for your classroom use are						
2. Available workbooks to accompany basic text are						
3. Available supplementary textbooks in the classroom are						

	Nearly Nonexistent But *Needed*	Nearly Nonexistent *Not* Needed	Excellent	Good	Fair	Poor
4. Available teachers' guides accompanying textbooks are						
5. Available programed instructional materials are						
6. Available non-projected visuals (posters, charts, flannel boards, etc.) are						
7. Available overhead projector transparencies are						
8. Available filmstrips and slides are						
9. Available motion pictures are						
10. Available educational TV programs (i.e. Channel 12) are						
11. Available closed-circuit TV is						
12. Available instructional recordings and instructional tapes are						
13. Available facilities for the production of audio-visual aids are						
14. Available materials for the production of audio-visual aids are						
15. Available personnel for the production of audio-visual aids are						
16. Available library resources are						

B. *In-Service Education—Professional Personnel*

	Nearly Nonexistent But *Needed*	Nearly Nonexistent *Not* Needed	Excellent	Good	Fair	Poor
17. The amount of time provided during school hours for the study of new curricular offerings is						
18. Opportunities to participate actively in classroom research projects that test new ideas are						
19. The number of workshops and conferences (held within the system) providing new ideas on materials, content, and methodology is						
a. The caliber of such workshops and conferences held within the school system is						
b. The number of such workshops and conferences or institutes attended OUTSIDE the system is						
c. The caliber of such OUTSIDE institutes, etc. is						

	Nearly Nonexistent But *Needed*	Nearly Nonexistent *Not Needed*	Excellent	Good	Fair	Poor
20. Programs provided to keep the staff up-to-date on the psychological aspects of education (child development, testing, etc.) are						
21. The opportunities provided to study and visit schools using newer techniques and organizational patterns (team teaching, nongrading, etc.) are						

C. *Curriculum Evaluation and Development*

22. Provisions in the curriculum for educating the gifted are						
23. Provisions in the curriculum for educating the average pupil are						
24. Provisions in the curriculum for educating the slow learner are						
25. Specialists available to assist in developing the curriculum are						
26. Specialists available for helping the classroom teacher to improve instruction are						
27. The methods used by the system in evaluating the effectiveness of the curriculum are						
28. The degree to which teachers participate in curriculum evaluation and development is						
29. The educational contributions of the state department of education to your district's program of curriculum development are						
30. The educational contributions from National sources (N.E.A., U.S. Office of Ed., etc.) are						

D. *Adequacy of Consultant Services*

31. The availability of consultant services in techniques of teaching is						
32. The adequacy of special education services (speech correction, partially-sighted, brain damaged, etc.) is						
33. The degree to which the system is providing teachers with consultant services in the areas of child growth and development is						

	Nearly Nonexistent But *Needed*	Nearly Nonexistent *Not Needed*	Excellent	Good	Fair	Poor
34. Provisions for consultants to assist with pupils who have psychological or related problems are						

E. *Educational Information Services*

35. The degree to which sufficient data is *disseminated* to the teacher regarding current changes in education (techniques, content, psychology of learning, etc.) is						
36. When a problem is to be researched for such a purpose as method planning, the quantity and quality of available resources are						
37. In the area of curriculum development, provisions made for making available curriculum guides (showing what other schools are doing) are						
38. The extent to which a curriculum library is provided for teachers is						
39. The availability of data processing services to the system and its personnel is						

F. *Other Needs: Please list other services and/or materials (not presently available and not listed in this questionnaire) which you deem desirable for your professional work.*

CONSULTANT'S EVALUATION FORM FOR DETERMINING REGIONAL SERVICES

Education Service Center, Chester and Delaware Counties.

	Local District Able To Provide Effectively	Can Be Provided More Effectively By Cooperative Organization	Priority
A. *Instructional Materials*			
1. Available basic textbooks for your classroom use are			
2. Available workbooks to accompany basic text are			
3. Available Supplementary textbooks in the classroom are			
4. Available teachers' guides accompanying textbooks are			
5. Available programed instructional materials are			
6. Available non-projected visuals (posters, charts, flannel boards, etc.) are			
7. Available overhead projector transparencies are			
8. Available filmstrips and slides are			
9. Available motion pictures are			
10. Available educational TV programs (i.e. Channel 12) are			
11. Available closed-circuit TV is			
12. Available instructional recordings and instructional tapes are			
13. Available facilities for the production of audio-visual aids are			
14. Available materials for the production of audio-visual aids are			
15. Available personnel for the production of audio-visual aids are			
16. Available library resources are			
B. *In-Service Education—Professional Personnel*			
17. The amount of time provided during school hours for the study of new curricular offerings is			
18. Opportunities to participate actively in classroom research projects that test new ideas are			

	Local District Able To Provide Effectively	Can Be Provided More Effectively By Cooperative Organization	Priority
19. The number of workshops and conferences (held within the system) providing new ideas on materials, content, and methodology is			
a. The caliber of such workshops and conferences held within the school system is			
b. The number of such workshops and conferences or institutes attended OUTSIDE the system is			
c. The caliber of such OUTSIDE institutes, etc. is			
20. Programs provided to keep the staff up-to-date on the psychological aspects of education (child development, testing, etc.) are			
21. The opportunities provided to study and visit schools using newer techniques and organizational patterns (team teaching, nongrading, etc.) are			
C. *Curriculum Evaluation and Development*			
22. Provisions in the curriculum for educating the gifted are			
23. Provisions in the curriculum for educating the average pupil are			
24. Provisions in the curriculum for educating the slow learner are			
25. Specialists available to assist in developing the curriculum are			
26. Specialists available for helping the classroom teacher to improve instruction are			
27. The methods used by the system in evaluating the effectiveness of the curriculum are			
28. The degree to which teachers participate in curriculum evaluation and development is			

	Local District Able To Provide Effectively	Can Be Provided More Effectively By Cooperative Organization	Priority
29. The educational contributions of the state department of education to your district's program of curriculum development are			
30. The educational contributions from National sources (N.E.A., U.S. Office of Ed., etc.) are			

D. *Adequacy of Consultant Services*

31. The availability of consultant services in techniques of teaching is			
32. The adequacy of special education services (speech correction, partially-sighted, brain damaged, etc.) is			
33. The degree to which the system is providing teachers with consultant services in the areas of child growth and development is			
34. Provisions for consultants to assist with pupils who have psychological or related problems are			

E. *Educational Information Services*

35. The degree to which sufficient data is *disseminated* to the teacher regarding current changes in education (techniques, content, psychology of learning, etc.) is			
36. When a problem is to be researched for such a purpose as method planning, the quantity and quality of available resources are			
37. In the area of curriculum development, provisions made for making available curriculum guides (showing what other schools are doing) are			
38. The extent to which a curriculum library is provided for teachers is			
39. The availability of data processing services to the system and its personnel is			

Appendix 4

GUIDELINES FOR ESTABLISHING A COOPERATIVE LEARNING RESOURCES CENTER[1]

1. The primary objective of every audio-visual program is the improvement of learning, of teacher effectiveness. Dependence upon a casual catch-as-catch-can film rental basis for the provision of teaching materials can hardly be considered a characteristic of an effective instructional program. A well-planned, well-organized, and adequately financed audio-visual program must be provided. For the thousands of smaller and medium-sized school systems in both rural and urban areas, participation in some form of cooperative audio-visual program offers the possibility of high quality service at low cost.

2. Cooperative audio-visual programs should be established within the administrative framework of an already existing public school institution—county school system, an intermediate unit (possibly embracing two or more counties), a county or regional junior college, or a regional teacher education institution. Where the existing institution is inadequate to undertake such a program, first efforts should be made to modify and strengthen it.

3. In an area where no existing institution can undertake the organization and operation of a cooperative program, an intermediate level agency should be created by organizing a legal body to act as a governing board. A centrally located public school facility may be used as the service center.

4. Legal authority for providing funds and for making policy may be granted by state legislative enactment, state board of education action, county board of education action, or by the joint action of the individual governing bodies of participating school districts.

5. The organizational structure of a cooperative program should be defined in state law, by a constitution, set of bylaws, and/or through a contractual agreement between the cooperative's governing board and the participating districts.

[1]Henry R. McCarty and Horace C. Hartsell, *The Cooperative Approach to Audio-Visual Programs* (Washington, D.C.: Department of Audiovisual Instruction and Department of Rural Education, National Education Association, 1959), pp. 64–69.

6. Each cooperative program should be governed by a board of education, board of directors, or board of trustees. Representatives of all the participating schools or school districts should be involved in the determination of policies dealing with actual operation of the program.

7. The area served by a cooperative program should be large enough to assure the economical use of materials; it should be small enough to enable the efficient and prompt distribution of materials and service. County and state boundaries should not be permitted to deter the organization of an effective program. In some areas a pupil population base of 10,000 to 25,000 seems to be adequate; in others a minimum base of 50,000 appears desirable. It is doubtful that an efficient program could operate on a base less than 10,000 pupils.

8. Cooperative programs must have an equitable and continuing system of financial support. Financial responsibility should be shared by local, county, and state school agencies or by other governing bodies responsible for contributing to the support of education in the particular area or locality.

9. Finance provisions based upon an annual per-pupil allowance should be determined locally on a basis of the objectives established for the program. Such expenditures can be expected to vary from one area to another.

10. A full-time professionally qualified audio-visual director should be appointed by the cooperative's governing board to direct the operation and administration of the center.

11. Provisions should be made for an adequate technical and clerical staff for the performance of such functions as scheduling, processing, shipping, maintaining, and producing audio-visual materials.

12. The budget for the cooperative program should include all costs of operation—salaries, operation and maintenance costs, and allocations for the purchase and production of materials.

13. A continuous program of inservice education in the effective use of audio-visual materials should be carried on for teachers, building coordinators, and administrators. The staff of the cooperative audio-visual center, together with specialists in other curricular and teaching fields in local districts, county programs, teacher education institutions, and the state education agency should be involved in, and responsible for, such an inservice program.

14. An effective corps of audio-visual building coordinators should be organized to coordinate the requests and use of audio-visual materials in each school building with the cooperative center.

15. Each participating school district in a cooperative program should assume responsibility for equipping each of its buildings for the convenient and efficient use of audio-visual materials. Darkening facilities and a sufficient number of projectors and other equipment should be readily available to each teacher.

16. The emphasis of the cooperative audio-visual program should be on the provision and distribution of those materials and services which the local schools cannot provide with equal economy and efficiency. The major investments for materials by the cooperative center should be in 16mm educa-

tional films and in the materials and equipment for such production services as tape duplication, photography, graphic art, and radio and television programming. Many of the less expensive materials—filmstrips, recordings, flat pictures, charts, and exhibits should be provided from each school's audio-visual center as local schools are able to accept this responsibility. The cooperative audio-visual center may prepare and produce many of these materials at the request of teachers and local schools, but they should be deposited in and distributed from the local school's materials collection.

17. Provisions should be made for the transportation or distribution of audio-visual materials to and from each classroom with the minimum involvement of the school's building coordinator and teachers. Frequent distribution through a pickup and delivery service, express or parcel post. Center-provided pickup and delivery service is most convenient and efficient. Where parcel post can provide 24-hour service, it may be favored because of its economy.

18. Simple and efficient methods for requesting materials should be established. A complete, up-to-date, and well-designed catalog of the audio-visual materials available from the center should be provided for every teacher.

19. Where such a procedure is possible, the selection of materials to be purchased for distribution through the cooperative center should be made by committees of experienced teachers who represent all subject fields and grade levels. Selection should be based on the curricular needs of the instructional programs of the schools served and the students involved.

20. The director of a cooperative center (and such other professional staff as may be provided) should work closely with curriculum specialists to determine specific audio-visual and materials needs and to develop guides and study outlines for teachers in the various subject areas and grade levels in the use of audio-visual materials.

21. The directors of cooperative centers should have sufficient time available for visiting the schools served by the program in order to (a) consult with teachers on the use of audio-visual materials, conduct conferences and workshops, demonstrate materials, and provide other inservice education activities; (b) assist teachers in previewing and selecting materials; and (c) assist teachers in developing and producing teacher-made or school-made materials.

22. There should be a continuous evaluation of every cooperative program in order to realize the highest quality of service possible and a maximum use of the materials available. Only by continuous evaluation can the program be kept in tune with ever changing instructional needs.

Appendix 5

INTRODUCTION

This Evaluative Checklist is based on the assumption that there are fundamental elements of an educational media program which will facilitate the improvement of instruction. The elements around which this Checklist was developed were assumed to be common to most educational media programs. These include: 1) administrators and teachers are committed to the proper use of educational media for instructional purposes, 2) educational media are an integral part of curriculum and instruction, 3) an educational media center is accessible to the faculty, 4) the physical facilities are conducive to proper use of educational media, 5) the media program is adequately financed, and 6) the staff is adequate and qualified to provide for the educational needs of all faculty members.

The status of an educational media program is not likely to be known without periodic evaluation. The use of this Checklist should greatly facilitate such an evaluation by providing useful guidelines for making judgments on program elements.

The term "educational media" as used in this instrument means all equipment and materials traditionally called "audio-visual materials" and all of the newer media such as television, overhead projectuals, and programed materials. Likewise, the terms "media" and "educational media" are used interchangeably to mean both instructional equipment and instructional materials.

Before completing the Checklist, the evaluator may want to become

[1]W. R. Fulton, University of Oklahoma, Norman, Oklahoma. This instrument is a part of a study performed pursuant to a contract with the United States Office of Education, Department of Health, Education and Welfare, under the provisions of Title VII, Public Law 85–864.

familiar with the inventory of educational media and pertinent physical facilities of the program being evaluated. He may also want to study the criteria relating to the elements covered in the Checklist.

EVALUATIVE CHECKLIST

DIRECTIONS:

   Mark *one* of the spaces at the left of the statement that most nearly represents the situation in your school system. If a statement accurately describes your school, mark the *middle space* to the left of that statement. If you feel that the situation at your school is below what is described, mark the *lower numbered space*; if above, mark the *higher numbered space*. In any case mark only *one* space.

EXAMPLE:

| 1 | | 2 | | 3 | There is no full-time director of the media program.
| 4 | | 5 | | 6 | There is a full-time director in charge of the media program.
| 7 | | 8 | | 9 | There are a full-time director and a sufficient number of clerical and technical personnel.

I. School System Educational Media Services

Criteria

   *A school system should have a program of educational media services administered through a school media center, and building centers if such are needed, which provides teachers with an adequate supply of appropriate instructional materials.
   *The educational media center should be a separate service unit that operates at the same level as other major services.
   *A school system should have clearly defined policies, procedures, and plans for its educational media program, including short-range, and long-range goals.
   *There should be a sufficient number of professional media staff members to administer the educational media program and to provide consultative services to teachers throughout the school system.

A. *Commitment to the Media Program*

| 1 | | 2 | | 3 | The school's educational media program consists of services from a media center managed by clerical and technical staff members. The services are not well coordinated and no one person has been given administrative responsibility for system-wide media activities.

| 4 | | 5 | | 6 | The school's educational media program consists of a media center with clerical and technical staff. The program is directed by a staff person who has some educational media training but not enough to qualify him as an educational media specialist. He reports to the administrative officer in charge of instruction.

| 7 | | 8 | | 9 | The school has an educational media program including an educational media center and necessary building media centers directed by an educational media specialist who reports directly to the administrative officer in charge of instruction. He is provided with facilities, finances, and staff essential in meeting the media needs of the instructional program.

B. *Commitment to Educational Media as an Integral Part of Instruction*

| 1 | | 2 | | 3 | The school provides some educational media and services for teachers who request them, but teachers are not particularly encouraged to use the services.

| 4 | | 5 | | 6 | A variety of educational media and services are generally available and some attempts are made to acquaint teachers with the services, and to encourage their use.

| 7 | | 8 | | 9 | The school provides the quantity and variety of educational media and services needed by all buildings and encourages teachers to use media as integral parts of instruction.

C. *Commitment to Providing Educational Media Facilities*

| 1 | | 2 | | 3 | Although some new and remodeled facilities provide for the use of some types of educational media, the school gives little attention to media utilization at the time buildings are planned.

| 4 | | 5 | | 6 | The school provides most new and remodeled buildings with light control and other facilities necessary for the use of some types of educational media.

| 7 | | 8 | | 9 | All new buildings are equipped for the greatest possible use of educational media and are designed to permit adaptation for new developments in media. Old buildings are being modified as fast as possible to provide for effective use of media.

D. *Commitment to Financing the Educational Media Program*

| 1 | | 2 | | 3 | Finances for the educational media program are inadequate to provide the services that teachers need and are prepared to use. There are no written policies relative to allocations, income sources and charges against the budget.

| 4 | | 5 | | 6 | Finances for the educational media program are sufficient to maintain the status quo, but the current media services are not sufficient to meet the instructional needs. Long-range curriculum plans do not include provisions for financing needed educational media services.

| 7 | | 8 | | 9 | The educational media program is financed entirely from regularly appropriated school funds. The budget reflects to some degree long-range educational media plans and includes provisions for special media for unusual curriculum problems. The budget is prepared, presented, and defended by the director of the media services in the same manner as that of any other budget unit.

E. *Commitment to Staffing the Educational Media Program*

| 1 | | 2 | | 3 | The responsibility for educational media services is assigned to various staff members whose primary commitments are in other school jobs.

| 4 | | 5 | | 6 | The responsibility for educational media services is delegated to a person who has had some training in educational media. He is provided with some clerical and technical assistance.

| 7 | | 8 | | 9 | Leadership and consultative services are provided by an educational media specialist and a qualified professional staff. An adequate clerical and technical staff is also provided.

II. Educational Media Services—Curriculum and Instruction

Criteria

*A school system should engage in a continuous evaluation of its educational media program as it relates to the instructional program.

*Continuous inservice education in the use of educational media should be carried on as a means of improving instruction.

*The faculty and the professional media staff should cooperate in planning and developing the parts of the instructional program that make provisions for the use of educational media.

*Professional educational media personnel should be readily available for consultation on all instructional problems where media are concerned.

A. *Consultative Services in Educational Media Utilization*

|1| |2| |3| Educational media personnel render consultative assistance in the instructional application of educational media when they are asked to do so and are free from other duties.

|4| |5| |6| Educational media personnel are usually available and are called on for consultative assistance in the use of educational media.

|7| |8| |9| Educational media professional personnel work, as a part of their regular assignments, with teachers in analyzing teaching needs and in designing, selecting, and using educational media to meet these needs.

B. *Inservice Education in Educational Media Utilization*

|1| |2| |3| Inservice education is left entirely to building instructional units and is limited to their own capabilities and such other resources as they can find.

|4| |5| |6| Professional educational media staff members are available on request to assist teachers and supervisors in inservice education activities relative to the use of educational media.

|7| |8.| |9| Professional educational media staff members are involved in planning and conducting continuous inservice education activities concerned with the selection, development, production, and use of all types of educational media.

C. *Faculty-Student Use of Educational Media*

|1| |2| |3| Only a few teachers make any use of educational media in their classrooms. Students rarely use media in class presentations.

|4| |5| |6| Quite a few teachers make occasional use of educational media in their classrooms. Students occasionally use media in class presentations.

|7| |8| |9| Most teachers use appropriate educational media in their classrooms. Students use appropriate media for individual and group study, as well as for class presentations.

D. *Involvement of the Media Staff in Planning*

|1| |2| |3| The professional educational media staff is seldom involved with teachers in planning for the use of educational media.

|4| |5| |6| The professional educational media staff is occasionally involved with teachers and supervisors in planning and producing materials for use in the instructional program.

|7| |8| |9| The educational media specialist and his professional staff are usually involved with teachers, supervisors and other curriculum workers in planning for the use of and in experimenting with educational media in the instructional program. He is also regularly involved in decision-making activities relating to the integration of educational media with the curriculum and instruction.

III. The Educational Media Center

Criteria

*Educational media centers should be organized around the concept of offering a wide variety of services and media to all instructional and administrative units of a school system, with leadership, consultative help, and other services provided by professional media specialists and other media center personnel.

*The instructional program should be supported by an adequate supply of educational media and a system of making them accessible to the faculty and students.

*The educational media center should provide such media services as procurement, maintenance, and production of appropriate educational media to support the instructional program.

A. *Location and Accessibility of Educational Media*

| 1 | | 2 | | 3 | The location of the school's educational media center is such that media are not accessible to most teachers. The school's educational media center is not supplemented by building centers where media are placed on long-term loan.

| 4 | | 5 | | 6 | The location of the school's educational media center is such that media are not very accessible to teachers. The school's educational media center is supplemented by a few building centers that provide some media and services not available from the school media center, but merely duplicate others.

| 7 | | 8 | | 9 | The location of the school's educational media center and the presence of necessary building centers make media highly accessible to all instructional units. Both the school's and the buildings' educational media centers are adequately equipped to support a quality instructional program.

B. *Dissemination of Media Information*

| 1 | | 2 | | 3 | Information concerning educational media is seldom disseminated to prospective users, but there are no definite plans or channels for such dissemination.

| 4 | | 5 | | 6 | Information concerning educational media is disseminated to teachers and staff members on an occasional basis or when requested.

| 7 | | 8 | | 9 | Information concerning all educational media and programs is frequently disseminated to teachers and staff members as a matter of policy.

C. *Availability of Educational Media*

| 1 | | 2 | | 3 | The quantity of educational media is so limited that significant delays occur between requests for materials and their availability. Reservations must be made on a "first come, first served" basis, and the media must be picked up by the user.

| 4 | | 5 | | 6 | The quantity of educational media and the distribution system makes it possible for media to be delivered to teachers on relatively short notice.

| 7 | | 8 | | 9 | There is a sufficient quantity of educational media and an adequate distribution system to insure the delivery of all media to teachers on any day during the week in which they are requested.

D. *Storage and Retrieval of Media*

| 1 | | 2 | | 3 | Media storage facilities are available but are inadequate for some types of educational media, and personnel have difficulty in locating and retrieving specific items.

| 4 | | 5 | | 6 | The school's educational media center and all building centers have enough storage shelves and drawers for currently owned instructional materials. The retrieval system is adequate most of the time.

| 7 | | 8 | | 9 | Adequate storage space, including space for future expansion, is provided in the school's educational media center and in all building centers, with proper humidity control where needed. The school's educational media center has a master retrieval system for immediate location of all media.

E. *Maintenance of Media*

| 1 | | 2 | | 3 | Educational media are cleaned and repaired when complaints regarding their operable condition are made by users.

| 4 | | 5 | | 6 | Educational media are cleaned and repaired whenever the maintenance staff has time to do so.

| 7 | | 8 | | 9 | All educational media are inspected after each usage and are cleaned and repaired on a regular basis or when inspection indicates the need.

F. *Production of Media*

|1| |2| |3| Limited production facilities are available for teachers to produce their own materials.

|4| |5| |6| Educational media personnel, as well as teachers, produce some educational materials, but the media staff is limited to the extent that all demands for production cannot be met.

|7| |8| |9| Educational media personnel, as well as teachers, produce a variety of educational media not otherwise available, and meet most production demands for such media as films, filmstrips, slides, graphics, and recordings.

IV. Physical Facilities for Educational Media

Criteria
*Each classroom should be designed for and provided with essential facilities for effective use of appropriate educational media of all kinds.
*Each classroom should be equipped with full light control, electrical outlets, forced ventilation, and educational media storage space.
*Classrooms should be equipped with permanently installed bulletin boards, chalkboards, projection screens, map rails, and storage facilities needed for the particular type of instruction conducted in each classroom.

A. *Physical Facilities in Existing Classrooms*

|1| |2| |3| A few classrooms have been modified for use of educational media. However, no systematic plans have been made to adapt all classrooms for the use of educational media, except that some departments have made such plans for their own classrooms.

|4| |5| |6| Some classrooms have been modified and equipped with such physical facilities as light control and electrical outlets and others are partially equipped. A plan for systematically equipping all classrooms is in operation.

|7| |8| |9| All classrooms have been modified and equipped for optimum use of all types of educational media.

B. *Physical Facilities in New Classrooms*

|1| |2| |3| Some new classrooms are provided with physical facilities such as light control and electrical outlets, but only in special cases are provisions made for the use of a wide variety of media.

|4| |5| |6| Most new classrooms are provided with physical facilities that make possible optimum use of educational media.

|7| |8| |9| All new classrooms are designed for and equipped with physical facilities that make possible optimum use of all types of educational media by faculty and students.

V. Budget and Finance of the Educational Media Program

Criterion
*Financing the educational media program should be based on both the school system's long-range goals and immediate educational needs. The budget should reflect a recognition of long-range goals, and be sufficient to support an adequate media program for optimum instructional improvement.

A. *Reporting Financial Needs*

|1| |2| |3| The financial needs of the educational media program are reported to the administrative officer in charge of instruction only when immediate expenditures are urgently needed.

The financial needs of the educational media program are regularly

| 4 | | 5 | | 6 | reported to the administrative officer in charge of instruction.
Regular reports reflecting the status and needs of the educational
| 7 | | 8 | | 9 | media program, including facts about inventory, facilities, level of
utilization, and effectiveness of the media program, are made to the
administrative officer in charge of instruction.

B. *Basis for Budget Allocations*
The educational media budget is based on an arbitrary allotment of
| 1 | | 2 | | 3 | funds irrespective of need.
The educational media budget is based almost entirely on immediate
| 4 | | 5 | | 6 | needs, though some consideration is given to long-range goals.
The educational media budget is based on both the immediate needs
| 7 | | 8 | | 9 | and the long-range goals of the school and reflect clear-cut policies
concerning allocations, income sources, and budget practices.

C. *Development of Media Budget*
Each building instructional unit develops its own educational media
| 1 | | 2 | | 3 | budget without consulting an educational media specialist.
The budget of the educational media program reflects the media
| 4 | | 5 | | 6 | needs of most building instructional units. However, some buildings
have their own media budget which has no relationship to the educational media program.
The budget of the educational media program reflects the media
| 7 | | 8 | | 9 | needs of the entire school system and is developed by the professional
media staff in consultation with financial officers, principals and other
school administrators.

VI. Educational Media Staff

Criterion
*The educational media program should be directed by a well qualified full-time
media specialist who is provided with sufficient professional, clerical, and technical staff to provide adequate media services to the entire school system.

A. *School System Media Staff*
A staff person has been assigned to look after the media program.
| 1 | | 2 | | 3 | He performs more as a clerk and a technician than as a professional
media person.
A professional media person with some special training is in charge
| 4 | | 5 | | 6 | of the educational media program and has some professional, clerical,
and technical assistance. He and his assistants are primarily oriented
toward the mechanical and technical aspects of the program.
The educational media program is directed by a well qualified media
| 7 | | 8 | | 9 | specialist who is provided with sufficient professional, clerical, and
technical staff to provide adequate media services from the school
media center. Professional media staff members are oriented toward
curriculum and instruction.

B. *Building Media Staff*
Some buildings have a teacher, a clerk, or someone else assigned to
| 1 | | 2 | | 3 | help obtain materials and care for equipment, but no released time
is granted from other jobs to coordinate media activities in the building.
Most buildings have a teacher, or a member of the professional staff
| 4 | | 5 | | 6 | assigned to coordinate media activities, but he has not been given
sufficient released time from other school tasks, or enough clerical and
technical assistance to permit him to render media services needed
in the instructional program.
A full-time professional educational media coordinator serves each

|7| |8| |9| building. Buildings that do not have sufficient teachers and media utilization to warrant a full-time coordinator share his services. He is provided sufficient clerical and technical assistance to supply all media services needed in the building. He reports to the school's educational media director and works closely with the media staff, supervisors, and other curriculum workers.

PROFILE SHEET

To develop a Profile image of your program, transfer your mark from each item of the Evaluative Checklist to this sheet. Connect the marked squares by straight lines. Then turn the sheet to a horizontal position. This will pictorially demonstrate the "peaks" and "valleys" of attainment for your program.

		Weak						➤	*Strong*		
Section I										
	Item A	|1|	|2|	|3|	|4|	|5|	|6|	|7|	|8|	|9|
	B	|1|	|2|	|3|	|4|	|5|	|6|	|7|	|8|	|9|
	C	|1|	|2|	|3|	|4|	|5|	|6|	|7|	|8|	|9|
	D	|1|	|2|	|3|	|4|	|5|	|6|	|7|	|8|	|9|
	E	|1|	|2|	|3|	|4|	|5|	|6|	|7|	|8|	|9|
Section II										
	Item A	|1|	|2|	|3|	|4|	|5|	|6|	|7|	|8|	|9|
	B	|1|	|2|	|3|	|4|	|5|	|6|	|7|	|8|	|9|
	C	|1|	|2|	|3|	|4|	|5|	|6|	|7|	|8|	|9|
	D	|1|	|2|	|3|	|4|	|5|	|6|	|7|	|8|	|9|
Section III										
	Item A	|1|	|2|	|3|	|4|	|5|	|6|	|7|	|8|	|9|
	B	|1|	|2|	|3|	|4|	|5|	|6|	|7|	|8|	|9|
	C	|1|	|2|	|3|	|4|	|5|	|6|	|7|	|8|	|9|
	D	|1|	|2|	|3|	|4|	|5|	|6|	|7|	|8|	|9|
	E	|1|	|2|	|3|	|4|	|5|	|6|	|7|	|8|	|9|
	F	|1|	|2|	|3|	|4|	|5|	|6|	|7|	|8|	|9|
Section IV										
	Item A	|1|	|2|	|3|	|4|	|5|	|6|	|7|	|8|	|9|
	B	|1|	|2|	|3|	|4|	|5|	|6|	|7|	|8|	|9|
Section V										
	Item A	|1|	|2|	|3|	|4|	|5|	|6|	|7|	|8|	|9|
	B	|1|	|2|	|3|	|4|	|5|	|6|	|7|	|8|	|9|
	C	|1|	|2|	|3|	|4|	|5|	|6|	|7|	|8|	|9|
Section VI										
	Item A	|1|	|2|	|3|	|4|	|5|	|6|	|7|	|8|	|9|
	B	|1|	|2|	|3|	|4|	|5|	|6|	|7|	|8|	|9|

Appendix 6

STANDARDS FOR SCHOOL MEDIA PROGRAMS. HOW DO YOU RATE?[1]

	Standards For School Media Programs (Selected Categories)	Present Media Standards in your State or District	Present Achievement in your School
ENROLLMENT	Standards for elementary schools with enrollment of 250 or more		
STAFF	1 media specialist per 250 students 1 technician and 1 media aide per media specialist		
FACILITIES	Reading room—Space based on 15% of student enrollment at 40 square feet per student. Seating capacity of 30%–40% for individual study areas equipped with power Additional space—Small group viewing and listening; conference; office; workroom; maintenance and repair; media production; dark room; materials, equipment, and magazine storage; stacks		
COLLECTION	Books—6,000–10,000 titles representing 10,000 volumes or 20 volumes per student, whichever is greater		

[1]John Rowell, "AASL and DAVI Issue New Standards for Media Programs," *The Instructor*, LXXVIII, No. 3 (1968), pp. 82–83.

	Standards For *School Media Programs* *(Selected Categories)*	*Present Media* *Standards in your* *State or District*	*Present* *Achievement* *in your School*
COLLECTION, *Continued*	Magazines—For grades K–6: 40–50 titles; for grades K–8: 50–75 titles (includes adult but not professional periodicals)		
	Newspapers—3–6 titles		
	Filmstrips—500–1,000 titles representing 1,500 prints or 3 prints per student, whichever is greater		
	8 mm Films (single concept) —1½ films per student with at least 500 titles supplemented by duplicates		
	16 mm Films—Access to minimum of 3,000 titles supplemented by duplicates and rentals		
	Recordings (tape and disc)— 1,000–2,000 titles representing 3,000 recordings or 6 per student, whichever is greater		
	Slides—2,000		
	Art prints (reproductions)— 1,000		
	Pictures and study prints— Access to 15 sets per teaching station and 25 sets in media center, plus individual pictures and study prints		
	Globes—1 per classroom and 2 in media center		
	Transparencies—2,000		
FACULTY LIBRARY	Books—200–1,000 titles		
	Magazines—40–50 professional titles		
	Additional materials, including: Courses of study, curriculum guides, teacher's manuals, state and local educational releases, and so on		

Index

Acoustical conditions. *See* Sonic
   environment
Administration
   definition of, 12
   evaluation of, 156, 161–62, 164
   rationale of, 8–9, 12–37
   responsibilities of, 54–66
   See also Leadership
Administrative council, district, 55, 59
Aesthetic environment, 85, 86, 118
Alexander, William M., 39
American Association of School
   Administrators (AASA), 22, 158
Appraising, administrative process and,
   24, 35
Architect, role of, 84–86, 122
Assistant superintendents
   for business, 59–61, 65, 66
   in charge of instruction, 40–42, 46, 51,
     55–61, 63–65, 76, 77, 81, 137, 139,
     140, 152, 161–62
Audio-visual media
   budget for, 139–40, 142, 150–53
   evaluation of, 49, 52–53, 158–59
   role of, 4, 10, 67, 71–73, 76, 80, 122,
     123, 126–29
   source for, 46–47, 52
   See also specific media
Audio-Visual Service Center (San Diego),
   129–31

Bass, Bernard H., 13n
Bell, Norman, 112n
Beynon, John, 110n
Boardman, Thomas H., 140n, 142
Books. *See* Textbooks
Brick, E. Michael, 107n
Brickell, Henry M., 142–43
Brown, James W., 26, 75–76, 81

Budget
   administration of, 55, 58–60, 65, 77,
     78, 135–55
   definition of, 135–36
   evaluation of, 156, 163, 165
   financing of, 135, 138, 142–49, 153–54
Burr, James B., 13n, 14n, 25n
Bushnell, Don D., 30, 31n

Carlson, Mildred A., 45
Caravaty, R., 93n
Castetter, William B., 136, 137
Central storage, need for, 74
Chief school administrators. *See*
   Superintendents
Child, evaluation of, 158–60, 165
Childress, Jack R., 136n
Climate control. *See* Thermal
   environment
Coffield, William H., 13n, 14n, 25n
Cogswell, John F., 32
Collins, George J., 143, 150
Community support for learning
   resources, 13, 32–35
Computer-assisted instruction (CAI),
     2–8, 10, 64, 65, 68, 69, 80, 111–13,
     118, 124, 128
   See also Systems approach
Consultant services, 84, 116, 118
   adequacy of, 175–79
   cooperative approach to, 121, 124, 127,
     133
Cooperative Research Act of 1954, 145, 146
Coordinators
   of curriculum, 41, 56–58, 64, 65, 76, 78
   of elementary education, 58
   of learning resources, 40, 41, 45–48,
     52, 53, 55, 57–58, 60, 61, 63, 65,
     76–78, 80–81, 84, 138, 162

Coordinators (*cont.*)
  of secondary education, 58
  of subject area curriculum, 40, 45–46,
    48, 52, 57, 58, 60–62, 65, 66
Coulson, John E., 32
County superintendents, 59
Criteria. *See* Evaluation
Curriculum
  design of, 9, 38–53, 72, 122–27
  evaluation of, 121, 123–24, 126, 156,
    162–63, 165, 175, 178–79
  sources of, 43
Curriculum Area 9, 120–27
Curriculum council, district, 40–43,
  48–52, 55, 57, 58, 61–63, 65, 161,
  162
Curtis, R., 104n, 105

DeBernardis, Amo, 115n
Decision making, administrative process
  and, 22–24, 35
Deliberating, administrative process and,
  21–24, 35
Design
  of curriculum, 9, 38–53, 72, 122–27
  of school plant, 9, 83–119, 130–31, 156,
    163–65
Development services, cooperative
  approach to, 121, 123–24
Dial access systems, 68, 70, 74, 80, 81,
  128, 161, 164
Display facilities, 83, 86, 113–15, 118
Doll, Ronald C., 44n

Echols, Dan, 103, 104n
Economic Opportunity Act of 1964, 145
Edenvale elementary school (San Jose),
  114
Educational Facilities Laboratories,
  72–73, 108
Educational Information Services, 121,
  124, 127
Educational television
  administrator and, 21–24
  cost of, 140, 150–52
  evaluation of, 157–60
  guidelines for, 18, 36
  as learning aid, 1, 8, 10, 38, 45, 64, 68,
    74, 76, 80, 81, 121, 126, 128
Educational Television Facilities Act,
  145–46
Egbert, R. L., 30, 31n
Electrical and electronic facilities, 74,
  83, 114–15, 119
Elementary and Secondary Education Act,
  67, 102, 104, 124, 125, 145, 146, 151,
  154

Ellsworth, Ralph E., 73n, 108
Evaluation
  checklist for, 182–90
  definition of, 159, 160, 165
  of educational needs, 173–76, 178–79
  of instructional materials, 167–70,
    173–74, 177
  of learning resources program, 156–66
Evans, N. Dean, 39n, 56n, 60n, 85n, 171n

Facilities. *See* Design
Fayol, Henri, 19–20
Featherstone, Richard, 112n
Fensch, Edwin A., 25
Films as learning aids, 1, 2, 8, 38,
  45–50, 58, 61, 62, 67–69, 71–73,
  122, 126, 128, 129, 134, 140, 145,
  150–52, 168–69
Fitzwater, C. O., 54n
Foundation for Economic Education,
  49–50
Foundations, funds from, 142, 149
Fountain Valley School District
  (California), 107
Fox, Robert S., 40n
Freeman, 50
Frey, Sherman H., 141n
Fulton, W. R., 139n, 164, 183n

Games, sources for, 48, 121
Garber, Leo O., 149n
Gassman, M., 93n
Gauerke, Warren E., 136n
Getschman, Keith R., 141n
Getzels, J. W., 17n
Gibson, Charles Dana, 91–92
Globes, evaluation of, 167–68
Government as partner, 12, 33, 39, 58,
  131, 142–48, 154
Greater Cleveland Area Research Council,
  148
Green, A., 93n, 107n, 116n
Griffiths, Daniel E., 20, 27, 36
Guba, E. G., 17n
Guidance services, director of, 41

Halpin, Andrew W., 28n
Hanlon, James M., 26
Harry Fulton School, 107
Hartsell, Horace C., 128, 129n, 180n
Haviland, D., 93n
Horner, W., 104n, 105

Indiana State University, multimedia
  classroom at, 110–11
Industry, education and, 148–49